Chicken Soup for the Soul®

Our **101** BEST STORIES

Like Mother, Like Daughter

Chicken Soup for the Soul® Our 101 Best Stories:
Like Mother, Like Daughter; Stories about the Special Bond between Mothers and
Daughters by Jack Canfield, Mark Victor Hansen & Amy Newmark

Published by Chicken Soup for the Soul Publishing, LLC   www.chickensoup.com

The publisher gratefully acknowledges the many publishers and individuals who
granted Chicken Soup for the Soul permission to reprint the cited material.

Cover photos courtesy of Jose Luis Pelaez Inc / Getty Images and Jupiter Images/photos.
com. Interior Illustration courtesy of iStockphoto.com/Janedoedynamite.

Cover and Interior Design & Layout by Pneuma Books, LLC
For more info on Pneuma Books, visit www.pneumabooks.com

Distributed to the booktrade by Simon & Schuster. SAN: 200-2442

Publisher's Cataloging-in-Publication Data
(Prepared by The Donohue Group)

Chicken soup for the soul. Selections.
    Chicken soup for the soul : like mother, like daughter : stories about the special
bond between mothers and daughters / [compiled by] Jack Canfield [and] Mark
Victor Hansen ; [edited by] Amy Newmark.
    p. ; cm. -- (Our 101 best stories)
  ISBN-13: 978-1-935096-07-8
  ISBN-10: 1-935096-07-9
1. Mothers and daughters--Literary collections. 2. Mothers--Literary collections.
3. Daughters--Literary collections. 4. Mothers and daughters--Conduct of life--
Anecdotes. I. Canfield, Jack, 1944- II. Hansen, Mark Victor. III. Newmark, Amy.
IV. Title.
PN6071.M7 C484 2008
810.8/092052   2008930431

PRINTED IN THE UNITED STATES OF AMERICA
on acid∞free paper
16 15 14 13 12 11 10 09   05 06 07 08

Chicken Soup for the Soul®

Our **101 BEST STORIES**

Like Mother, Like Daughter

Stories about the
Special Bond between
Mothers and Daughters

Jack Canfield
Mark Victor Hansen
Amy Newmark

CSS

Chicken Soup for the Soul Publishing, LLC
Cos Cob, CT

Chicken Soup
for the Soul

Contents

A Special Foreword by Jack and Mark xi

❶
~The Magical Bond~

1. The Club, *Susan B. Townsend* 1
2. Replicas, *Melissa Arnold Hill* 3
3. Missing Pieces, *Lizanne Southgate* 5
4. The Look, *M. M. English* 10
5. The Bike Trip, *Peggy Newland* 12
6. Roses for Tara, *Tara Steele as told to Heather Black* 18
7. Princess, *Kristy Ross* 23
8. The Little White Chapel, *Dawn Rambin* 26
9. I Love You More, *Christie A. Hansen* 29
10. Stranded on an Island, *Beverly Beckham* 31

❷
~Mutual Support~

11. The Birth of Daughters, *Karen C. Driscoll* 37
12. Pennies from Heaven, *Holly Jensen Hughes* 40
13. Mothers and Daughters, *Patricia Bunin* 42
14. Cellular Love, *Amy Hirshberg Lederman* 44
15. Growing Up, *Lisa Duffy-Korpics* 47
16. Running Role Model, *Mindy Pollack-Fusi* 52
17. The Power of My Mother's Love, *Shana Helmholdt* 55
18. Mama's Lesson, *Nicole Plyler Fisk* 59

❸
~Learning from Each Other~

19. What Mothers Teach, *Ferna Lary Mills* 65
20. The Sweater, *Pamela Albee* 69
21. Toast Means Love, *Toni Hall* 72
22. A Couple of Cacti, *Kelly E. Reno* 74
23. My Mother's Greatest Gift, *Marie Ragghianti* 77
24. Chasing Butterflies, *Karen Majoris-Garrison* 82
25. The Little White Shoes, *Catherine Monserrat, Ph.D.* 85
26. Moving in with Mom, *Carol Sjostrom Miller* 89
27. Mother's Silver Candlesticks, *Liesel Shineberg* 92
28. Thanksgiving Dinner and Infant Seats,
    Frances Firman Salorio 95
29. Things I Learned from My Mother, *Sylvia Rosa-Casanova* 98
30. A Cup of Coffee, *Barb Huff* 102

❹
~Always There for Each Other~

31. Marissa, *T. J. Banks* 109
32. Abigail's Dove, *Karen Majoris-Garrison* 112
33. Divorce—Cut and Dried, *Kelly McLane* 116
34. A Perfect Skate, *Nancy E. Myer* 119
35. Planting Day, *Beth Pollack* 122
36. The Prom That Almost Wasn't, *Kate Clabough* 125
37. Help Mom, I Need You! *L. Maggie Baxter* 128
38. A Hug for Your Thoughts, *Brenda Nixon* 133
39. Climb On, *Judy Henning* 135
40. My Turn, *Barbara Jeanne Fisher* 139
41. The Bear, *Zulmara Cline* 141
42. Marathon Women, *Susan Fishman Orlins* 144

❺
~Gratitude~

43. Your Friend, Mommy, *Patricia J. Lesesne* 151
44. It Runs in the Family, *Jarralynne Agee* 153
45. My Mother's Cure, *Jean Jeffrey Gietzen* 156
46. She Came Back Bearing Gifts, *Luann Warner* 160
47. The Reunion, *Kathy N. Jublou* 163
48. A Peace Corps Mama, *Cheryl Reece Myers* 167
49. Cinderella, *Tekla Dennison Miller* 168
50. The Most Precious Gift, *Linda Rivers* 173
51. Happy Birthday, Baby, *Kim Childs* 176
52. Never Enough, *Laurie Kalb* 179
53. An Angel in Disguise, *Alice Lundy Blum* 181
54. Happy Returns, *Jane Robertson* 185
55. The Mother Who Matters, *Kristy White* 189

❻
~Saying Goodbye~

56. I'm Okay, Mom and Dad, *Lark Whittemore Ricklefs* 195
57. To See You, *Cynthia M. Hamond* 198
58. A Name in the Sand, *Elizabeth Stumbo* 200
59. Angel Escort, *Elissa Hadley Conklin* 203
60. Joan's Bouquet, *Julie Messbarger as told to
    Charlotte Adelsperger* 207
61. Thirsty, *Nancy B. Gibbs* 209
62. The Red Sweater, *Stella Shepard* 211
63. Tough Love, *Mary Harrison Hart* 214
64. Anticipating the Empty Nest, *Bonnie Feuer* 217
65. A Rose for Mother, *Maria E. Sears* 219
66. Leaving Home, *Beth Copeland Vargo* 223

❼
~Through the Generations~

67. Lessons on Napkins, *Caurie Anne Miner* 229
68. The Gift of Memory, *Sally Friedman* 232
69. Yellow Irises, *Marion Owen* 235
70. It's a Date! *Carol McAdoo Rehme* 239
71. Pantyhose Hair, *Annette Marie Hyder* 241
72. Sandwich Generation, *Tricia Short* 244
73. Of Satin and Ceremonies, *Carol McAdoo Rehme* 246
74. I Never Saw My Mother Do a Sit-Up, *EllynAnne Geisel* 248
75. Sweet Sixteen, *Shelly Teems Johnson as told to
    Gloria Cassity Stargel* 250
76. Two Grannies in the Kitchen, *Patricia Lorenz* 255

❽
~Like Grandmother, Like Mother, Like Granddaughter~

77. Sticky Memories, *Mary Ann Cook* 263
78. The True Lesson of Homework, *Sally Friedman* 266
79. Becoming a Grandma, *Robin Lim* 269
80. Crinkles and Crow's Feet, *Anne Culbreath Watkins* 270
81. Travels with Grandma, *Phyllis W. Zeno* 273
82. "What's in a Name?" *Patty S. Sullivan* 276
83. Babies, Boredom and Bliss, *Janet Hall Wigler* 279
84. Beach Talk, *Judith Marks-White* 283

❾
~Special Mother-Daughter Moments~

85. Thumbs-Up Smiley Face, *Patricia Buck* 289
86. Light, *Jacquelyn Mitchard* 291
87. Looking for Love(s), *Kathleen Kersch Simandl* 296
88. Teddy Bear Tonic, *Bonnie Walsh Davidson* 299

89. She Did It Her Way, *Julie Firman* 303
90. The Queen of Coleslaw, *Annmarie Tait* 305
91. The Impossible Dream, *Peggy Spence* 308
92. A Family Christmas Carol, *Michelle Anzelone* 311
93. Honey's Greatest Gift, *B. J. Reinhard* 313
94 The Green Pajamas, *Marion Bond West* 316
95. Secret Weapon, *Jennifer Oliver* 320

⑩
~Funny Mother-Daughter Moments~

96. The Littlest Daughter, *Julie Firman* 327
97. Starring on the Six O'Clock News, *Erin K. Kilby* 329
98. Mommy Needs a Raise! *Regina Wiegand* 332
99. Clothes Closet Reflections, *Patricia Lorenz* 333
100. Catfishing with Mama, *Lin Sutherland* 335
101. Heave Ho, *Betty A. King* 340

MORE CHICKEN SOUP 344
WHO IS *JACK CANFIELD?* 359
WHO IS *MARK VICTOR HANSEN?* 361
WHO IS *AMY NEWMARK?* 363
ACKNOWLEDGMENTS 365

Chicken Soup for the Soul

A Special Foreword

by Jack and Mark

For us, 101 has always been a magical number. It was the number of stories in the first *Chicken Soup for the Soul* book, and it is the number of stories and poems we have always aimed for in our books. We love the number 101 because it signifies a beginning, not an end. After 100, we start anew with 101.

We hope that when you finish reading one of our books, it is only a beginning for you too—a new outlook on life, a renewed sense of purpose, a strengthened resolve to deal with an issue that has been bothering you. Perhaps you will pick up the phone and share one of the stories with a friend or a loved one. Perhaps you will turn to your keyboard and express yourself by writing a Chicken Soup story of your own, to share with other readers who are just like you.

This volume contains our 101 best stories and poems about that special and often mysterious bond between mothers and daughters. We share this with you at a very special time for us, the fifteenth anniversary of our *Chicken Soup for the Soul* series. When we published our first book in 1993, we never dreamed that we had started what would become a publishing phenomenon, one of the best-selling series of books in history.

We did not set out to sell more than one hundred million books, or to publish more than 150 titles. We set out to touch the heart of one person at a time, hoping that person would in turn touch another person, and so on down the line. Fifteen years later, we know that it has worked. Your letters and stories have poured in by the hundreds of thousands, affirming our life's work, and inspiring us to continue to make a difference in your lives.

On our fifteenth anniversary, we have new energy, new resolve, and new dreams. We have recommitted to our goal of 101 stories or poems per book, we have refreshed our cover designs and our interior layout, and we have grown the *Chicken Soup for the Soul* team, with new friends and partners across the country in New England.

How often have you seen a teenage girl pretend to be perturbed, but secretly smile, when she is told that she acts or looks just like her mother? This new volume includes our 101 best stories and poems about mothers and daughters from our rich fifteen-year history. We chose stories written by mothers about their daughters and stories written by daughters about their mothers. They all celebrate that special, sometimes magical, relationship between mothers and daughters.

We hope that you will enjoy reading these stories as much as we enjoyed selecting them for you, and that you will share them with your families and friends. We have identified the 32 *Chicken Soup for the Soul* books in which the stories originally appeared, in case you would like to continue reading about motherhood and families among our other books. We hope you will also enjoy the additional titles about families, parenting, and women in "Our 101 Best Stories" series.

With our love, our thanks, and our respect,
~*Jack Canfield and Mark Victor Hansen*

Chapter

1

Like Mother, Like Daughter

The Magical Bond

The truth is that when one woman gives birth to another,
to someone who is like her,
they are linked together for life in a very special way.
~Nancy Friday

The Club

My mom is a never ending song in my heart of comfort, happiness, and being.
I may sometimes forget the words but I always remember the tune.
~Graycie Harmon

The doctor cuts the umbilical cord at birth, but I believe it remains an invisible connection throughout the lives of both mother and child. In utero, the cord that joined my mother and me flowed with blood, rich in food and oxygen. After birth, my mother provided me with emotional and spiritual sustenance. When my mother died and our connection was severed by her removal from the physical world, I floundered. I felt displaced and disoriented. There are still times, years later, when I feel deprived and bewildered without that invisible cord in place to nurture and nourish me.

I recall the day my mother joined the club. I was eleven and had come home from school for lunch. That day, as with many days that preceded it, I had been followed home by two girls who teased and taunted me every step of the way. I was crying by the time I reached my door and I needed my mother. I rushed blindly into the kitchen and fell into her arms, sobbing and trying desperately to tell her how hurt I was. I saw my father and wondered why he was home in the middle of the day. I then looked up into my mother's face and saw it streaked with tears and contorted with her own misery. I thought, Wow, she is really upset about the teasing, too!

My father broke the silence and announced, "Your grandmother died this morning." Only after I joined the club years later did I begin to comprehend the wrench she was feeling that day at lunch. The cord to her mother had been cut, and she was struggling to breathe on her own for the first time.

I have heard that time heals all wounds. I do not believe this. The person who has lost a limb never stops missing the arm or leg that is gone, but somehow time permits that person to cope eventually with the loss. The cloud of grief that isolates, suffocates and blinds us will lift.

I was a mother of two when my mother died. There have been three babies born since, and sometimes the pain of not being able to share the smallest and most insignificant moments that I know she would understand paralyzes me briefly, and I feel angry and cheated.

My mother is physically gone, but she still sustains me. A glance at an old photograph, the sight of her handwriting on a recipe card or the remembrance of a moment long ago can evoke a memory so powerful and vivid, I swear sometimes I can hear her calling my name. Her obvious presence in my five children continues to inspire and motivate me even when I am tired, lonely and scared. One's meticulous attention to detail, another's smile and another's unflagging optimism resurrect her when I need her the most.

My mother has not left me, even though the cord has finally been cut, and I have joined the club I never knew existed.

~Susan B. Townsend
Chicken Soup for the Mother & Daughter Soul

2

Replicas

The moment a child is born, the mother is also born.
She never existed before. The woman existed, but the mother, never.
A mother is something absolutely new.
~Rajneesh

After one last agonizing push, my baby is here. All I can see are bright red, squirming legs and feet as one doctor passes her to the next, and she disappears amongst the teal green clothing of the medical personnel.

I try to see what is happening over on that table under the light, but it is impossible from my angle. But my mother is here.

"Oh, she's beautiful!" she tells me, and grabs my hand.

I believe my husband is in shock. He stands behind the nurses and doctor staring in disbelief at our little creation.

Seconds later, a bundled up little person is placed in my arms. And now, for the first time, I look into the face of my daughter, a perfect, innocent human being who has never been exposed to hate, sorrow or cruelty. To my surprise, she isn't crying, but is making a sound somewhere between a hum and a coo. Whatever it is, it sounds beautiful to me. Her eyes are dark and round — she has my eyes!

As my eyes meet the tiny replicas of my own, "Oh my gosh" are the only words I can mutter before I begin to cry.

She looks like an angel. A tear drops from the tip of my nose and lands on her bright pink cheek. She blinks.

"Sorry," I whisper as I wipe my tear from her cheek.

Her skin is so soft; it feels like velvet. Her hair is tinged with blood and looks dark from the wetness.

Caught up in this serene moment, I have forgotten my husband and mother at my side. They both have tears in their eyes.

I look at my husband and say, "This is our baby."

He kisses my forehead.

My attention is once again directed solely to this miracle in my arms and the rest of the world disappears again. Her eyes are looking about now, and her tiny lips are slightly moving as if she is trying to tell me a secret. Her little nose is covered with tiny white bumps that look as if God carefully placed them there. A little hand emerges from the white blanket. It is a bit purple and oh so tiny. With my index finger, I stroke her palm. She grasps my finger and holds on tight. My heart melts. She looks at me again.

"Hi," I say, with a big smile.

"Honey, we've got to run a few tests and give her a bath. I'll bring her right back," a nurse says out of nowhere.

"Okay," I say with a sigh.

I look back down at my daughter and say, "I love you, Summer."

The nurse carefully takes her from my arms. As she is leaving the room, I watch the blanket move from the wiggling of my baby's feet.

Minutes later, my mother and I are alone in the room. She hugs me all at once, and I notice she has tears in her eyes.

"There is no love like the love you have for your child," she says, looking into my eyes, replicas of her own.

"I know," I say, and smile.

~Melissa Arnold Hill
Chicken Soup for Every Mom's Soul

Missing Pieces

Children and mothers never truly part
Bound in the beating of each other's heart.
~Charlotte Gray

When I got pregnant at seventeen, the circumstances could not have been worse. The father was a thirty-eight-year-old police officer. He was furious at the news of "my" problem. Life at home with an alcoholic parent and abusive stepparent was lonely and precarious.

Childishly, I tried to ignore these facts. I crocheted small pink blankets (I knew the baby was a girl) and scoured yard sales for tiny dresses and parenting books, determined to be a "good" mother. My daughter would be loved, and I, at last, would have someone to love me.

Reality reared its ugly head. Nights I didn't work were spent in my car or at a movie to avoid my parents' drinking and the fighting that ensued. Finally, I could no longer push away the thought that tormented me: My child could not live like that. The mere thought of bringing her into that house made me physically ill; the idea of losing her broke my heart. My only other family was a grandmother who refused to have anything to do with me once she found out I was pregnant. There was no way to escape with the baby. There was no place to go.

But there was a way out for her.

Not surprisingly, my OB/GYN knew an attorney with clients waiting for a baby. His clients had enough money to smooth out any obstacles in a child's life. He met me at a pie shop, carrying a sheaf of papers for me to sign. I had no idea what they said, tears blinded me and I was sure I was going to throw up. Obediently, I signed every place I was told to. He paid for my pie and left.

Hours after I delivered, the new parents arrived at the hospital. "No need for you to hold her," said the nurse, whisking the baby from me.

Alone in the hospital room, I called my mother. Angry at being deprived of the welfare check the baby would have "entitled" us to, she told me never to come home and hung up. Somewhere in the plastic hospital bag that contained my clothes was my worldly fortune of thirteen dollars and twenty-eight cents.

The parents stopped by my room the next day. They were smiling and happy, just popping in for a quick visit to let me know they were grateful and in a hurry. Then they were gone, taking my daughter to a better life.

In desperation, I called a coworker who took me in. That night, I stood in the shower, watching the water, blood, milk and tears swirl down the drain and wishing the rest of me would go, too.

But the heart lives on hope. No matter what those papers had said, I was convinced I would see her again. Clinging to that, I let time propel me forward. The bleeding stopped, the milk dried up, the tears slowed and hardened into a lump that settled in my chest.

The loving logic that forced the "right" decisions for my child did nothing to heal the shambles of my heart. The loss remained with me, a discreet open wound that bled quietly, steadily through the years.

Life went on. I went to work, married, had five more children and, eventually, divorced.

The children have always known they have an older sister. Although they watched me send out information to reunion organizations and conduct searches on the Internet for her, they never knew that I choked inside whenever someone asked how many children I had. The socially acceptable lie, "I have five," brought a wave of grief every time it left my lips.

"My" children are seventeen, twelve, eleven, ten and eight. At thirty-seven, my life appeared rich and full. So, how do I make sense of the fact that I have lived with a hole in my heart these many years, that nineteen and a half years ago I swallowed my screams and they still echo inside?

Since the birth of my first child, a shadow person accompanied me, an infant who grew through the years, a blurry outline with a face that I could not see, a face I was sure I would recognize if given the chance. She stood just out of sight at every birthday or holiday and as I dried dishes or washed my face. And she took from me any sense of completeness, for she held a piece of my heart.

Every year on November 27, her birthday, I wrote her a letter and then threw it away. I wondered and grieved. Before she turned eighteen, I registered with every adoption reunion service. Perhaps she would not want to find me; maybe she didn't know she was adopted. Maybe she knew and would hate me forever. So I waited, with the knowledge that any phone call, any knock on the door could heal my heart or break it again. Worst was the thought that I might wait forever.

On April 19, we were leaving for church. The flag on the mailbox was raised, which was odd for a Sunday. Inside lay a small piece of lined paper torn from a notebook.

"Lizanne S.: The daughter you gave up for adoption, Aaron [sic], is looking hard for you. Her number is...." A North Carolina phone number followed. Below that was printed a man's name and a local phone number.

Sure that this was a cruel hoax my first reaction was grief and fury. In tears, I called the local number. The writer lived on the same country road as we do. All he could tell me was that a young woman had called him from North Carolina, saying she was my daughter and that she could not find my phone number. So she pulled up listings for all numbers on the same road and began calling them to ask for help in contacting me.

I was stunned. My stomach knotted as hope and fear battled within. The six of us continued on to our church in complete silence.

Our service had guest musicians that day. We sat down as a woman's clear voice began the first song: "I will never forget thee, I will never forsake thee." In the instant her words hung in the air, my fear and doubt vanished.

There was no answer at the Charlotte number, so I left a message on the answering machine. I waited for two long hours before the telephone rang. "Mom..." the voice said hesitantly, "Mom," and she began to cry. My daughter had found me.

Over the next hours, we boosted profits for AT&T and the makers of Kleenex. Her summer break was four days away, and she would leave for a month-long internship in Central America in nine days. Unable to wait so long to meet her, I was on a plane from Portland to Charlotte the following day.

During the interminable flights and layovers, I sifted through years and memories, searching for the pieces she would care about, weaving a chain of my life to give her.

Erin stood, tall and blond, at the gate, holding a teddy bear and balloon. Hugging and crying, we held on to each other, trying to make up for almost twenty years in one fierce embrace. Over the next few days, we talked, laughed, hugged, stared at each other and cried more. Piece by piece, we filled in details of the shadowy picture we had of each other.

We share the same coloring, fierce competitive drive and anger at any injustice. Both of us have cold hands and feet, skin that burns at the first ray of sun, and an addiction to caffeine. Given an option, neither of us believes in mornings that start before ten. Currently, each of us is enrolled in a Spanish class, studying law and spending time weight training. However, the saddest commonality is the core of hurt, the sense of incompleteness and the "missing piece" in our hearts.

For the last month that I carried her, when I knew I would lose her, I grieved. And that was part of the legacy she carried away. No legal paper could sever that tie.

Erin has a good life with parents who love her and have given her everything money could buy. She is happy and healthy. For that, I am grateful.

This summer she is spending time with me and her newly found siblings. Her five brothers and sisters are ecstatic, stunned, confused and sometimes, I suspect, a bit jealous. So they talk about it, ask questions and adapt, throwing open their hearts to a stranger who has always held a place in mine. I watch them play and wrestle together, a jumble of arms, legs and giggles. Late at night, I creep down the hall and watch her sleep.

As she fills out the application to transfer from college in Charlotte to Oregon State, I can feel my heart relax. For nineteen and a half years, I have held my breath, held my loss, held my tears. Now, I can let it all go.

All our lives are better now that we can share them with each other. The core of heartache is gone. Our shadows have faces — familiar, tear-streaked, laughing faces. The search for the missing part of us is over.

~Lizanne Southgate
A 6th Bowl of Chicken Soup for the Soul

The Look

It happens to the best of us. We plan for a baby, and for a few blissful months that is exactly what we have—a soft and usually sweet-smelling baby who looks adorable in eyelet and ribbon and who endearingly dampens the shoulders and laps of those enslaved by the dimpled wee knuckles and the gentle gurgles. That's how it all begins.

At some point, however, the baby who we had planned for, all sweetness and light, becomes a person with complex thought processes and with means of expressing herself. This is something we had not planned for.

A few days ago, I answered a question from my daughter with what I thought was a terribly clever and witty remark. I turned to see the reaction from my beloved and was met with The Look. Those of you who have never had the unique privilege of living with a nine-year-old girl may not be familiar with The Look (this may be viewed as a sexist remark, but I find that my daughter is ever so much more accomplished at giving The Look than my son).

The Look involves a slackening of the jaw, a downward tilt of the head and a 180-degree roll of the eyes. The Look is often accompanied by a forceful exhalation of breath indicating: a) disgust, b) disbelief, c) exasperation, d) embarrassment, e) all of the above. The Look occurs more frequently in public, where the youngster must never be seen to approve of anything the parent does, says, likes, thinks or is.

And so I had been fixed with The Look. It was meant, of course, to indicate the extreme disapproval of the actions of the parent (me) on the part of the child (my daughter). It was meant to whip me into line, to check my inappropriate behavior, but I thought it was really quite funny. My laughter brought on another Look and the icy comment, "Not amusing, Mother."

Now the child's grandmother finds this is all very humorous. She sarcastically says that things will only get better. She says she can hardly wait until my daughter turns thirteen. She says she is most delighted to see that the Ultimate Mother's Curse ("I hope you have a child who is just like you!" which was first cast over me when I was, perhaps, three) has finally come true. The child's grandmother offers no sympathy. Instead, she laughs gleefully and begins to point out the many ways in which my daughter and I are alike.

I fix her with The Look and try to pretend she's not my mother.

~M. M. English
Chicken Soup for the Mother & Daughter Soul

The Bike Trip

My mother's life was one huge story, and a major chapter was "the bike trip." In 1956, my mother, June, rode a three-speed Schwinn from New York City to California, not because she wanted to be a wild girl, not because she wanted to prove anything, but because she wanted to see the Pacific Ocean.

As a child, I'd sit on my mother's lap and say, "Tell me the stories."

And she'd start with the beginning: about how she couldn't afford a plane ticket or a train ticket to see the country, so she decided to ride her bike. About her girlfriends thinking she was crazy; girls didn't do those things; it was unsafe. About convincing a Girl Scouting friend, Teri Foster, to ride across with her. "We didn't really think we'd do it, riding bicycles across the country! But then Schwinn sponsored us, and then the Today Show heard about us, and then we had to. It was a lark, really, something to make my friends laugh, and now here we were, two girls on bicycles wanting to ride to California."

"What did you have to pack?" I said, leaning back into her.

"I didn't know what I'd need, so I brought along a little of everything." And she'd describe how she packed a bathing suit, cocktail dress, high heels, pearls, some shorts and shirts, red lipstick and a Bible. "A bathing suit for hot days, an old wool sweater for cold and always my saddle shoes because they were the best. They held up in the heat, stayed warm in the rain and still looked nice at the end of the day."

She still has them.

"But why'd you bring a cocktail dress and high heels?" I asked, and this would always make her laugh, make her pull out red lipstick from her shirt pocket and smear it on her lips.

"Back then, you couldn't go out to eat in shorts or sandals. You dressed for dinner, and we were invited out quite often. By cowboys, businessmen, but usually preachers from the local churches. We were celebrities."

There was no talk about fear or worries about the unknown. She simply got on her bike and rode. She didn't have an itinerary, no specific route, other than pointing her bike west and riding.

"They didn't have motel chains back then, so we just asked farmers or preachers, mayors or policemen if we could sleep in city parks, front yards or barns." The towns they passed through called them "celebrity girl cyclists" and they were given keys to cities, parades and new tires. "Sometimes we got to sleep in an extra bedroom of a kind person, but usually we requested camping under the stars. We had our sleeping bags and always made a campfire. We invited anyone who passed by to sing Girl Scout songs with us."

She sang in hoedowns in Colorado, and was a chambermaid in the Grand Canyon "when money got low. I didn't have a credit card, and there were no ATMs back then for money." And she talked about the West being some place dyed in red and rock, with sunsets that held the sky.

My favorite part was watching her face when she talked about California. "We finally got there; we were set up on blind dates. Guess who my date ended up being?" she'd always ask, and I'd always answer loudly, "Dad!" They were married three months later.

I came along six years after that.

And always, I craved being inside her stories. I wished to run my fingers over the edges of the Rockies, along the glowing yellow fields of Iowa, wished to splash inside the ponds of New England under stars. I wanted to touch her life, know her inside this special place she called her "adventure of a lifetime."

As I grew older, I stopped sitting on my mother's lap, listening to the old stories of her three-speed, her bicycle bell, the steak and

Manhattan dinners in her cocktail dress, that ride across the country. I had other things on my mind, places to go, people to see and didn't have time to listen to her past. I moved away from home after college and traveled in my Chevy Malibu, this lime green dream of a car that held six and went fast, always on the highway. I had my life, or so I thought, until trips back home were filled with worries: Dad with another stroke, Mom counting her blood pressure pills, organizing doctor visits and falling asleep in her old rocking chair, the one that held us together when I was a child. I'd go into the garage where her dusty bike leaned and ring its rusty bell, the old flag still hung lopsided from the handlebars.

On one trip, I found her journal, and I sat with the deteriorating pages, closing my eyes after reading her descriptions of sunsets, early morning hill climbs, cowboys wrangling broncos, aspen trees in fall, how she rode each hill with a friend in mind. And I became her journey. I was the celebrity girl cyclist in her words. I held that journal tightly in my hands and decided then that I needed to go. I would ride my bike across the country.

But no one wanted to go. Friends, coworkers, cousins shook their heads at me, called me loony. "Take a car!" "You'll be run off the road!" "Why do you want to waste time doing that?" they said. It took me three years to find someone to go with me. I met Brian at my brother's house, this man with curly hair and green eyes who played a guitar and had a dream to ride across the country on a bicycle. When I found out he knew bike maintenance, we had to get married. We started our life together making plans not for children but for bike routes, bike gears, tires and high-performance Lycra. It was all so very romantic.

In 1996, Brian and I started off on our trip, packed for fifty-five days of riding on 24-speed Schwinns. We'd trained for months up mountains in Utah, up and down elevations that would leave us spent and excited at the same time. We didn't know if we'd have our jobs when we got back from the trip, we had nothing saved in the bank, we had mortgage and college loans to pay for, but it didn't matter. We had credit cards. We were ready to go.

Mom was there for the first day of our trip. Of course she had comments.

"Why are you wearing all that rubber stuff?" Mom asked. "I didn't wear that when I went." We were standing in Rockefeller Plaza after our appearance on the Today Show with Bryant Gumbel, for our send-off. People walked past us in suits and heels, staring at us in bike shorts and helmets. Mom was coiffed like I'd never seen her before, her usual green eyeshadow and red lipstick replaced by sculpted pink cheeks and lined eyes, hair blown up and over her forehead.

"I told you before Mom. It wicks the sweat away. It's Lycra."

"So wear your bathing suit. I did."

"I don't want to wear a bathing suit."

"You're going to fall off your bike with those shoes."

"They click on and off. I've practiced."

"They frighten me."

"Lots of things frighten you."

"Like now. This," she waved her hand around at the bustling city of New York. "The world has changed from when I went."

"We'll be careful," I said. "We're staying in motels every night."

"I camped. Why aren't you camping? Just ask a nice policeman to guard you in a city park."

We stared at each other, her lined face to my expectant one, and then we laughed with her holding the handlebars. The day was like us, brilliant blue and then blown clouds, and I see how love can be between mother and daughter—this confusing place between rain and sun that often goes unnoticed until it's there in your face.

"I love you," I said, hoping she didn't think that I was canceling out her comments.

"I love you more."

"I'll call you."

"Every night." Her eyes were hard, and I knew then as I know now that she sits by the phone sometimes waiting for me to call.

"Absolutely."

And we were off, in a blaze of tears and blessings and thrown rice from a passerby as if it were a honeymoon we were going on instead of a cross-country ride.

As we rode, there were times when I wanted to give up: in the humidity of the East, my eyes covered in sweat; when the wind in Nebraska blew me straight across the road; through food poisoning and 130-mile days; a blizzard in Colorado and men throwing empty beer bottles against our bike frames. But I didn't. I'd see her face, fragility balanced out with spunk and spice, and keep pedaling on. I couldn't give up or give in because I was her girl; I'd heard the bike trip stories so many times that they were inside my veins, running in and out of my heart, these stories a heartbeat that pounded me over the Poconos, across the fields and plains, up the Rockies, the Sierra Nevadas to the Pacific Ocean. These stories were whispered urgings, prayers uttered in my mother's name to finish, keep at it. I could do it, and would do it.

San Francisco Bay was beautiful on our last leg of the trip, sailboats careening past the bridges, the city in the haze of an indigo sky. The fact that my mother was singing "She'll be comin' round the mountain" at the top of her lungs did not deter us as we dipped tires into the Pacific Ocean. As Brian went up to the boardwalk to drink celebratory wine, Mom and I stared out past the breakers to the sun dipping toward the sea.

"It's all just beginning, isn't it?" she asked. And I didn't know if she was talking about my life or our lives together, this new shared story of time. I didn't want to ask because to me, it didn't matter.

"We did it," I said.

"We sure did." And I knew she was talking about us, mother and daughter. I realized that life is not about accomplishing or finishing but experiencing moments like these and holding them close — my mother's hand in mine, her long gaze over my face as if wanting to memorize me, and the waves rolling over us and up the beach, leaving our feet covered in sand.

I hope my six-year-old daughter finds a road. It might not be along her grandmother's route of 1956. It could take her away from the back roads Brian and I took in 1996, and in fact, maybe she will want her own path apart from ours. But the important thing is the journey, the adventure, a favorite story you want to repeat aloud at night over and over again until it threads itself, a colorful quilt of love, around her heart.

~Peggy Newland
Chicken Soup for Every Mom's Soul

Roses for Tara

A mother's treasure is her daughter.
~Catherine Pulsifer

I t was a simple, two-page application, but I knew it could change my life forever. Name: Tara Steele. Birth Date: October 1, 1978. Place of Birth: North Vancouver, B.C.

Ever since I could remember, I'd always known I was adopted. But now that I was an adult, Canadian law said I could register to have my records opened and maybe find my birth mom.

Does she look like me? Would she even want to meet me? I wondered, as I sat on my bed proofreading every line. Then I folded the form and tucked it away in my purse... for the next five months I carried it around, wondering if I'd ever have the nerve to mail it.

• • •

We were only seventeen and still in high school. My boyfriend, Fred, and I were too young to raise a child. We could never give a baby the life she deserved, but I still cried the day my mom and I went to the adoption agency and a caseworker showed us pictures and bios of four prospective couples.

The moment I read the third bio, I knew they were the ones. They were both teachers, and they'd already adopted a little boy.

"Maybe my baby won't feel so different with a brother who was also adopted," I said. As my mom and I were leaving, the caseworker acciden-

tally let slip their name, "Steele," so I always knew at least that much about the baby girl I called Natalie Rose.

"I'll always love you," I whispered the day the social worker took her away, and every night I prayed that God would give my baby all the happiness life could offer.

● ● ●

My mom and dad split up when I was four, but my brother, Regan, and I always knew they loved us. After all, they'd picked us out special. But there was a part of me that never stopped wondering about my birth parents. Where did they live? What did they look like? Did I have any brothers or sisters?

Everywhere I went, I studied total strangers, wondering if they could be the ones. "What if I met them somewhere and didn't even know it?" I asked my mom. On my sixteenth birthday she gave me a letter the social worker had passed along when she carried me home from the hospital.

"We brought you into this world out of love. Please keep me in your heart," I read, my eyes brimming with tears.

"I bet she's thinking about you this very minute," Mom said.

● ● ●

Every year on her birthday, I bought roses for my Natalie Rose and cried listening to Joni Mitchell sing about the baby she'd given up for adoption.

It broke my heart whenever I went to the mall and saw moms and daughters shopping together. Fred and I broke up before the baby was born and never saw one another again. I later married a different man and had a wonderful son named Christopher. But Natalie Rose was never out of my thoughts.

When Christopher was twelve, I told him he had a half-sister somewhere. "Can we go find her?" he asked, excitedly.

But I said no. "We have to wait till she's ready and hope she wants to find us," I explained, knowing there was a chance my daughter might hate me for what I'd done and never want anything to do with me.

My sister Dawn was also eager to find the niece she'd never known. "You have to register with the agency so if she wants to find you she can," she insisted. But Dawn did more than just rally me on—she became the instrument God used to fill the gaping hole in my heart.

• • •

After I graduated from high school, I moved from Burns Lake—a small northern British Columbia town—to North Vancouver to live with my dad and try to break into movie production work. I carried that application in my purse. I had it with me when I went to my job at the costume shop, visited friends or swam at the rec center pool with Dad and my half-siblings, Brendan and Michaela, from his second marriage.

And then one day Dad went swimming alone, and when he came home he pounded on my bedroom door. "Tara! Come quick! I have something incredible to tell you!"

• • •

Dawn works at the rec center, and she always noticed Charles Steele because she knew that was the surname of my baby's adoptive parents. "He has a son and a daughter, but she's too young," she told me once, but then one day Charles brought another daughter with him... Dawn took one look at her and knew.

"She's just the right age, and I'd recognize those strong hands anywhere," my sister called to tell me. "They're your hands, Theresa. I think I found your daughter."

"No, it's too incredible," I said, refusing to get my hopes up only to have them dashed.

Dawn waited until a day when Charles came alone to the rec center, then cautiously asked, "By chance, do you have an adopted daughter?"

"Yes, her name is Tara," Charles replied, and when he said her birthday was October first, Dawn knew for sure.

•••

I hugged my dad, then grabbed the phone to call my mom. "I found my birth mom!" I sobbed in near hysterics.

Mom was thrilled for me because she already knew something I was just now learning for myself—that there was a giant piece of me that had been missing all my life. I hadn't kept that application in my purse so long because I was nervous about meeting my birth mom. I'd kept it because I was terrified it might not help and then I'd never, ever find her.

•••

Dawn arranged for Tara to call me, and as I paced the floor I didn't know what to expect. A lifetime of questions were about to be answered, and I felt overwhelmed with joy, wonder and worry.

I'm not ready for this, I panicked, and just then the phone rang. I don't even remember what Theresa and I talked about that first night. All I remember is the sound of her voice.

"It's the voice that's been ringing inside my head my whole life," I told my mom later. "She's everything I always imagined."

Tara has my eyes and her father's nose. "You're beautiful," I sighed the day we met and fell into one another's arms. And later when I met Charles and Sharon, Tara's mom and dad, I knew I'd made the right decision all those years ago. "You've given her the life I never could have and raised a beautiful daughter," I said.

I tracked down Fred and told him about Dawn's miracle. He told me he'd been looking for her on the Internet, and when Sharon met Tara's birth dad she touched his chin and laughed, "Now I know where she got her dimples."

Theresa lives about an hour and a half from North Vancouver, and every time we get together we learn about even more things we share in common. We walk alike and gesture alike. We both love camping and swimming and bike-riding.

I loved meeting all my new uncles and aunts, my half-brother Christopher and my cousins. I couldn't wait for my twenty-second birthday when we threw a big party and everybody was there.

"I finally get to give you these in person," Theresa wept, handing me a big bouquet of roses.

Natalie Rose. I think it's such a beautiful name. Maybe one day, if I have a daughter of my own, that's what I'll name her, too.

~Tara Steele as told to Heather Black
Chicken Soup for the Christian Teenage Soul

Princess

Within your heart, keep one still, secret spot where dreams may go.
~Louise Driscoll

The dress hides far in the back of the closet, behind years of accumulated plastic-sheathed memories. Carefully, I pull it from the dark recesses, past layers of archived prom dresses, granny gowns and jean jackets that mark a fabric trail of my increasingly distant and often troubled youth. As the dress faces the morning light for the first time in many years, tiny sparkles wink at me through the dusty garment bag hiding its loveliness. Removing it from its transparent covering and holding it to my cheek, I smell its fragrance and the musty perfume of the past.

My mother bought the dress more than forty years ago for a cocktail party at the general's house. As the wife of an army captain, she experienced alternating pangs of excitement and worry at the extravagant purchase. The dress hung for many days, weighed down by assorted tags, while she fought a silent battle with herself. The precarious balance between womanly desire and financial practicality shifted in favor of one position, then the other.

Self-absorbed like most ten-year-olds, I didn't understand my mother's budget dilemma. I knew only that something black and wonderful had entered her closet and hung in solitary splendor amidst the flowered housecoats and practical day dresses.

I don't think she actually decided to keep the dress until the day of the party. When I crept into her room late that afternoon, the offending tags finally lay discarded in the trash. My mom hummed happily from behind the closed bathroom door. Eager with anticipation, I slipped back out the door.

After what seemed like hours, my mother's voice beckoned me into her room. What I saw when I bounced through the doorway took my breath away! My sensible mother, who made me eat my vegetables, ironed my father's shirts instead of sending them out, drove me to Brownie meetings, and baked chocolate chip cookies, was transformed into an elegant beauty clad in a soft ebony cloud.

"What do you think?" she asked as she turned slowly in front of the mirror.

I stood mute in wide-eyed wonder and then reverently delivered the highest compliment I could think to give. "You look like a princess."

And she did.

The dress tightly enclosed her slim waist, then flared out in a bell-shaped skirt. The black taffeta underskirt rustled as she twirled, and lamplight bounced off silver and blue confetti-sized sparkles strewn over the black organza overskirt. The dress shimmered like stardust scattered by a fairy godmother. It was a dress fit for a princess, and that night, in my eyes, my mother ruled the kingdom.

Years later when my mother and I found the dress in the back of her closet smothered with layers of her past, she told me that the night of the general's party was one of the most memorable nights of her life. Not because of the dress, but because of the admiration she saw in my ten-year-old eyes and the compliment I had given her. Then she repeated the words I had said more than three decades ago as she had stood regally before her mirror dressed in stardust and midnight.

I wanted to cry. Not tears of joy for the poignancy of the moment, but tears of sadness for the many years lost to us because of the complexities of adolescence. Because that special year, the year I discovered a princess in my mother's lamp-lit bedroom, was the last year of my childhood when we fit together snugly and comfortably like two interlocking pieces of a puzzle.

In the intervening years between that long ago moment of love and our reminiscing, the bond forged between my mother and me in my early childhood was sorely tested. During my rebellious teens and early twenties, she saw little in my eyes but anger and heard little in my voice but recriminations.

Though as adults my mother and I slowly built a strong relationship, I longed to take back those hurtful years of my youth and replace them with memories of love and kindness. But I couldn't. I couldn't change the past any more than I could iron out the wrinkles etched deep in her face or restore to her the vitality of her youth. I could only stand beside my beautiful seventy-year-old mother and whisper, "I love you, Mom."

And she could only smile and reply, "I've always known that."

As I stand in my bedroom smelling the past from deep within the folds of my mother's dress, I am thankful I have it to remind me of the strength of a mother's love and the power of a moment. But I am most thankful my mother and I still have time to build enduring memories that will sweeten the past with their musty perfume.

~Kristy Ross
Chicken Soup for Every Mom's Soul

The Little White Chapel

Miracles happen to those who believe in them.

~*Bernard Berenson*

I love to go on road trips. It doesn't matter where.

One Sunday afternoon, my best friend Evelyn and I decided to drive from our hometown of Phoenix, Arizona, to a gem and mineral show a couple of hours away. Evelyn was excited about expanding her rock collection. I was just thrilled to be heading out on a new adventure.

After a while, we turned onto a deserted stretch of highway and passed a large white sign on the side of the road. It stated simply: Pause, Rest and Worship.

"What's that?" Evelyn asked. It was strange to see a sign like that in the middle of nowhere. What did it mean?

About a quarter mile down the road, we spotted a small white chapel sitting by itself in a field. As we drove past, we wondered: Who would build this tiny church out here— and why? We turned the truck around to find out.

As we started down the dusty trail and got closer, we noticed how small it really was. It wasn't much bigger than a playhouse, maybe eight feet across and twelve feet deep. There were little flowers planted around the outside and a little white cross was perched on top. There wasn't a sign or any literature telling us what it was called or describing its history. Was it in fact a church? Were we on private property? Should we be here? Would it be all right if we went inside?

Cautiously, we got out, looked around and walked toward the chapel's tiny door. It was open. We stepped inside.

There were four wooden pews, each would seat two people. I sat down. As I admired the simplicity and the beauty of the little chapel, I beheld its beautiful stained glass windows. A sense of profound calm came over me. All was quiet. Still. Peace.

I noticed a plaque hanging on the front wall. I got up and walked toward it. It was from the man who had built the chapel.

This was his farm. He had built this chapel to celebrate all of the many blessings that God had given him in his life. He had lived a very long and happy life, blessed with a wonderful wife, many healthy children and a farm where he had worked and lived.

On the altar at the front of the chapel lay a guest book with its pages open. Written at the top was a note: "Rest, pray, enjoy the chapel. Stay as long as you like."

As I turned the pages, I noticed the countries: Japan, Israel, France, Brazil... people from all over the world had found their way to this little white chapel.

I looked around for a place to leave a donation. There wasn't one. This man just wanted to share his special place with strangers who might need a brief respite on their long journey.

It has now been two years since my visit to the little chapel, and this is my first Christmas without my mother. I lost her last year to heart failure. We were very close and I miss her so very much.

As I was out shopping for presents, I suddenly stopped and the reality sunk in. Mom wasn't going to be here to get her present this year. She wasn't going to help me cook the turkey. She wasn't going to look across the table and smile at me as if to say everything would be all right.

I wanted to see her face when she opened up her gift. I wanted to cook with her and receive her warm smile. For the first time, I would spend this holiday without my mother, and it would be that way for the rest of my life. I was feeling very alone and wasn't sure how I was going to make it through the season.

At that moment, I looked up and right in front of me, on a display table, stood a small white ceramic chapel.

Immediately, I was taken back to my little white chapel in the dusty desert. Once again, I could feel the peace of its refuge, the strength of its love. I recalled the man who had built it out of gratitude for life's blessings, and then I remembered my own life's blessings. Suddenly, I felt myself smiling my mother's smile, and like the little chapel, I know that she, too, would always be there with me on my journey through life.

~Dawn Rambin
Chicken Soup for the Traveler's Soul

I Love You More

Meet my daughter, Amanda. Four years old and a fountain of knowledge. The other day she was reciting a list of all the facts and tidbits she has memorized. "One plus one is two. If you mix yellow paint with blue you get green. Penguins can't fly…." On and on she went.

Finally, she finished. "Mom," she said, looking very smug, "I know everything."

I acted as if I believed her, but chuckled to myself thinking of all the this-and-thats that a four-year-old child couldn't possibly know. Comparing her four years to my almost three decades of life experiences, I felt sure I knew what she knew and then some.

Within a week, I would learn I was wrong.

It all began as we were standing in front of the bathroom mirror while I fixed Amanda's fine blonde hair. I was putting the final elastic on a spunky pair of ponytails and finished with, "I love you, Amanda."

"And, I love you," she replied.

"Oh, yeah," I taunted, "well I love you more."

Her eyes lit up as she recognized the cue for the start of another "I love you more" match. "Nuh-uh," she laughed, "I love you the most."

"I love you bigger than a volcano!" I countered—a favorite family phrase in these battles of love.

"But, Mom, I love you from here to China." A country she's learning about thanks to our new neighbors up the street.

We volleyed a few favorite lines. "I love you more than peanut butter.... Well, I love you more than television.... I even love you more than bubble gum."

It was my turn again, and I made the move that usually brings victory. "Too bad, chickadee. I love you bigger than the universe!" On this day, however, Amanda was not going to give up. I could see she was thinking.

"Mom," she said in a quiet voice, "I love you more than myself."

I stopped. Dumbfounded. Overwhelmed by her sincerity.

Here I thought that I knew more than she did. I thought I knew at least everything that she knew. But I didn't know this.

My four-year-old daughter knows more about love than her twenty-eight-year-old mom. And somehow she loves me more than herself.

~Christie A. Hansen
Chicken Soup for the Soul Celebrates Mothers

Stranded on an Island

The two most important things a parent can give a child are roots and wings.
~Hodding Carter

hen she was little she clung to me and said, "You're my best friend in the whole wide world."

She used to cry when I went away, for a night, for a weekend. "Why can't you take me?" she would ask.

And I would explain, "Because this party is for grown-ups. Because this is a business trip. Because you'd be bored."

"No, I wouldn't, Mommy. I'd never be bored around you."

Such absolute, unconditional love.

"Someday you'll go away and leave me," I would tell her. "You'll spend a night at a friend's, and then maybe a weekend and pretty soon you'll be going off for weeks at a time and before you know it you'll be traveling all over the world and then you'll move to Japan and you won't miss me at all."

"I'd never move to Japan without you," she would say, laughing. The idea of growing up and living in Japan always chased away her tears. It was something said offhandedly to divert sorrow, but it became a tradition. Whenever she would grumble about my leaving, I would tease her about her leaving me to go to Japan.

She's only fourteen now, and she hasn't left yet. Not physically, anyway. But mentally she's prepared to go, though she doesn't know it and I didn't know it either until the other day.

She came home from school with a homework assignment: Choose six people, dead or alive, real or fictional, with whom you would choose to be stuck on a deserted island. Her English class had just finished reading Lord of the Flies, a story about a group of stranded children on just such an island.

I never thought for a minute that I wouldn't make the list. It didn't cross my mind. Didn't she say I was her best friend in the whole world? Didn't she know I would love her and take care of her better than anyone ever could?

And yet that night, when she recited the names of the people she would take, there was no mention of me. There was the fictional Mafatu, a boy from Call It Courage who had survived life on an abandoned island. "He would know what to do," she said. "I'd take him because he's been through this before." And there was Mary Poppins, "because she's nice and magical and could whisk us to places off the island if we got bored," she said.

And she chose her brother, Robbie, "because I love him, and he'd know how to make a boat," and John McLean, her godfather, "because he knows how to fix everything," and TV character Doogie Howser, "because he's a doctor and young and won't die soon," and Anne of Green Gables "because she's smart and imaginative and funny."

"But what about me? I can be smart and imaginative and funny, too," I said.

"Anne of Green Gables is young and can have babies, Mom. She's more useful."

I'm old, and I'm not useful. That's what she was trying to say. I immediately began to sulk.

"You're not serious, Mom, are you? This isn't real, you know. I'm not going to live on an island. I'm not going anywhere."

"Oh, yes you are," I wanted to say. "You just don't know it yet."

I moped around for a while, a little in jest but a little in earnest, too. I understood why she didn't choose me. It wouldn't have been a wise choice. What do I know about survival? I consider it a crisis when the electricity goes out during a storm. Her selections were all sensible.

The thing is, I would have chosen her. I wouldn't have been

sensible. I wouldn't have thought about what each person could contribute. I would have thought only about who I would most like to be with.

"If I could have picked only one person, Mom, I would have picked you," she reassured me the next day. But that's only because when she asked me to make her a grilled cheese sandwich, I suggested that Anne of Green Gables make it, and when she said she needed a ride to the mall, I hinted that Mary Poppins should take her.

"You know, Mom, you're being very immature," she told me.

I know I am. Very immature. But that's because our roles have suddenly reversed. The little girl who clung to me and called me her best friend clings no more. Instead I am the one watching her move on and asking, "Why can't you take me?"

~Beverly Beckham
Chicken Soup for the Mother's Soul 2

Like Mother, Like Daughter

Mutual Support

Sweater, n.: garment worn by child when its mother is feeling chilly.
~Ambrose Bierce

The Birth of Daughters

I am finally and victoriously pregnant after seven years of marriage. I am also absurdly worried about what my mother will think. I've recently gone back to school for a master's degree. My husband is not quite finished with a Ph.D. program. I feel as if we're being a little reckless, as if we have no business even thinking about a child, let alone strategically planning the optimal conditions to make one.

So I nervously rehearse the "big news." My worst fear is a raised eyebrow asking, "And just how do you think you're going to raise this child on a student's income?" Asking, in fact, the very question that I'm nervously asking myself—What are you? Crazy?!

I end up telling my parents by inviting them to Thanksgiving dinner even though it's only Easter. "Well, it's a little far ahead to make plans..." my dad says. I tell him I already know what I'll be doing—getting ready to deliver his first grandkid. He looks surprised, but definitely not elated.

My stomach starts to sink.

I think I wince as I look to my mother for her response. It's my turn to be surprised. She rockets off the couch, doing a little victory dance, exclaiming, "I knew it! I knew you were pregnant! I'll be right back!"

And she runs off upstairs. She returns with a little gift bag. "Here!" she says, thrusting it at me, "Presents for the baby! I just knew you were pregnant! I was wondering when you'd tell us. I've had this stuff for over a month."

I've only known for a month myself.

I admit to my mom that I was expecting a lecture from her regarding our financial situation. I can tell that the thought has never even crossed her mind. I hear the words, "Oh, don't worry about the money. Everything will work out just fine."

Now I find out we are not expecting a baby. We're expecting two. It took a while to sink in. This time, my mother, a twin herself, is the first person I called. From that moment on, she's my constant pregnancy companion.

Looking back, I'm embarrassed by my ignorance, but I guess I thought maybe she'd pat me on the head, tell me to eat saltines when I felt like barfing, and send me some flowers in the hospital.

Instead she acts like she's just won the lottery. She tells everyone who will listen that she's going to be a grandmother of twins. She buys me maternity clothes. She "picks up" things for the babies. ("Hi, honey, I just bought a couple of wardrobes for your embryos.") She sends me cards.

She calls me regularly.

I go into labor early and unexpectedly. Mom sounds nervous but thrilled.

I wish she could be with us, but we're hundreds of miles apart.

About six hours later, the nurse tells me I have a visitor in the waiting room. In walks Mom. I actually think that fatigue and pain are making me see things.

"How did you get here?" I ask incredulously. I know she can't possibly have driven—there hasn't been enough time.

"I flew, and then I took a taxi," she tells me matter-of-factly, as if this is the kind of thing she does on a daily basis. She, like me, hates to fly, probably even more than she hates to drive. "Did you think I'd miss this for the world?" she asks me.

"All I know is I really wanted you to be here."

"I know that, honey, that's why I came."

When she sees her tiny, squalling granddaughters for the first time, she makes it as far as my husband. She hugs him and starts to cry. It's as if she'll never stop. And I know her tears are tears of deep relief. I know they are tears of intense joy and intense love. I know they are the tears that a mother cries for a child. I know it because I can taste it in the salt of my own tears.

I offer her up two tiny bodies and feel the ties that connect us bind tightly as she takes her granddaughters into her arms for the first time.

"There are some things you'll never understand until you have kids. You'll see," she has always told me. And sitting there in that hospital bed, totally exhausted and emotionally raw, seeing my mother holding my two impossibly light brand-new daughters, I think I do see. I see that becoming a mother has not only given me the gift of loving a child with an intensity that I never knew existed, but also the gift of my own mother — and the sudden realization that I am, and have been all my life, loved the same way.

May the circle be unbroken.

~Karen C. Driscoll
Chicken Soup for the Mother & Daughter Soul

Pennies from Heaven

You never will finish being a daughter.
~ Gail Godwin

My friend Jill and her mom had a very close relationship. Of the many things they enjoyed together, they often talked about Jill's wedding day and what it would be like to plan together. But losing a battle with cancer would keep Jill's mom from ever seeing her daughter get married. Her death was devastating.

A few years later, Jill got engaged and began to plan her wedding. Every nuptial detail brought mixed emotions during this bittersweet time. Yet, despite her loss, Jill amazed me with her strength and faith.

Soon after her mom's death, a peculiar thing began happening. Jill would find pennies at odd times in familiar places.

Sometimes she would go to shops and restaurants where she and her mom had spent time together. Miraculously, she'd find a bright, shiny penny. Occasionally she'd leave a room only to come back and find one right in the middle of the floor, knowing it wasn't there earlier. In the midst of stressful situations or struggles with her grief, a penny would pop up.

Jill believed they were signs from her mom.

"They're her way of letting me know she'll always be with me. They're my 'pennies from heaven.'"

On the day of the wedding, the bride, her other attendants and I went to Jill's favorite salon to get our hair done. The stylist did Jill's hair first, creating an elegant "up-do" with her blond locks. The rest of us followed, taking turns in the stylists' chairs. The morning was pleasant, with lots of laughter, smiles and even a few tears of love and happiness.

While Jill was in another room getting her makeup done, the stylists softly asked how she was holding up, knowing it was an emotional day.

"She's doing great," I said, "thanks to her 'pennies from heaven.'"

The two stylists looked perplexed, so I explained the phenomenon.

Astonished, one replied, "You're not going to believe this. But when we opened the shop this morning, there was a single, shiny penny in the middle of the floor. I know it wasn't there when we closed up the night before."

He directed us to the corner where he had swept the untouched penny. As he placed the polished copper coin in my hand, we stared at each other. All of us decided we would plan a special moment to present this token to Jill.

After the wedding reception, we anxiously waited for all the guests to leave.

"Close your eyes and stretch out your hand," I nervously asked. Grinning from ear to ear and with goose bumps tracing my spine, I gently placed the symbolic coin in Jill's palm.

She opened her eyes and stared in amazement.

While we explained where we found the penny, tears welled in her eyes. Jill squeezed the comforting coin and brought it close to her heart. Then she smiled and opened her hand again to admire her wedding memento.

"She's been here all day, hasn't she?" I fondly asked my friend.

With remarkable calm, Jill answered, "Yes, Mom didn't miss a thing."

~Holly Jensen Hughes
Chicken Soup for the Bride's Soul

Mothers and Daughters

A mother understands what a child does not say.
~Jewish Proverb

"You won't forget to bring the potato masher, will you?" I said to my mother on the phone after telling her I had to have a mastectomy. Even at eighty-two, and three thousand miles away on the long distance line, she knew what I meant: soupy mashed potatoes.

This was what she had made for every illness or mishap of my childhood—served in a soup bowl with a nice round spoon. But I had been lucky as a child and was rarely sick. Most often the potato medicine soothed disappointment or nourished a mild cold. This time I was seriously ill.

Arriving on the midnight plane from Virginia, Mom looked fresh as a daisy when she walked through the front door of my house in California the day after I came home from the hospital. I could barely keep my eyes open, but the last thing I saw before I fell asleep was Mom unzipping her carefully packed suitcase and taking out her sixty-year-old potato masher. The one she received as a shower gift, the one with the worn wooden handle and the years of memories.

She was mashing potatoes in my kitchen the day I told her tearfully that I would have to undergo chemotherapy. She put the masher down and looked me squarely in the eye. "I'll stay with you, however long it takes," she told me. "There is nothing more important I have to do in my life than help you get well." I had always thought I was the stubborn one in my family, but in the five months that followed I saw that I came by my trait honestly.

Mom had decided that I would not predecease her. She simply would not have it. She took me on daily walks even when I couldn't get any farther than our driveway. She crushed the pills I had to take and put them in jam, because even in middle age, with a grown daughter of my own, I couldn't swallow pills any better than when I was a child.

When my hair started to fall out, she bought me cute hats. She gave me warm ginger ale in a crystal wineglass to calm my tummy and sat up with me on sleepless nights. She served me tea in china cups.

When I was down, she was up. When she was down, I must have been asleep. She never let me see it. And, in the end, I got well. I went back to my writing.

I have discovered that Mother's Day doesn't happen some Sunday in May, but on every day you are lucky enough to have a mother around to love you.

~Patricia Bunin
Chicken Soup for the Mother's Soul 2

Cellular Love

A daughter is the happy memories of the past, the joyful moments of the present, and the hope and promise of the future.
~Author Unknown

My mother called tonight while I was cooking dinner. Again, for the third time today. I knew it was her because the words "Mom's cell" lit up my own cell phone like a marquee on Times Square. I lay down my cutting knife and shook the pieces of onion and red pepper from my hands. Mom with a cell phone; boy, have things changed!

There was a time in my life, B.C. (Before Cell phones), when my mother would become anxious, depressed or even mildly hysterical if she couldn't reach me by phone. No matter that I worked full-time and ran a marathon life shuttling kids, groceries and the dog from one end of town to the other. If she called the house, and I didn't answer, something had to be wrong.

"Where are you? I've tried a hundred times but you don't answer. Is anybody there?" were the plaintive words I'd find on my answering machine after returning home from a long day at work. If my mother got lucky, she'd reach my daughter and tell her to leave me a message, which I'd usually find about a week later, written in crayon on the back of the phone bill. "Call Gramma. She wants to know if you still live here."

I move about the kitchen banging pots, the cell phone balanced precariously between my cheek and raised left shoulder. I make a mental note to cancel the chiropractic appointment I made for neck pain and resolve to buy a headset instead.

I toss the salad as my mother shares the events of her day: a doctor's appointment for my father who can't see as well as he thinks but she lets him drive anyway, lunch with a friend whose husband has Alzheimer's disease, and an exercise class for osteoporosis even though she's sure the teacher has shrunk two inches since she began taking the class. It doesn't really matter what we talk about. What matters most is the invisible line of connection we create in spite of the time and distance between us.

A friend is dying of cancer, and my mother wants to know if she should visit her or wait to be asked.

"You should go," I tell her.

What about Eleanor's husband, the one with Alzheimer's. Should she invite them to dinner or would it be too hard?

"For whom?" I ask.

At seventy-eight, my mother now lives in a country whose borders are defined by mountains of fear. Its landscape is restricted by age, illness and the loss of much of what and whom she has cherished and known. The roads she traveled on so easily in her youth have become more treacherous as she loses confidence in her ability to navigate through the world we live in today. Yet she faces these obstacles with a will of iron, determined to fill her life with meaning and purpose. At times, this translates into trying to control a part of mine.

"Did you use that Silver Palate spaghetti sauce recipe I sent you? It has all the essential vitamins and lots of black olives, which are good for your system," she counsels.

"Oh, yeah, it was great!" I fib as I stir a jar of store bought marinara sauce into the pasta. When I was a new wife and mother, this type of domestic micromanaging drove me crazy. Now I'm just grateful that someone is still worried about my vitamin intake and regularity.

"I'm sending you some articles about skin care. I think you should do something about those little brown spots on your face," she says with the authority of a dermatologist.

I look in the mirror and notice a blotch of spaghetti sauce on my chin.

When I left for college, I didn't realize that my departure would trigger an emotional spiral downward that took my mother months to overcome. She began marking her life by the events that occurred in mine: the afternoon I graduated from law school, the evening of my wedding, the morning my son was born. She needed so much more assurance once I was gone, and sharing the everyday events in our lives was the salve that soothed her loneliness. If I was preoccupied or too tired to talk, I would simply listen to her stories while I folded clothes or packed school lunches for the kids.

An outsider listening to our conversations might think them trivial, but in reality, they are the bedrock upon which our deeper and more profound understandings occur. I hear in her words the true concern she has about my father's failing eyesight and her fear that many of her lifelong friends will soon be gone. I know that underlying her recipes and medical advice is the fear that I'm working too hard or not taking care of myself. In discussing the more banal whats, whos and whys of our lives, we open doors to an intimacy we both want from our relationship.

Several years ago, I sent my mother a Mother's Day card that still hangs on her refrigerator door. On the cover, a woman is applying red lipstick in the rearview mirror of her station wagon while driving the kids to school. The caption reads: "Oh my God, I think I've become my mother!" Printed on the inside are the words: "I should only be so lucky."

I hang up just as my husband walks through the door, cell phone falling from my ear like an oversized clip-on earring. He picks it up off the floor as I acknowledge, "My mother just called." Whatever the cost, whenever the time, she has my number. It's called cellular love.

~ Amy Hirshberg Lederman
Chicken Soup for Every Mom's Soul

Growing Up

My mother had been reading me the story of *The Borrowers*, tiny visitors who hid in the nooks and crannies of a house. Captivated, I had set up a tiny dining room under a bookcase with dollhouse furniture. For weeks, I'd left out crumbs and a little bowl of water—the cap of the ketchup bottle—before I went to bed. Each morning before school, I would check to see if the Borrowers had returned. The water and crumbs would be gone. Sometimes there would even be a minuscule thank you note left for me.

At nine, I should probably have been too old to really believe in the Borrowers. And though I suspected that my tiny visitors might be my mother's doing, I still held on to my belief that they just might be real. Then one day I came home from school, and my mother was gone. So were the Borrowers.

"Mommy is very sick," my father said to me, his usually bright blue eyes looking tired and sad. "She's going to be in the hospital for a while until she gets better. Her kidneys aren't working right, and the doctors are going to make her better, but it's going to be a few weeks until you can see her because the doctors need that time to fix everything, okay?"

At first it seemed almost like a holiday. Everyone was especially nice to me; my father made my favorite meals or we would go out to dinner. He would bring home letters from my mother, "Make sure you ask Daddy to help you brush your hair; once the knots start, they are so hard to brush out." My hair, fine and wavy, was prone to tangles.

"Why can't I go and see Mommy?" I would ask him.

But his answer was always the same, "Not yet. She's too weak right now... but soon."

It was difficult to imagine my mother weak. We went swimming together every day in the summer, walking the five or so miles to the community pool and back again. Sometimes we chased each other around the house playing tag until the downstairs neighbors became so aggravated they would bang on the ceiling for us to stop. Then we'd collapse on the floor from laughing so hard, each of us trying in vain to be quiet.

And no matter how busy she was, she always had enough time to sit on the floor and play dolls with me. In her games, my dolls were never just going to parties, they were architects or doctors, or even running for Congress! I was probably the only nine-year-old whose mother introduced her to *Jane Eyre* and *Gone with the Wind*. I would read a bit of the book each day, and we would sit and discuss it over tea and cookies.

"The women in these books are strong, Lisa. They go through very difficult situations and learn that they can take care of themselves," my mother would tell me. She admired the strength in Jane and Scarlett, and she wanted me to value it as well.

But then things had begun to change. More often I would get up in the morning to fix my own breakfast, or come home from school to find a neighbor waiting to bring me to her home after school. Sometimes my parents would be in their bedroom talking with the door closed. The day the Borrowers stopped coming, I knew something was really wrong.

With my mother gone, I noticed that my father rarely went into my parents' bedroom anymore. I'd sometimes get up in the middle of night and find him lying asleep on the couch in the flickering light of the television, still in his work clothes. Pulling the blanket up over him and turning off the TV, I was a girl who was growing up. A girl who no longer believed in the Borrowers.

"Daddy?" I asked my father one day, "Is Mommy going to die?" He looked at me for what seemed forever, then grabbed my arms and pulled me to him. "Maybe," he said and then lowered his head and began to weep. I wrapped my arms around his neck and held him close. We sat there and cried, for the first time, together.

Then he told me that my mother had been diagnosed with end-stage renal failure, which meant that her kidneys had failed and that unless she had a kidney transplant, she would probably die. In the early 1970s, dialysis as a treatment for renal failure was in its early stages. My mother was at the County Medical Center where they had access to new medical technology. It had been touch-and-go for several weeks, and at times it appeared as though they might have waited too long to be able to help my mother. I told my father I wanted to see her.

At the hospital, my father shouted at the nurse at the desk in the intensive care unit, "I don't care if it's not allowed."

"It will be too disturbing for the child," the nurse said to my dad in a low voice, motioning for him to lower his voice as well.

My father walked over to me where I was sitting on a bench against the wall. "Listen, Honey, I'm going to go and talk to the chief of staff about you seeing your mommy. Sit here and draw me a picture, and I'll be back in a few minutes, okay?" I nodded my head and watched him walk off down the hall with the nurse.

The large double doors had the words "Only Medical Staff Allowed" written on them in large bold letters. A sign in front of the bench said "Children under fifteen not admitted." The sounds coming from behind the double doors frightened me and the thought that my mother was in there frightened me even more.

But as I sat there, my fear dissolved and I became angrier and angrier. Who were these strangers to keep me away from my mother? Scarlett O'Hara wouldn't have sat by and let people tell her what she could and couldn't do. My mother was behind that door, and I was going to go in and find her.

Putting both hands on one side of the ICU door, I pushed as hard as I could. Inside, bright fluorescent lights illuminated the room, people in white scurried around and loud beeping filled the air. Without knowing how I knew, I turned to my right and started to walk toward a bed where most of the activity was being focused. No one seemed to notice me.

The woman on the bed seemed very small and was surrounded by tubes and machines with blinking lights. She looked like my mother, except paler and smaller than I remembered. Her eyes were closed and her long dark hair was spread out on her pillow.

"She's not responding!" a white-coated man shouted.

"Her pressure is too low," a nurse shouted back to the man in the white coat.

"Mommy," I said quietly, then again louder. "Mommy?"

People started running over to me. "Get her out of here!" bellowed the man in the white coat.

"Wait!" shouted the nurse and motioned for me to come over. As I walked over to my mother, everyone stepped back except for the man in the white coat who tried to grab my shoulder. The nurse standing by the bed put her hand up to stop him.

"Look," she said, glancing down at my mother.

My mother had opened her eyes. "Lisa?" She turned her head to look at me and smiled. The frenetic beeping seemed to slow down.

"Mommy, it's me." I stood next to the bed, wanting to crawl in beside her despite the machines and tubes all around her.

"Come here." She raised her arms, and I let her wrap her arms around me. "Don't be scared by all of this. These machines are going to make me better. We'll have one in our house, and I'll be able to come home to stay." Frowning ever so slightly, she added, "Has anyone been helping you brush your hair?" Laughter from behind me reminded me that we weren't alone. Doctors and nurses were standing around watching us, many with tears in their eyes.

They knew, though I didn't, that only moments ago my mother had actually died. Later she told me that she remembered seeing a young woman lying on a hospital bed connected to tubes and machines. She felt very sorry for the woman until she realized that she was looking at herself and, for the first time in months, she felt no pain or discomfort. In what seemed like a movie, she remembered seeing people rush over to her to try and resuscitate her.

"I felt such peace, such happiness. I didn't want to be that woman on the bed anymore until I heard a girl's voice that said 'Mommy?'"

When she realized that the voice was mine, she knew that she had to come back. I'm sure that if I hadn't violated hospital policy and been there to call her back, things would have turned out very differently.

Soon after, my mother came home, along with a dialysis machine that became a permanent part of our family. And although the Borrowers never returned, I didn't need them anymore. I was a girl who could brush the tangles out of her own hair. I could fix a meal or two without any help. I was a girl who still had her mother. And that was the most important part.

~Lisa Duffy-Korpics
Chicken Soup for the Mother's Soul 2

Running Role Model

She never quite leaves her children at home,
even when she doesn't take them along.
~Margaret Culkin Banning

I admit it—I did it purely for myself. Well, at first I did it because I'd lost a bet. After my best friend completed her ninth Tufts 10K, I bet her that if she would run the Boston Marathon, I, a non-runner, would run Tufts next time. I posed this idle bet because I never thought she'd really do it. Guess what? She did it!

Preparing to make good on my wager, I began my training in earnest, and I quickly fell in love with the solitude, the fresh air and sunshine, the singing birds, and the capabilities of my thirty-eight-year-old body. During those first few runs, however, I couldn't shake feelings of guilt about pursuing self-gratification. Wasn't I supposed to be home taking care of my family?

My guilt peaked when, after one particularly long run, I returned home to soak sore muscles in a leisurely hot bath and left my "off-duty" sign posted a while longer. Lying in my Epsom salts, I heard Melissa, my three-year-old, whimper, "Where's Mommy?" My husband distracted her—while I gritted my teeth and grasped the sides of the tub, torn between the desire for time by myself and the urge to comfort my child. In that moment, I understood that with each run, I needed to train not only my body, but my mind—to allow myself this private time to seek the selfhood I was entitled to! Besides, if I were reenergized, I'd be better able to handle the demands of motherhood.

Indeed, my two daughters quickly adjusted to my long weekend runs. They'd casually acknowledge that I was leaving. "Going running, Mom?" Gina, my eight-year-old, would ask as she watched me lace up my running shoes. "Have a nice run," Melissa would add.

I'd kiss them and leave, and they'd be all smiles, knowing this was a chance for them to be alone in the house, while Dad worked in the garden, one ear on them. (Mother Nature programmed men with far fewer guilt genes, and women are finally taking heed.) Moreover, I think they recognized that I came back from my runs nicer than when I left!

Finally, it was time for my first practice race—a 5K. Off I went with a number pinned to my chest—my heart pounding behind it. My family cheered me on from the sidelines, and when I finished the race, they lunged to hug me, despite my sweaty body.

"Did you win?" asked Melissa. (I couldn't believe she hadn't noticed that four million people crossed the finish line before me.)

"Sorry you didn't win, Mom," said Gina. (She'd noticed!)

"Girls, I finished!" I proudly announced, briefly explaining that this was a personal victory. Yet even in the excitement of my own triumph, I noted with pride that my daughters, at such a young age, accepted as quite natural that women can—and should—be winners. When I was a child, the message I got was that nice girls don't compete.

Months later, I successfully completed the Tufts 10K, and instead of abandoning running with this fulfilled obligation, I surprised myself and continued.

Not too long ago, I ran my third Tufts 10K. Each has been as triumphant as the one before. But that year, the scene was more magical than ever. Melissa, then six, wore a running suit her sister bought her with her own money. Gina, then eleven and nearly my size, wore my commemorative shirt from my first Tufts 10K.

As I ran alongside six thousand other women, I thought of my two most loyal fans—my daughters—awaiting me at the finish line. With them was my adoring husband, who admits he gushes with pride when the starting gun fires and I run past with the pack. And that year, my best friend, sidelined by an aggravated injury, watched the race with my family. No bets necessary: I was running for all of us.

As I approached the finish line, my daughters jumped off the curb and ran to meet me. Holding hands, we raced the final tenth of a mile together.

Afterwards, I stretched my tired legs, wiped my sweaty face and chowed down on snacks. Meanwhile, my daughters animatedly and repeatedly announced that several children, including a seven-year-old, had run the race. I suspected what was coming.

"Can I run with you next year? Can I start training with you now? Can we? Can we?" I heard over and over again as I slipped out of my sweaty T-shirt into a dry one.

I considered their request: Training with them would mean giving up my time to rejuvenate and be alone amid fall leaves, nature paths and singing birds. Training with them would mean being a teacher, as usual, instead of, for a change, the one being taught. Training with them would mean sharing the hot water three ways at the end of each run. However, training with my daughters would also mean that I have helped these two future women tackle an obstacle, learn a skill and take pride in their own accomplishments.

"Of course," I announced. In part, I waged this idle threat because I never thought they'd really do it, but I knew if they would it could only be a positive step for all of us. So we went home and attempted our first mile run together. Guess what? They did it!

~Mindy Pollack-Fusi
Chicken Soup for the Mother & Daughter Soul

The Power of
My Mother's Love

discovered the power of my mother's love the spring I was twenty-six years old. I was hard at work in graduate school, busily moving toward my doctoral degree in psychology. It was early spring, the grass still brown and crunchy beneath my feet, as I walked from my car to the hospital entrance. I had been sick for a month with infections so resilient that not even the most powerful antibiotics were able to eradicate them. I felt incredibly weak, but had so much to do, I was eager to be done with this appointment.

As I walked wearily through the sliding glass doors into the admissions area, I anticipated a diagnosis of anemia or some other vitamin deficiency, a lecture about improper eating habits, finishing with a new regimen of vitamin horse-pills and a strict diet. I could hear my mother's voice, "I told you—you should be eating more protein. You're just not taking care of yourself. You're studying too hard." Why is this happening now? I thought resentfully. It is so inconvenient.

After what seemed like hours of waiting, a doctor appeared from behind the sherbet-striped curtains and entered the cubicle where I lay stretched out on the gurney. Startled to find me alone, he inquired where my family was. I told him that my husband had to work that morning and that my mother and father were living in a different state. The concern on his face deepened.

"I have reason to believe that you have leukemia," he said. The statement hung in the air and then fell like a ton of bricks, shattering my world as I knew it and rocking me at my very foundation. My first question after that initial moment of shock was, "Am I going to die?"

The doctor explained his diagnosis needed to be confirmed immediately with additional testing. After that, chemotherapy treatments would start immediately. Bottom line, I would be admitted immediately to the hospital and would not be released for at least a month. My condition was life-threatening. He told me that if I had waited a day or two longer my condition could have been fatal. My body was shutting down because of the rampant takeover of the quickly proliferating white blood cells. I could still die—suddenly—at any time.

After a painful test that confirmed the diagnosis of acute leukemia, my family began to arrive. I remember vividly the expression of shock and anguish on my mother's face. She looked as if the world had dealt her a deathly blow, as if her world had been shattered as well. It was this sense of shared trauma that would see us through the ordeal of the following five months.

Time passed in a blur of treatments. There were three extended hospital stays, rounds of chemotherapy, endless waiting for blood counts to return to normal from the devastating effects of chemo, and even longer days and nights spent fending off the fever of infection. During this time, my mom was my rock, ever present and ever supportive. Every day, twelve to sixteen hours a day, she was there with me at the hospital.

One of the most trying parts of the hospital routine was the mask she was required to wear anytime she was in my room to protect me from the potential deadly germs of the outside world. Yet she wore her mask every day without hesitation or complaint, enduring with me the boring and cramped confines of the Isolation ward.

Later, I came to see that time of shared isolation as a time of immeasurable bonding, not unlike my time in her womb. I was dependent on her for life support, trusting that she would nourish and protect me. I came to appreciate the enormity of the responsibility she had taken for me years ago at my conception. And now, without a moment's hesitation, she had taken that responsibility again. The beauty and power of our bond and her commitment to care for me were profound healing forces in my recovery.

During those months, my mother and I had many rituals that came to sustain us. Each morning, I would awaken early and sit by the window waiting for my mother's familiar red car to tool down the street and into the visitor's parking lot. When I spotted her car, I immediately felt that I could make it through another day—as if she were my guardian angel, guiding and protecting me through the most difficult battle of my life. As she walked from the parking lot to the hospital I would wave at her. Each morning she looked up and cheerfully waved back. She was happy to see me as well.

During that time, I began to understand that a mother does what she needs to do to nurture and protect her child, even if that means enduring horrible conditions herself. Those long days at the hospital, I later learned, were very stressful for my mom. There were days when she broke out in itchy, painful hives and went downstairs to the emergency room for treatment. She hid it so well that I never knew she was in discomfort. Most of the time, she sat by my bed and we talked, played cards and watched "Oprah" together. Other times, she read quietly and watched me sleep.

My mother had no other purpose in those days except to tell me she loved me with her presence. I especially felt her love the times she reached out and rested her hand on top of mine. Such a small gesture, but one that immediately brought me calm and peace—a sense that the world was all right and that I was okay.

I also cherished our evening ritual. Many nights I experienced panic and anxiety when I knew it was time for Mom to leave. My mother would kiss me goodnight and assure me I would see her tomorrow. Again, I would perch in the windowsill and wait until I saw her walking into the night, toward her car. She would turn as she neared the end of the sidewalk and look up into the darkened windows of the hospital and find me, waving to her. She would give one last wave before getting into the car. Then I'd watch the taillights of her car fade into the dark, knowing that in the morning, we would start our rituals all over again. This is how we survived those challenging months—together.

Eventually, I recovered from my leukemia and have been in remission for seven years now. Battling for my life was painful in every way, yet sharing that ordeal with my mother produced some of the most precious moments in our relationship. I experienced first-hand the overwhelming power of a mother's love to bring peace and healing in even the most difficult of life's circumstances.

~Shana Helmholdt
Chicken Soup for the Mother's Soul 2

Mama's Lesson

The stars are constantly shining,
but often we do not see them until the dark hours.
~Anonymous

My mother and I have always had a very special relationship, a bond that few people can comprehend. Ever since I was a little girl, I remember her teaching me about a mother's love: constant and unconditional. She would remind me of an old Polish proverb: The greater love is a mother's, then comes a dog's, then a sweetheart's. During my trying teenage years, specifically ninth grade, my mom was my best friend.

Everything was going great — at least it was for a while. I was a straight-A student who enjoyed school. Being an only child, I loved having a good time with classmates my age. A few weeks after my freshman year started, though, things began to change. I became the target of a bully. I don't know why; I had actually been his friend the year before. But nevertheless he made it his personal goal to make me miserable. I had always had a lot of friends, but as his daily attacks grew worse, more and more of my classmates joined him in laughing at me. I became the class joke. The self-esteem and assertiveness that I once enjoyed diminished with each passing day. I drew into myself and became timid, silently enduring his hurtful remarks.

I would climb into the car after school, look at Mama and burst into tears. I'll never forget the tenderness with which she rubbed my hand and the compassion with which she listened to my stories day after day.

I now know the pain she went through right along with me. How she cried as soon as she was done assuring me that it would get better—for she had no way of knowing if it ever really would. How she stayed up at night trying to think of advice she could give me—comeback lines to try—that would end it all. Mama never gave up. She was always coming up with solutions to my problems. Some of her advice worked; some of it didn't. But I remember it all. Mama started having a special prayer time from 11:55 to 12:45 every day—fifth period. Just knowing that Mama and God were thinking about me strengthened me.

One day, I snapped out of my self-pity when I found this letter on my desk after school:

Nicole,

As I look out your window I can see a little girl hanging out her doll clothes, a fifteen-year-old with the weight of the world on her shoulders and a young woman, successful at whatever she chooses to do with her life. The most difficult thing I have had to deal with is seeing the hurt in your eyes. But we're lucky because, for a lot of people, life is much tougher.

You are a beautiful, talented, smart, young, Christian woman. You have morals and concern for other people. These things aren't taught in school, but from a loving family and a loving heart.

Sit back, relax and know that there is some good in every day. Don't worry so much about what others think and say, but instead think about the things that make you special. You will not be remembered as being mean and hateful. You will be remembered as being pretty, caring, smart and compassionate. We all have our high school memories. People will not remember you with negative thoughts.

You have plans, and you have dreams. Hold on to those. I know many of them will become a reality for you. No matter what you do, you are always loved. I know two very successful people who were bullied. They got through high school, and so will you!

You have everything going for you. Stop feeling sorry for yourself. That is the worst thing you can do. You've got what it takes, and we all know it.

Love,

Your Proud Mom

Her words of love and support changed everything. After that, all the bullies in the world could not have dampened my spirit. I saved her letter, and it's still part of my strength. It has helped me be a lot of what I am today. I love it most because it's from my mother.

Oh, and incidentally, the bully eventually gave up on me, and two years later he asked me out on a date!

~Nicole Plyler Fisk
Chicken Soup for the Christian Teenage Soul

Chapter 3

Like Mother, Like Daughter

Learning from Each Other

*How far you go in life depends on your being tender with the young,
compassionate with the aged, sympathetic with the striving,
and tolerant of the weak and strong.
Because someday in life you will have been all these.*
~George Washington Carver

What Mothers Teach

It takes two to speak the truth — one to speak, and another to hear.
~Henry David Thoreau

Many years ago, when my daughter Sara was in the fifth grade, she came to me with a life-gripping problem. As tears welled up in her big brown eyes, she began explaining her dilemma.

"Marcy hates me!" she cried. "She hates me because Kathy is my friend, too. She wants me to be her friend and nobody else's." Sara choked back her tears and said, "She won't play with me if I hang out with Kathy. But, they are both my friends!"

I tried my mommy-best to console her and let her know that we cannot control how others feel and react. Even though we should understand feelings, there are some things that are out of our control, and some decisions we can only make for ourselves.

As I was trying to decide what motherly advice I could give her, she stumped me with, "You talk to Marcy. You tell her that I like her and want to be her friend, but I can have other friends, too!"

Oh boy. I sat there staring at her for a few moments trying to figure out how I got into this mess, when suddenly the idea came to me. I excused myself and left the room, telling her I would be right back. My mind raced. It was obvious that she needed to learn that there are just some things you need to do for yourself. Only, how could I teach her this without her feeling like I had failed her?

Picking up two wicker baskets from the living room, I quickly tossed their contents onto the floor and walked back into Sara's room. She stared at me like I was nuts.

"What are those for?" she asked with big, surprised eyes.

"It's a life lesson for you," I explained. "Just sit down and let me explain."

She sat on the edge of the bed with a wary eye. Placing the smaller basket inside the big one, I placed the handle of the big basket over my arm and began to slowly walk around the room as I explained.

"When everyone is born, God gives them a little basket. This little one here is yours. The big one is mine. As you grow, so does the basket. But if you notice, your little basket is inside mine. Why do you think that is?"

She just glared at me. Nope. Not getting through yet. Not even close.

I continued. "Your little basket is in mine because when you were born, there were too many things you couldn't do for yourself. I had the responsibility of feeding you, changing you, bathing you, and doing everything else you couldn't do on your own. So I put your basket in mine and carried them both for a while."

She nodded, but so far still thought I was crazy.

"Well, as you grew older and began to do some things on your own, I began placing a few more things in your basket. When you learned to tie your shoes, that went in your basket. You wouldn't want me tying your shoes now, would you?"

She bowed her head a second and said softly, "No, that would be stupid. I can tie my own shoes."

"Right," I said. "And when you learned how to put on your own clothes, I put that in your basket. You don't even like me telling you what to wear now, never mind dressing you."

She agreed with a small nod.

"As you grow older, there will be more and more things you must do on your own." As I spoke, I gradually took her basket out of mine and handed it to her. "You will eventually carry your own basket with things only you can do, like deciding who you want to be friends with, who you will date, what college you will go to, who you will marry."

She looked up at me and said, "I understand. There are some things that I have to do for myself because they are in my basket."

Hallelujah! The light came on! "Yes," I squealed, "but it's even better than that because you decide the things that belong in your basket or someone else's. Like now, you decide who you want to be friends with. If Marcy doesn't like your decision and gets angry, whose basket needs to carry her anger?"

She smiled. "Marcy's. Right?"

I hugged her and continued with the story. "You're absolutely right. Marcy's responses aren't in your basket. They are in hers. Now, one last thing you need to understand before the basket story is over." She was smiling big now and really getting into my little skit.

I stood there for a moment, thinking of my own mother and grandmother who were living with us, reminiscing about the things they used to do for me that now I do for them. Even though it tugged at my heartstrings, I held up the big basket and said, "One day when I'm much older, there will be things I can no longer carry in my basket. When that time comes, eventually you will begin taking things out of my basket and placing them into your own. Just like I do now for Grandma and Momma. Eventually, the things that are in my basket will be taken out, for I won't always be strong enough to carry everything I'm carrying right now."

I reached over and gently took the small basket from her hands and traded with her. As she felt the large handle of the big basket and watched me take the little one, she understood.

Softly, I said, "Life is a circle."

As she smiled and gave me a big hug, she said, "Mom, I think I can put much more in my basket. Don't worry about Marcy. I can do this."

As I put the magazines and the potpourri back into the baskets in the living room, my own mother entered and asked me what I was doing. Smiling, I gave her a quick overview of my impromptu skit, feeling quite smug and proud of myself. Mom just smiled.

A few days later, I was surprised to see one of the tiniest baskets I've ever seen, sitting on the top of my computer desk. It was small enough to hide in the palm of my hand. Underneath it was a note, in my mother's handwriting that said simply, "Just remember, your basket isn't nearly as big as you think it is. Love, Mom."

~Ferna Lary Mills
Chicken Soup to Inspire a Woman's Soul

The Sweater

Our power is just the force of our love for our children and grandchildren.
~Barbara Weidner

I t was too late when I realized I'd made a mistake. I'd been so blinded by my own grief at the rapid decline and death of my father that I hadn't thought through how his death would affect my daughter.

For months, Dad had been complaining of pain in his shoulder, "a pinched nerve"—or so we thought. When he fell ill on vacation and was diagnosed with progressive, primary prostate cancer, we were all shocked.

My dad was one of those special people who was born with a twinkle in his eye. I've never met anyone who didn't think the world of him. Little children, especially, were drawn to him like candy. He would clasp his hands together and grin with such joy that kids would come running. During a visit with my sister in Ireland, he taught the village children how to play American football. The Irish children would often come by in the evenings to ask, "Can Grandpa come out and play?"

So it was no surprise that he was especially close to my five-year-old daughter, Jodi, the last of his grandchildren to reside near him in the United States. They would giggle and laugh together for hours, making up stories and feeding pretend animals in the backyard.

By the time they found Dad's cancer, it had spread to his bones and things went quickly. When we went to visit him, Jodi sat quietly next to the bed, pretending to read from a book to him—there were no more boisterous games. I had explained to her that Grandpa was very sick and that he couldn't play the way he used to, but it was hard for her five-year-old mind to comprehend.

Toward the end, I didn't take Jodi along, because I didn't want her to be frightened by Dad's gaunt frame and the look of pain and suffering on the face of the vital man we all adored.

After he died, I didn't know if Jodi understood the finality of death, or if she just thought that Grandpa was out of town, "on vacation." But as the weeks went by, she became very quiet and withdrawn, crying frequently at things I thought odd.

One evening, I sat with her on my lap and gently stroked her hair.

"You seem very sad, Pumpkin," I said. "Can you tell me what's wrong?"

She was silent for a few moments and then broke into sobs.

"I didn't get to say goodbye to Grandpa," she said.

That's when I realized that in my well-meaning way, I'd made a mistake.

Through a haze of mutual tears, we sat and rocked, and talked about Grandpa and all the wonderful times we'd had with him.

"Would you like to say goodbye to Grandpa now?" I asked.

She looked at me as if I were a little strange.

"Close your eyes. Now picture Grandpa's face right in front of you. When he smiles, you can talk to him."

Suddenly she got a huge grin on her face. "He's smiling so big at me!"

"Then tell him whatever you want to tell him."

"Grandpa," she said, "I love you and I miss you so much. I want to say goodbye for now. Goodbye, Grandpa."

Then I remembered the gifts I'd taken for myself when my mother packed my father's clothes away. I had asked her for a couple of his old cozy sweaters that he loved to hang around in on the weekends. I went and got the two blue sweaters and offered one to Jodi.

"These are special sweaters of Grandpa's. If we are sad or missing him, we can put them on and feel as though he is hugging us."

We both wept again as we each pulled one over our heads. Then I held her as she gently drifted off to sleep. For the first time in weeks, she seemed at peace, a slight smile on her face.

Both sweaters were well used over the years. Frequently if Jodi was having a hard time, she retreated to her room. When I checked on her later, usually I'd find her stretched out on her bed with Grandpa's old blue sweater wrapped around her—sleeping peacefully with just the slightest hint of a smile on her face.

Jodi is eighteen now and still loves to wear Grandpa's sweater. Somehow, it always fits perfectly. You see, it's the size of a hug.

~Pamela Albee
Chicken Soup for the Mother's Soul 2

Toast Means Love

Do not squander time, for that's the stuff life is made of.
~Benjamin Franklin

Without a doubt, my favorite food is toast. Not just any toast; it has to be slathered with butter and placed under the broiler until it's just right. I love it when it is perfectly browned and a small circle of melted butter gathers in the center. Toast reminds me of love.

When I was a little girl, we would all cuddle up in my mother's bed and eat toast together. We sat there under the blankets—my mother, my sister, my brother and me—munching our hot, crispy squares and telling why we loved each other. Not big things, just little everyday things: cute dimples, funny laugh, wavy hair.

When I was in college, my friends teased me about my love for toast. I decided to find out why I loved toast so much. I called my brother and asked him if he loved toast as much as I did. He laughed and said that we all ate toast back then because we were poor. He doesn't eat toast anymore. So I called my sister. She said that when we were little, since we didn't have any other food to eat, we ate toast. She despises toast.

Finally, I called my mother. As I began to quiz her about my toast obsession, she interrupted. She said, "Honey, we ate toast because I was twenty-three years old at the time. Your father left us, and I didn't have a job. I went to the welfare office, and the social worker that I talked to said, 'The country didn't give you those babies.' I got mad and walked out of there, and I got myself a job. Sometimes, all we had was bread, but I wanted to make it nice. I needed to have you three nearby me because I was scared back then, and I needed your comfort and your love. I'm sorry."

"But Mom," I wailed, "I thought toast meant love!"

She was silent for a moment, then said quietly, "It does, sweetie. It does."

~Toni Hall
Chicken Soup for the Single Parent's Soul

22

A Couple of Cacti

On a sweltering afternoon, my mother came home from grocery shopping. She stumbled through the door with several paper sacks in one hand and a small, brown paper bag in the other. "Help with these!" she called.

Being a rebellious sixteen-year-old, I slowly sauntered over to her rescue and took the smallest bag from her.

"Be careful with that!" she warned.

"What's in it?" I asked with mild curiosity.

Mother set down the groceries and beamed proudly. "They had a close-out sale on some cacti—poor, pathetic little things. I thought I might try to nurse this one back to health."

I watched as she carefully extracted a sickly fuzzy cactus from the paper bag and set it down gently on the kitchen counter.

I burst out laughing at the fuzzy nub of a plant. "Mom! It looks like Charlie Brown's Christmas tree! I hope you kept your receipt!"

Mother just rolled her eyes at me and carefully set the cactus by the sun window, cooing softly to the ridiculous thing.

By the second week, the fuzzy little cactus had perked up just a little. I didn't pay much attention to it. High school had started, and I was busy with classes and my budding social life. Boys were starting to ask me out on dates, and I was absorbed in a thrilling, but often confusing, new world.

One day, on my way out to school, I found a paper bag sitting on the front steps. My heart sank as I read the brief note. It was a gift from a boy who had a crush on me. I hadn't been very nice to him but didn't know what else to do. I knew I didn't want to go out with him.

I took the bag in the kitchen and, to my surprise, there was another tiny cactus inside. This one was green and straight with lots of prickly spines on it.

"Oh no!" I groaned. "Look, Mom, that guy gave me a cactus! How weird!"

Mother laughed. "Maybe he's trying to tell you something."

"Yeah, something," I mumbled. I knew the two of us weren't meant for each other.

Mother inspected the cactus carefully. "This is perfect. Now the other cactus will have a friend."

"Like, whatever, Mom," I said, mustering up as much sarcasm as I could. I left for school. Mother fussed with the spiny thing and set it next to the other one in the kitchen window.

A couple of months later, I was eating a piece of toast in the kitchen one morning. I glanced at the cacti and noticed that they'd both started bending toward each other like two green bananas. I laughed because they looked sort of... happy.

Through the winter, Mother and I watched those two cacti growing closer and closer to each other. They were both bending dramatically and had nearly formed a U shape.

I was a typical teenager, and sometimes our household got pretty turbulent back then. But those two green cacti were always the subject of pleasant conversations between Mother and me. We'd laugh and joke about the imaginary romance they were having.

Mother would be the fuzzy one, and I'd be the spiny one. We'd throw silly one-liners back and forth between the cacti. I'd say things like, "Hey, baby, what's a nice girl like you doing in a pot like that?" Mother would answer, "Hey! Keep your stickers to yourself, young fellow!"

One morning that spring, I went into the kitchen and something truly amazing caught my eye. My spiny cactus had grown a hot pink flower on the top of its head, closing the gap between the two cacti and completing the union between them.

Tears came to my eyes. I realized in that moment that these two cacti had bonded in their own special way. I ran upstairs to get Mother. We both stood there staring at those cacti as big, soggy tears ran down our cheeks.

Later that day, Mother and I went to the garden center. After much discussion, we settled on a beautiful pot, big enough for the two of them.

Without disturbing the cacti's delicate union, we carefully transferred them into their new pot. We were so proud and happy for them. They were in love.

I survived high school and, soon after graduating, moved away to the city and started my own life. Mother kept the two cacti, and I'd always ask how they were doing when I called. "They're still together," she'd tell me.

I felt a sense of security, knowing that our little green couple was happy and healthy.

One day, Mother called to inform me that the fuzzy one had died. "I did everything I could," she told me, "but I just couldn't revive her."

Fighting back tears, I said, "That's okay, Mom. You're the one who saved her ten years ago, remember? Besides, she had a long, happy life... and she experienced true love."

The spiny one became ill just months later and passed away. I cried a little when I heard the news. Then I laughed, remembering the happy times Mother and I had enjoyed, watching our spiky sweethearts reach out to each other in our kitchen window. They had helped us keep our hearts connected, too, during my own prickly years.

~Kelly E. Reno
Chicken Soup for the Gardener's Soul

23

My Mother's Greatest Gift

I don't think of all the misery but of the beauty that still remains.
~Anne Frank, The Diary of a Young Girl

I was ten years old when my mother was left paralyzed by a spinal tumor. Prior to that, she had been a vital, vibrant woman — active to an extent most people found astonishing. Even as a small child, I was awed by her accomplishments and beauty. But at thirty-one, her life changed. And so did mine.

Overnight, it seemed, she was flat on her back, confined to a hospital bed. A benign tumor had incapacitated her, but I was too young to comprehend the irony of the word "benign," for she was never to be the same.

I still have vivid images of her before the paralysis. She had always been gregarious and entertained frequently. She often spent hours preparing hors d'oeuvres and filling the house with flowers, which we picked fresh from the gardens that she kept in the side yard. She would get out the popular music of that era and rearrange the furniture to make room for friends to abandon themselves to dance. In fact, it was Mother who loved to dance most of all.

Mesmerized, I watched her dress for the evening's festivities. Even today, I remember our favorite dress, with its black skirt and midnight-lace bodice, the perfect foil for her blond hair. I was as thrilled as she the day she brought home black lace high-heeled pumps, and that night my mother surely was the most beautiful woman in the world.

She could do anything, I believed, whether it was play tennis (she won tournaments in college) or sew (she made all our clothes) or take photographs (she won a national contest) or write (she was a newspaper columnist) or cook (especially Spanish dishes for my father).

Now, although she could do none of these things, she faced her illness with the same enthusiasm she had brought to everything else.

Words like "handicapped" and "physical therapy" became part of a strange new world we entered together, and the child's rubber balls she struggled to squeeze assumed a mystique that they had never before possessed. Gradually, I began to help take care of the mother who had always taken care of me. I learned to care for my own hair—and hers. Eventually, it became routine to wheel her into the kitchen, where she instructed me in the art of peeling carrots and potatoes and how to rub down a good beef roast with fresh garlic and salt and chunks of butter.

When, for the first time, I heard talk of a cane, I objected: "I don't want my pretty mother to use a cane." But all she said was, "Wouldn't you rather have me walk with a cane than not walk at all?"

Every accomplishment was a milestone for us both: the electric typewriter, the car with power steering and brakes, her return to college, where she earned a master's degree in special education.

She learned everything she could about the disabled and eventually founded an activist support group called The Handicappers. One day, without saying much beforehand, she took me and my brothers to a Handicappers meeting. I had never seen so many people with so many disabilities. I returned home, silently introspective, thinking how fortunate we really were. She took us many other times after that and, eventually, the sight of a man or woman without legs or arms no longer shocked us. My mother also introduced us to victims of cerebral palsy, stressing that most of them were as bright as we were—maybe brighter. And she taught us to communicate with the mentally retarded, pointing our how much more affectionate they often were compared to "normal" people. Throughout all of this, my father remained loving and supportive.

When I was eleven, Mother told me she and Daddy were going

to have a baby. Much later, I learned that her doctors had urged her to have a therapeutic abortion—an option she vehemently resisted. Soon, we were mothers together, as I became a surrogate mom to my sister, Mary Therese. In no time at all, I learned to change diapers, bathe and feed her. Though Mother maintained maternal discipline, for me it was a giant step beyond playing with dolls.

One moment stands out even today: the time Mary Therese, then two, fell and skinned her knee, burst into tears and ran past my mother's outstretched arms into mine. Too late, I glimpsed the flicker of hurt on Mother's face, but all she said was, "It's natural that she should run to you, because you take such good care of her."

Because my mother accepted her condition with such optimism, I rarely felt sad or resentful about it. But I will never forget the day my complacency was shattered. Long after the image of my mother in stiletto heels had receded from my consciousness, there was a party at our house. I was a teenager by then, and as I saw my smiling mother sitting on the sidelines, watching her friends dance, I was struck by the cruel irony of her physical limitations. Suddenly, I was transported back to the days of my early childhood, and the vision of my radiant, dancing mother was before me again.

I wondered whether Mother remembered, too. Spontaneously, I moved toward her, and then I saw that, though she was smiling, her eyes were brimming with tears. I rushed out of the room and into my bedroom, buried my face in my pillow and wept copious tears—all the tears she'd never shed. For the first time, I raged against God and at life and its injustices to my mother.

The memory of my mother's glistening smile stayed with me. From that moment, I viewed her ability to overcome the loss of so many former pursuits and her drive to look forward—things I had taken for granted—as a great mystery and a powerful inspiration.

When I was grown and entered the field of corrections, Mother became interested in working with prisoners. She called the penitentiary and asked to teach creative writing to inmates. I recall how they crowded around her whenever she arrived and seemed to cling to every word, as I had as a child.

Even when she no longer could go out to the prison, she corresponded frequently with several inmates.

One day, she asked me to mail a letter to one prisoner, Waymon. I asked if I could read it first, and she agreed, little realizing, I think, what a revelation it would be to me. It read:

Dear Waymon,

I want you to know that I have been thinking about you often since receiving your letter. You mentioned how difficult it is to be locked behind bars, and my heart goes out to you. But when you said that I couldn't imagine what it is like to be in prison, I felt impelled to tell you that you are mistaken.

There are different kinds of freedom, Waymon, different kinds of prison. Sometimes, our prisons are self-imposed.

When, at the age of thirty-one, I awoke one day to find that I was completely paralyzed, I felt trapped—overwhelmed by a sense of being imprisoned in a body that would no longer allow me to run through a meadow or dance or carry my child in my arms.

For a long time I lay there, struggling to come to terms with my infirmity, trying not to succumb to self-pity. I asked myself whether, in fact, life was worth living under such conditions, whether it might not be better to die.

I thought about this concept of imprisonment, because it seemed to me that I had lost everything in life that mattered. I was near despair.

But then, one day it occurred to me that, in fact, there were still some options open to me and that I had the freedom to choose among them. Would I smile when I saw my children again or would I weep? Would I rail against God—or would I ask Him to strengthen my faith?

In other words, what would I do with the free will He had given me—and which was still mine?

I made a decision to strive, as long as I was alive, to live as fully as I could, to seek to turn my seemingly negative experiences into positive experiences, to look for ways to transcend my physical limitations by expanding my mental and spiritual boundaries. I could choose to be a positive role model for my children, or I could wither and die, emotionally as well as physically.

There are many kinds of freedom, Waymon. When we lose one kind of freedom, we simply must look for another.

You and I are blessed with the freedom to choose among good books, which ones we'll read, which ones we'll set aside.

You can look at your bars, or you can look through them. You can be a role model for younger inmates, or you can mix with the troublemakers. You can love God and seek to know Him, or you can turn your back on Him.

To some extent, Waymon, we are in this thing together.

By the time I finished Waymon's letter, my vision was blurred by tears. Yet for the first time I saw my mother with greater clarity. And I understood her.

~Marie Ragghianti
Chicken Soup for the Unsinkable Soul

24

Chasing Butterflies

I love my mother as the trees love water and sunshine—
she helps me grow, prosper, and reach great heights.
~Adabella Radici

I remember the day well—the turning point in my relationship with my daughter. It began on a hot July morning, the sun beating down upon our small country home. Outside, sitting in the shade of a maple tree, I sketched pictures of my five-year-old daughter, Abigail, as she chased butterflies. Moments like these kept me safe in her world. She was rapidly changing—becoming more and more like the butterflies she'd chase—always in motion. Today, however, I relished being the center of her kingdom and stifled my growing concern that the future would lessen our closeness.

"Look, Mama!" she shouted, waving toward the dirt road. "It's Rachel. Hi, Rachel!" Our neighbor's daughter waved back, and I gasped in disbelief. What had happened to that cute eight-year-old girl selling Girl Scout cookies on my doorstep six years ago? Surely, she isn't this tattered-looking teen sporting an eyebrow ring and purple hair! I watched as Rachel rounded the corner of our yard to head onto a path leading into the woods. She stopped only once to light a cigarette. Even though rumor had it that Rachel and her mother hadn't spoken to each other for two years, I had dismissed the gossip as just that—gossip. Now, after seeing Rachel, I gave it more credibility.

Abigail watched her, too, before turning to me. "Mama, was that a cigarette Rachel had?"

I explained that it was, answering as many questions as I could, but seeing Rachel in her rebellious teenage persona had soured my mood. Insecurities about what the future held for my own daughter and me surfaced. Had I been equipping Abigail with what she'd need to survive in the world? Had I been laying the foundation in these formative years to ward off a relationship disaster such as Rachel's?

"How about if we go swimming?" I suggested, wanting to avoid seeing Rachel again. Abigail shouted in agreement and danced around the yard. Little things made her so happy, and my heart became a camera—freeze-framing every inch of her. At the public pool, she was afraid of the water and barely ventured from the baby pool.

"Okay," I told her. "I'm Ariel the Mermaid, and you're Melody, her daughter. We need to go over to the big pool and save Atlantica from Ursula." She hesitated, but then the promise of an exciting new game overcame her apprehension and she galloped toward me.

"Let's go!" she giggled, entwining her petal-soft fingers in mine as we entered the pool.

We played for an eternity, and as she relaxed, I inched her closer to the deep end. Soon, I began to see our lives as that intimidating body of water ahead. If I could teach her to swim, we could stay afloat through life's rough seas.

"Mama!" she cried when she couldn't touch the bottom any longer. "I don't want to go any further!"

"Trust me," I whispered into her ear, soothing away her fears. "Hold onto my neck and you'll see how much fun we can have together." Her tiny fingers choked me but I continued calming her and soon she relaxed and shouted in glee.

"This is fun, Mama! I'm floating! Whee!" I held on to her waist and spun her around. The water cascaded over her as she imagined herself a real mermaid.

"Mama!" she exclaimed, watching as other children jumped into the pool. "I want to do that. Can you catch me?" I moved her to the pool's concrete edge and lifted her out. She stood there, scared.

"I don't want to do it now," she told me, her face full of anxiety. "What if you don't catch me?"

"I will catch you, Abigail," I said, knowing that this was a monumental minute in our lives. "You must trust me." Our eyes locked and in a split-second, both of our different fears became one. She was so much like me. From the way she ate a Snickers bar to the way she comforted her dolls—I'd witnessed so much of myself in my daughter.

"Honey, I know that you're scared. Even Mama gets scared sometimes."

"What scares you?" she blurted, her tone suggesting that mothers were never afraid of anything.

"Well, right now, I'm scared that you won't trust me," I confessed. A flurry of emotions crossed her beautiful features as she digested my words. And then, in a moment frozen in time, she closed her eyes and jumped off the ledge. I hadn't expected it so soon, but then I seized the God-given opportunity and reached out for her. My hands clasped around her wet body, and I pulled her toward me—safe and secure.

"Mama! You did it!" she shouted, kissing my face. "I trusted you, and you caught me! Now we both don't have to be afraid anymore." Her excitement bubbled over. "Mom, I think we went on an adventure today!"

Her words sparked tearful promises of hope to my soul. Like the butterflies she would chase—never knowing which way they'd travel—I realized that an old adage still proved true. Life is an adventure to be lived and not a problem to be solved. Somehow, some way, she and I would get through the difficult seasons of life.

Later, after we'd pulled into our driveway, Abigail jumped out of the van and squealed in delight. Running over to the bush her father had planted to attract butterflies, she giggled and waved at me.

"Mama! Do you see them?" she asked, pointing at the brightly colored insects fluttering over the bush's blossoms. I nodded, capturing her enthusiasm and tucking it safely inside my heart. We're going to be just fine, I thought, smiling as my daughter turned away from me to begin chasing butterflies.

~Karen Majoris-Garrison
Chicken Soup for the Mother & Daughter Soul

25

The Little White Shoes

My ten-month-old baby daughter threw her arms around my neck and nuzzled her tear-drenched cheek against my chest, desperate to get away from the doctor who had just finished a painful examination. He was a kind man who spoke to me with warm reassurance, but his words were anything but reassuring, and it was all I could do to hold back my own tears as I stroked my child's downy blond hair. She had been born without a hip socket, and the fact that it was being diagnosed so late was crucial.

The doctor said, "I recommend two years in body casts, followed by at least one surgery. At that point, we'll be able to determine whether she will ever be able to walk normally. Most likely, she will always have a painful, heaving gait."

The essential issue was time; it was essential to begin her treatment immediately so the condition didn't worsen. But the situation was worse than the doctor knew: the cost of treatment was beyond anything my husband and I could afford. It was clear I'd never see this physician again.

In the car, I sat down and curled my precious child in my arms. Delighted to be out of the office, she was quickly consoled and began to happily tap her little toes against my stomach. Her unborn brother, due in just a few weeks, kicked back at her from within. Distracted by their sweet tapping rhythm, I glanced down at the new white "walking shoes" I had so optimistically purchased when she had begun to pull herself to a standing position. She would never be able to walk in those shoes. I was terrified she'd never walk at all.

For the next few days, I vacillated between despair and anger. For months I'd been telling my pediatrician there was something wrong with her legs. A longtime friend, he had patiently listened to me, but had found nothing amiss. Now it seemed my child was to suffer permanent damage because of the delays. I prayed we'd find the help she needed and vowed to do whatever it took to find resources — a process that turned out to be dismal. Doors seemed to close at every turn. Banks refused to lend us the funds for her treatment. Shriners Hospitals had long waiting lists. Far too often, I felt like giving up. But then my darling child would look at me with joy and trust, and I would realize she could not afford the luxury of my discouragement.

Finally, I received a call from the physician who had made the diagnosis. He had been concerned about us. How were we doing? Were we ready to begin the treatment? Embarrassed, I reported that our efforts to raise the funds had failed. After a pause, he said, "When I didn't hear from you, I feared that might be the case. So I took the liberty of making a few phone calls. I've learned that young families such as yours can often qualify for assistance from the Crippled Children's Services in our state. I think you should call them right away." I felt a soaring sense of optimism for the first time.

The ensuing weeks were arduous, but we were carried along on a wave of renewed hope. During that time, I gave birth to a wonderful new baby boy. I also waded through mountains of bureaucratic red tape to get the approval to go to the Children's Hospital for an evaluation.

Sitting in the waiting room of a hospital for "crippled" children turned out to be an extraordinary learning experience. The little children, faced with all manner of physical challenges — wearing braces and casts, on crutches and in wheelchairs — seemed to embody the spirit of optimism so necessary for their healing. They played, laughed and babbled with one another. In contrast, the parents wore worried, tired expressions. We all were burdened by "the facts" and had to work much harder to maintain a sense of faith.

When our turn came, I picked up my two babies and walked in

to meet the physician. My initial reaction was that this beaming man must be a lunatic. "Young lady," he bubbled, "I have absolutely wonderful news for you. I have reviewed your daughter's X-rays, and we are going to be able to provide her with state-of-the-art care. A young physician in a nearby state has been specializing in a new treatment for conditions like hers, and he has had incredible success. He has just made the decision to come to our hospital for a year and provide care here." The "door" had opened wider, and the future held even greater promise than I had imagined.

The visiting physician's treatment was indeed revolutionary. His surgical procedure was to put a chip of bone where the missing hip socket should have been, and after the surgery my daughter was put in a body cast and sent home with us. Unseen, beneath the thick layers of plaster, a miracle began to grow. Every time they took an X-ray, I could see that the small chip of bone was gradually growing and shaping itself into the form of a perfect hip socket.

The surgery was 100 percent successful. After the cast was removed, my little daughter walked pain free and without a limp.

I still remember the visiting nurse coming to our home for a follow-up visit a year later to see the child with the hip dislocation. I pointed to our daughter as she ran through the room squealing after her brother. "No," the nurse said patiently. "I'm here to visit the child who had surgery for her missing hip socket." Then the light dawned and she said, "This is amazing. I've never seen a child recover so fully and in such a short period of time."

My daughter is now a grown woman with a family of her own. We rarely speak of her experience. The only reminder is a small scar on the front of her hip, a scar so insignificant she has been able to successfully pursue a career in modeling. Recently, she and I went rollerskating with her young daughter. As my granddaughter launched herself confidently onto the skating floor, my daughter and I began our somewhat wobbly, but valiant effort at merging with the other skaters. When they called for a "couple's skate," she and I joined hands as we had so often when she was little. As I watched our feet gliding along, I was suddenly struck by the sight of her skates and remembered the little white shoes of the child who could not walk. As we skated along, they began to play "Just the Two of Us."

I, too, have been forever changed. Out of my despair of not knowing where to turn, I learned to trust. I appreciate the importance of listening to my own instincts. From persisting in the face of adversity, I discovered that many of life's possibilities are unseen, yet may be ready to materialize in the next moment. Despite appearances to the contrary, our bodies carry within them great wisdom and the ability to heal in miraculous ways, and somewhere there are always caring and capable people who are willing to lend support. Out of challenges that seemed too heavy for my twenty-one-year-old shoulders to carry, came lessons that have carried me throughout my life.

~Catherine Monserrat, Ph.D.
Chicken Soup to Inspire the Body and Soul

26

Moving in with Mom

Grown don't mean nothing to a mother. A child is a child.
They get bigger, older, but grown? What's that suppose to mean?
In my heart it don't mean a thing.
~Toni Morrison, Beloved, 1987

Five weeks before my daughter was due, I went into pre-term labor and was sentenced to bed rest. I could get up only for weekly doctor's appointments, twice-weekly non-stress tests and bathroom privileges.

While giving me my instructions, my doctor said that I shouldn't be alone; I needed someone to get me to the hospital at the first twinge of a contraction. My husband, Jack, had been saving his vacation days for after the baby was born, and we both hated the thought of using them up. We also found out that it would be impractical for me to return home since our bedroom is on the second floor—and going up and down stairs was on my list of forbidden activities.

As Jack and I were exhausting our possibilities, my mother (who hadn't left my hospital room) piped up. "Why don't you stay with me?" she asked in her here's-what-we're-going-to-do voice. Jack thought that was the perfect solution; my mother could be with me all day, she lives a block from the hospital, and she has a first-floor guest room. I was more doubtful. Like most daughters, I have had my share of conflicts with my mother, and I didn't know if I could handle weeks of constant togetherness. Eventually, though, I realized it was the best option and moved back "home."

I spent my days sulking—acting more like a surly teenager than a gracious houseguest. When Jack came after work, and my mother visited friends or ran the errands she couldn't do during the day, I cried. I wanted to go home. I wanted to be away from my mother. Most of all, I just wanted everything to be normal again. I snapped at my mother incessantly.

"Do you have to tell everyone about my medical problems?" I yelled when I overheard her phone conversations. "Can't I have any privacy around here?" I whined when she checked to make sure I hadn't fallen during my two-minute showers. My mother, who had never hesitated to tell me to "knock it off" when necessary, apologized.

Thanksgiving came a few days later. I wasn't feeling very thankful, but I was craving my mother's mashed potato casserole. The night before Thanksgiving, my mother went to the grocery store and bought everything I wanted.

The next day, I lay on the couch and watched my mother prepare a gourmet meal for three—even straining the gravy because the slightest lump would make me gag. I could see how difficult the day was for her; my father had died six months earlier, and this was our first "family" holiday without him. When dinner was ready, my mother sat and looked down at her plate for a long time. "Aren't you going to eat?" Jack finally asked her.

"In a minute," my mother said, tears glistening in her eyes. "I was just thinking about how thankful I am to have a grandchild coming. I never would have gotten through the past few months without this baby to look forward to. And I know you're going to love being parents as much as Daddy and I always did."

I realized then just how lucky I was. While my husband was working all day, then pulling all-nighters assembling the crib, setting up the swing and changing table, and getting everything ready for the baby, I had my mother to take care of me.

For the next ten days, I let my mother fuss over me—and I let myself enjoy her company. She told me stories about her pregnancy and my childhood. We read baby books and magazines together. We laughed at trashy talk shows and cried over sappy movies. We ate all my favorite foods. I got to know my mother as more than just my mother.

I can't say everything was perfect, though. I had to take an "anti-contraction" pill every six hours, including one at 2:00 A.M., and my mother had a tendency to wake me at 2:15—after I had already turned off my alarm clock, taken the pill and drifted back to sleep. She was convinced that if I raised my arms, I would strangle the baby (despite repeated assurances from my doctor that this would not happen), so she panicked whenever I reached for something. And she said things like, "Maybe after you have the baby, you'll shave your legs again."

I didn't mind. In fact, I thought it was kind of funny. And I was grateful. I knew my husband and I would have managed on our own if we had to. But having my mother around just made things easier.

When my mother took me to the hospital for my third non-stress test, the nurse said, "Come on in, Grandmom. Don't you want to hear the baby's heartbeat?" As the sound of my baby's heart filled the room, I heard another sound—the sound of my mother's sobs.

"Is the baby's heart okay?" she asked. "Is everything all right?" When the nurse said everything sounded great, I could see my mother beaming through her tears, and I was so glad she was there. My father had died of a heart attack, and I realized what a gift it was for my mother to hear her first grandchild's strong, healthy heartbeat. She squeezed my hand as we listened. Then she turned to the nurse and said, "And you're sure Carol is okay?"

"Yes, Carol is just fine," the nurse smiled. "You're taking good care of her."

"Well, she's my baby," my mother said and kissed my cheek.

At that moment I saw that, while I was putting my life on hold to do what was best for my baby, my mother was putting her life on hold to do what was best for her baby, too. And as I held my mother's hand, I knew that I would follow her example. Whenever my daughter needs me—no matter how old she is or how cranky she is—I'll be there, just like my mother taught me.

~Carol Sjostrom Miller
Chicken Soup for the Mother & Daughter Soul

Mother's Silver Candlesticks

y mother saw the candlesticks displayed on a shelf in the rear of a secondhand store in the tenement district of New York City. They were approximately ten inches tall and heavily tarnished, but a surreptitious rub revealed their possibility, and a glance at the base showed the magic word "sterling." How did they get there? What poor soul had hocked them to survive? Mother ached to buy them, but we had come to exchange the shoes I was wearing for another pair to fit my growing feet. First things came first.

New York, where we settled upon entering the United States, and the area where we lived bore little resemblance to the Goldene Medina, the golden land that many immigrants had envisioned in their dreams. However, it was a land of opportunities, where all might achieve their aspirations if they worked hard toward their goals.

"We can swim, or we can sink," declared Mutti, as I called my mother, "and I have always been a strong swimmer."

And swim we did! Dad peddled caramelized almonds, which we made each evening and packed into cellophane bags, up and down Broadway. Mother went to school in the morning to learn to be a masseuse and did housework for various families several afternoons a week. I attended school at PS-51. My sister, Lotte, went to the Institute for the Deaf in St. Louis, where she worked in an exchange program to learn English. Nights, Dad worked as a night watchman, Mother sewed leather gloves for a manufacturing firm, and I strung beaded necklaces for the Woolworth store for one cent apiece.

The fifth-floor walk-up apartment we shared on 150th and Riverside Drive was hardly what my parents had been used to in their native country, Germany. It really wasn't a walk-up—it had an elevator—but the man who ran it held out his hand for tips each time anyone wanted a ride. Who could afford donations? We walked upstairs.

The place consisted of a kitchen, bathroom, living room and one bedroom. My sister and I shared the double bed in the living room, until she went off to school. When we first viewed the apartment, my mom blanched at the filth of the place. But with determination and elbow grease we made it habitable.

During one of our nightly chats while working together, Mutti told me about the candlesticks.

"Let's see if we can manage to buy them. I think they could look good once we clean and polish them."

Together we schemed how to save enough money to purchase them for Daddy's birthday. Thinking back, it was not the gift my father would have chosen to receive. He was more interested in the war, what of his property he could salvage, and how we would eat and pay the rent. But Mom was desperate to have something of beauty in our dingy flat.

The candlesticks cost three dollars. We conceived our plan in March and discussed money-saving strategies.

"I'll see if I can talk our three elderly neighbors into letting me carry their trash down to the basement," I offered. "Plus, I could make money stringing necklaces."

"I'll buy large eggs for Daddy, and we'll eat the smaller and cheaper ones," said Mom.

In addition, she purchased three-day-old bread, instead of day-old, saving seven cents a loaf. A friend told her that wrapping a damp cloth around the bread and heating it in the oven would make it taste fresh again. It worked!

We turned saving pennies into a game. At the end of April, we made a fifty-cent down payment on our treasure. By September 23, 1940, we proudly "paid them off," and the proprietor even threw in some used candles.

We rubbed and polished the silver. Mother cut the used candles and scraped the outside until they looked almost like new ones. I will never forget the first Sabbath Eve when we lit the tapers. Tears ran down my mother's face as she recited the blessings. Despite the hardships, we were grateful to be together and, most of all, to be safe and sound.

When I married and moved to Wyoming, my mother gave me the candlesticks as a wedding gift, so that I might always share in their beauty. "You helped to buy them. You know how much they mean to me. I want you to have them and to someday pass them on to your daughter," she said.

The candlesticks now stand on top of the piano in my living room. We have used them at every memorable occasion of our family's life, both happy and sad. One day, I will pass them on to my daughter, as they were passed along to me. The Sabbath candlesticks are, and always will be, much more than candlesticks. They are symbols of faith, courage and love.

~Liesel Shineberg
Chicken Soup for Every Mom's Soul

Thanksgiving Dinner and Infant Seats

When you're in your nineties and looking back, it's not going to be how much money you made or how many awards you've won. It's really what did you stand for. Did you make a positive difference for people?
~Elizabeth Dole

I had visited a friend on the Friday before Labor Day and was turning in my visitor's pass at the hospital desk, when I overhead an argument between the receptionist and a distraught man. The receptionist was explaining that his newborn baby couldn't leave the hospital without a car seat.

He looked so dejected as he said, "Where can I get a car seat at this time and where can I get the money to buy one?"

"I'm sorry, sir, but this is now the state law. No one can take a baby out of the hospital without an infant car seat."

My hackles were rising. Were they going to ask this man (or the taxpayer) to cover an additional four days in the hospital for lack of an infant seat? But when the receptionist said, "Your wife can go home with you today, but the baby can't leave unless she's in a car seat," I had to intervene. Leaving a newborn baby in an impersonal hospital for four days without her mother because there was no car seat? I knew from my mother how important that early bonding can be for a baby—and the mother.

So, being the daughter of a woman who never hesitated to jump in and help strangers, I said, "Sir, I have an infant car seat in my house that my sister just returned to me. I'd be glad to give it to you, but I live about twenty-five minutes away." Beaming in amazement and relief, the man said, "I'll follow you in my car."

As I debated whether I had done the right thing or been foolish in inviting a stranger to my home, the flashback happened. I remembered being in my parents' apartment in New York City for Thanksgiving dinner. Lots of us were there and it was very festive. Too much food, of course, and laughs and good times — and my mother frequently peering out the window of the eighth-floor apartment.

"What's going on, Julie?" asked my father.

"That man has been sitting on the sidewalk all day. He looks cold and hungry. I'm going to take him a Thanksgiving dinner," said my mother. And the protests arose from the group. He may reject it, he will know where you live, he'll think you're a softie and may bother you later, it's not safe.

Undaunted, my mother packed up a big Thanksgiving dinner, complete with pie wrapped in foil, grabbed some utensils and napkins, a few Thanksgiving candies and a nice heavy wool sweater of my father's that he didn't wear much in their warm New York City apartment and charged out the door.

We all watched out the window. My mother walked right up to him and we could tell that they were talking. The man seemed agreeable, took everything and thanked my mother profusely. As she walked back to the building, we watched the man. He carefully placed the plates and things on the sidewalk, took off his thin jacket, put on the wool sweater and put his jacket back on. Then he opened the food and began to eat. We stopped watching, feeling we were invading his privacy. Later he returned the plate and utensils to the doorman, whom my mother had alerted.

When my mother got back into the apartment, she was obviously moved by the man's plight and his appreciation of her Thanksgiving gift. And so were all of us. The man never bothered her and the gift was exactly the right thing to do. It stayed with me for many years — and popped into my head as I stood at the hospital debating whether to offer this man my infant seat.

When we got to my house, I offered him other never-to-be-used again baby things. He accepted. But there was nothing abject about his receiving the gifts. It was as if he knew people give to people and it's the right way to live. And he accepted my baby equipment as a new father from a longtime mother.

They say what goes around, comes around, and I believe it's true. My mother's good example comes around again and again through me, her daughter who learned by watching her. Silently, I thanked her for the lessons in generosity that she had given me.

~Frances Firman Salorio
Chicken Soup for the Mother & Daughter Soul

Things I Learned from My Mother

And thou shalt in thy daughter see, this picture, once, resembled thee.
~Ambrose Philips

When I was sixteen, my best friend and I went to the neighborhood Woolworth, crammed ourselves into a tiny, curtained cubicle and, after paying a quarter, mugged wildly while a camera took four consecutive snapshots of us. The resulting pictures, a strip of black-and-white photographs of inferior quality, made us laugh for hours. Much later, when Marilyn and I were examining the pictures for what seemed to be the hundredth time, she said something that made me question whether the pictures were as amusing as I first imagined.

"You remind me of your mother in these pictures," Marilyn remarked.

I went home and threw the pictures into the trash.

Back then, there was nothing that could insult me more than being compared to my mother. The truth was, and it hurts me to admit it, I was ashamed of her. And so, throughout my teen years, I did everything possible to prove that I was the antithesis of what I perceived her to be.

I had not always felt negatively about Mami. As a little girl, I was nicknamed "El Chiclet" because one of our neighbors observed that I stuck to my mother much like a piece of gum stubbornly adheres to the bottom of a shoe. Whether my mother was shopping, washing clothes or catching a TV show at our neighbor's apartment, I was there with her. I was so attached to her, in fact, that I often spent hours perched on a stool watching her iron the men's shirts she took in to earn a few extra dollars. I would be mesmerized by the fluid movements of her hands as she spread each shirt flat, smoothed it with her palms and rhythmically ironed the wrinkles away.

Most times, Mami hummed or sang as she worked her way through dozens of shirts, but on occasion, if I begged long enough, she would tell me a story. Mami would entertain me with stories about Juan Bobo, the famous Puerto Rican simpleton, or her own versions of fairy tales. My favorite was one about a damsel who rode on the back of a mythical creature to rescue her true love. Mami loved board games and could play Parcheesi or Chinese checkers for hours. She always beat me at Chinese checkers. I asked her once why she never let me win. She said that when I finally learned to play well enough to win on my own, I would appreciate it all the more. To this day, I can't recall if that ever happened.

I don't remember exactly when my feelings for my mother changed. I do know, however, that by the time I was in high school, Mami and I spent most of our time bickering. I resented everything about her, even those things she had no control over. I was embarrassed by her appearance because she was short and overweight. I was ashamed of her pitiable lack of education and broken English. I was mortified whenever she went through other people's garbage and salvaged things like toasters and irons so she could fix them and have a "new" appliance. The things I resented most of all, however, were Mami's rules. At eighteen, I still had a midnight curfew, and I was never allowed to sleep over at any friend's house. I fought her on every rule she imposed. Our home was a battlefield because she would not give in to me, just like she'd never let me win at Chinese checkers.

I moved out of my house eight months after I graduated from high school. In the years that followed, my mother and I lived in relative, distant peace. We talked on the phone occasionally; we saw each other even less. I never revealed anything about my life to her that would cause conflict between us. We both liked it that way.

It was not until I had my first child that my relationship with my mother began to change. My sister's daughter, my mother's only other grandchild, was already ten, and Mami was thrilled to have a new grandson to play with. We started visiting each other more often, and I discovered that Mami instinctively knew how to grandparent. She gently guided me when I asked for advice, but she never interfered.

Shortly after my son celebrated his second birthday, Mami was diagnosed with acute leukemia and was hospitalized for eight months. Weakened by chemotherapy and now confined to a wheelchair, Mami was no longer able to live alone. My husband and I offered to bring her to live with us.

While my sister and I were sorting through Mami's possessions in anticipation of her move into my home, I discovered the sepia-toned strip of pictures that Marilyn and I had taken at Woolworth. Somehow, Mami had rescued them from the trash and saved them in her photo album. As I grinned at the silly snapshots, I still could not see the resemblance between Mami and me that had been so obvious to my friend.

If I were ever to categorize the periods of my life that have given me the most grief and the most joy, I would have to say that the time my mother lived with us would count as both. During those years, my husband and I sacrificed our privacy and built our lives around my mother's comfort and care. We took her to all of her doctor's appointments, drove her to chemotherapy sessions and shopped for special foods. I monitored her medications and learned to inject her with insulin to control the diabetes she developed from the chemotherapy drugs. And yet, I have many wonderful memories of that time as well.

I can remember Mami's excitement when my son, Nick, and I gave her a wheelchair tour of the Bronx Zoo, and she spotted a baby giraffe. I can still recollect her exhilaration when we took her to visit her family in Puerto Rico. And best of all, I can still recall the bickering between Mami and Nick when they played Chinese checkers. She complained that he cheated, and he whined, not surprisingly, that she never let him win.

Two years after coming to live with us, Mami passed away, leaving me with an unbridgeable chasm of grief that, in some ways, I still carry with me today. Every once in a while, I pull out my mother's old album and stare at that yellowed strip of photographs that my friend and I took so many years ago.

The young girl in those photos who was ashamed of her mother has grown up. Today I search to find a similarity with the woman who taught herself to read and write, who had to iron men's shirts to make ends meet, and who was the best darned small-appliance repairman on La Salle Street.

~Sylvia Rosa-Casanova
Chicken Soup for the Latino Soul

A Cup of Coffee

I heated up a cup of coffee today in the microwave. I wasn't sure if I should laugh or cry as I stood there holding the steaming cup for the second time this morning. My son woke up crying, and it took nearly an hour of singing, consoling and rocking to get him back to sleep. In the meantime, my coffee got cold. So, I heated it up in the microwave.

I grew up vowing never to be like my mother. She is a wonderful, strong woman, and anyone would be proud to be like her. But I wasn't going to be. No one in town seemed to know her name. To the teachers and students at the various schools her children attended, she was simply known as ____'s mom (fill in the blank with any one of her five children's names). At the grocery stores and around the auto parts stores and hardware places, they affectionately called her "Mrs. Dale" after my father's first name; and the folks at the bank, utility companies and other such important places addressed her with Dad's last name, as Mrs. Keffer. Mom answered to all of these with a smile and kind words.

I, on the other hand, was never as gracious about it. Often, I would tell the bagger at the grocery store, "Her name is Joyce, by the way," as he handed her the bag and told her to have a nice day using one of the aforementioned names. Mom would always smile and say, "You have a good day, too," as she shot me the mind-your-manners-I-taught-you-better-than-that look. When we would then get to the car, I would bicker at her for not standing up for herself. "You are your own person," I would retort. "You're not just an extension of Dad."

"I could be called a lot worse," she would always reply. "Besides, everyone knows your dad."

Everyone in this small town did know my dad. He was a friendly, hard-working man who liked to flirt with the checkout girls and give car advice to anyone who needed it. He could charm his way out of a speeding ticket and talk his way into a better deal with ease. He would not think twice about fixing a broken part on one of the neighbor kid's bikes. Or leaving in the middle of a cold winter night to change a frightened teen's flat tire.

But everyone knew my mom, too. While Dad was a great man in the community, Mom was equally special. She had her own way of talking herself into a good deal, and she loved to give friendly advice to people she met. When she would wake up on cold, snowy mornings to a house full of college kids who had been stranded in town, she would weave her way through the sleeping bodies and fix enough pancakes for all. If anyone was in need, my mom was right in the thick of the fight to help. She would collect items for a family who lost all in a house fire, canned goods for the church pantry, and clothes for a teen mother's baby when no one else would help.

As a teen, I never understood my mom. How could someone with so much to offer the world be content to stay home and be known as an adjunct to her husband or as someone's mother? Why wasn't she proud of who she was? Once upon a time, she wanted to be a nurse and join the Peace Corps. How could anyone give up her dreams for washing out dirty diapers and packing my father's bologna sandwiches?

All I knew was that this was not going to happen to me. I had big dreams of making a difference in the world—but with a bang, not a whimper. People would know me. I planned on working my way up through the ranks of the YMCA with a busy writing career on the side. My husband, if there was one, would be right behind me and, as for children, they would be cute and at their nanny's side. I would not be like my mother—I would be me. And people would know me as someone important.

Now here I was heating up my cup of coffee in the microwave

for the second time. Just as I had watched her do a million times after setting it down to pack a lunch, feed the cats, tie a shoe, retrieve a towel from the dryer, find a paper that needed returning to school, answer the phone and a million other possible interruptions. I dreamed of downing a good café latte for breakfast before another busy day at the office, and here I was drinking instant mocha from a "Happy Birthday" mug with colored balloons all over it.

I understand now. I understood eight months ago as I held my son for the first time. I understood when his tiny little hand wrapped around my finger and his big blue eyes looked into mine as he drifted off to sleep. I understood when the love I have for my husband tripled as I first saw the little body cuddled in his big, strong arms and saw the tears streak down his face. I understood it all instantly.

I look forward to the day that I will be known as Andrew's mom to the people in town and the children at school. Every day, as my husband returns home from work and his face lights up as his son holds out his hands, I am proud to be Mrs. Frank Huff. Just like my mom is proud to be called Mrs. Dale Keffer. Just like my mom. Those are four words that I thought I would never say proudly.

By the way, if you see her, her name is Joyce.

And now I need to heat up my coffee again.

~Barb Huff
Chicken Soup for the Mother & Daughter Soul

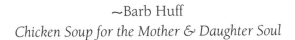

Chapter
4

Like Mother, Like Daughter

Always There
for Each Other

Remember, we all stumble, every one of us.
That's why it's a comfort to go hand in hand.
~Emily Kimbrough

Marissa

The more faithfully you listen to the voices within you,
the better you will hear what is sounding outside.
~Dag Hammarskjöld

arissa sat on the carousel horse, and I stood alongside her, my arms bracing her little long-legged body against the painted saddle. I glanced over at the crowd and saw my husband Tim watching us. And for a reason I didn't understand, I felt a terrible yearning, a need to freeze-frame the moment and etch every detail of him into my brain, from his pale and lightly-freckled face and intent blue-green eyes to his blue denim jacket.

Two weeks later, he was dead. And there I was, a thirty-four-year-old widow with a three-and-a-half-year-old daughter and a slew of people throwing advice at me. Some of it was good—a lot of it wasn't—and all of it said more about the folks hurling it at me than it did about me and my particular situation. One woman, however, sounded a note that proved to be just as prophetic as the yearning I'd felt on the carousel that cool June evening. "That little girl," she told me emphatically, "is going to be your salvation."

I rejected the notion. It's not fair to expect her to be all that, I remember thinking. I have to get through this on my own. And I set about trying to hammer out a new world from the debris of our old predictable one. I put Marissa in preschool three days a week, found a counselor I felt comfortable working with and forced myself to start writing again.

All of which were good, necessary things to do. But I was so intent on showing people—and myself—that I could handle, by myself, what life had thrown at me, that I had become more of an automaton than a person and a parent. I didn't neglect Marissa: I looked after her, gave her more toys than she needed and more animals than we both needed (our cat population shot up past the "sufficient" mark, and we acquired bunnies and even, for twenty-four hours, a pygmy hedgehog who loathed us). But my heart-spring was broken, and I couldn't respond to Marissa fully—then I would have to feel, and I wasn't ready to do that yet.

I resented having to be a two-in-one parent carrying the burden of all the responsibilities, while well-meaning friends and relatives got to take Marissa places and do all the fun stuff with her. I got tired, too, of feeling like I couldn't even have the luxury of being sick. I mean, if I did give into a sinus infection or a twenty-four-hour virus, wouldn't this Popsicle-stick-and-masking-tape world of ours simply fall apart?

"Oh, I know just how you feel," some of my friends in rocky marriages would say. "I'm like a single parent myself."

You're not! I always wanted to scream back. Your children's fathers are living and breathing. They might not help much, but they're there. It's not the same.

I was having an aggravated case of feeling sorry for myself. It was only natural, I suppose, but it wasn't getting us anywhere. So, as the numbness slowly receded, I made a conscious effort at being me again. Or, rather, a me who'd gone through a war and had the scars to prove it, but who was also tougher and more willing to try new things, both for Marissa and myself.

I'd been telling her ever since she was old enough to understand that "it's just the two of us now—we have to be a team." Well, now we truly started being one. I'd never been that wild about traveling—and I was more than a little daunted by the prospect of going it alone with my daughter—but now, I made a point of it. I'd never ridden a bike or been good at sports, but I bought Marissa a bike and pushed her along till she was ready to solo. We went horseback riding together for a year or so, then went on to doing Tae Kwon Do together. We dressed up for Halloween together, and she was on my business cards as my official partner when I was breeding Abyssinian cats. The secret, as I learned, was in focusing not on what we had lost but on what we still had: each other.

We no longer breed Abyssinians, and Marissa now prefers me to be a non-costumed, sensible mom on Halloween. But we play Scrabble, go for hikes, and watch Gilmore Girls together. I help her with her homework and her butterfly garden; she has introduced me to Harry Potter and Nintendo, and occasionally lets me hang out with her and play horses. We discuss my dates and her friends, and she sometimes contributes titles or suggestions for my stories and essays.

There are fights and tantrums—on both our parts—but there's a lot of clowning around and laughter, too. And when she won a tiny red and white cloth bear (known as Scarlett) at the carnival recently, she insisted on putting it in my room, saying it would be "our bear."

Sometimes when I look at her, I catch glimpses of the person she is becoming: a funny, intuitive, astute young woman with all her dad's directness. There's a reason that Gilmore Girls is one of our favorite shows: the playful verbal sparring and camaraderie between single mom Lorelei Gilmore and daughter Rory mirrors our own, uncannily. Marissa is my companion, my joy, my partner-in-crime and my comforter when I am down or sick. There's still a terrible yearning when I think back on that night on the carousel and what followed, but there is also Marissa. In short, that little girl has indeed been my salvation.

~T. J. Banks
Chicken Soup for the Single Parent's Soul

Abigail's Dove

It had been the worst snowstorm in ten years, and I'd been caught in it. After hearing earlier that it was supposed to snow later in the night, I had volunteered at our church to take groceries and medical prescriptions to elderly members in need. Since my husband was away on business, I called my mother and she immediately came over to my house to watch my three-year-old daughter, Abigail.

"Can't someone else help those people?" she had asked me, concerned for my safety. "I have a bad feeling about this, and it looks like it might snow at any minute."

I glanced out the window and had to admit that the sky looked threatening. I began to feel uncertain.

"Mama will be okay," my daughter smiled, taking her grandmother's hand. "She likes helping people. Besides, I'll be praying for her!"

My heart swelled at her words. We had such a close relationship that sometimes when I breathed, it was as though Abigail exhaled. I decided then that I had to act on what I'd been instilling in my daughter: that sometimes we just have to step out in faith and believe that God will keep us safe. Kissing my mother and daughter goodbye, I set out to make my rounds. On my last stop, the snow began to fall.

"You shouldn't have come here," Bill Watkins, a ninety-two-year-old member of our congregation, scolded. He coughed, trying to get out of bed, but the effort proved too taxing. Giving up, he settled back onto the pillows. "I told the pastor that I didn't expect anyone to come to the boonies for me."

"Nonsense," I grinned, positioning snacks and drinks by his bed. Beneath his gruff exterior, Bill was sweet as candy. His heart medication had to be taken every day, and living on a modest income without any surviving family members, he needed as much help as possible.

"Well, look what your stubbornness brought you," he said, pointing to the snow-covered road outside the window. His fingers clasped my hand. "Stay here, Karen. I want you safe."

I kissed the top of his head but decided to brave the road conditions. It would be worse later, I reasoned.

"I'll be okay," I told him, remembering my sweet daughter's words before I left. Thoughts of Abigail made me more determined to get home. I missed her already.

I got into my Volkswagen and gradually tried making it down the steep hill. Remembering old instructions about driving in the snow, I kept the compact car in second gear. The wind increased, creating waves of blinding white. As I squinted through the windshield, holding my breath, I screamed and jerked the wheel, narrowly missing the deer that stood frozen by my headlights.

The Volkswagen hit the embankment, plummeted off the side of the road, and skidded to the bottom of a ravine below. When the rolling motion finally stopped, I opened my eyes and realized that I had been unconscious for some time. Night had arrived—and with it the forecasted accumulation of snow. Panicking, I tried opening the door, but it wouldn't budge against the resisting snow. Sliding over to the passenger's door, I realized that the door had been jammed shut by a tree. I turned the key to start the engine, but the battery was dead. My hopes of rolling down the power windows to crawl out vanished. Without heat and adequate clothing, I curled up on the back seat and waited for help.

The frigid air enveloped me. Shivering, I chastised myself for not preparing for a circumstance like this. My toes and fingers were already numb. An eternity seemed to pass, and as I listened to the wind and snow hitting against the car, I prayed for my family, who would be sick with worry by now. Abigail would probably be drawing pictures for me when I arrived home. Since she'd been old enough to hold a crayon, she'd drawn pictures to brighten the days of her loved ones.

To calm my growing concern about my safety, I closed my eyes and concentrated on pleasant thoughts. Drifting into sleep, I saw Abigail. Abigail in the warm sunlight, laughing as she held out a beautiful white dove to me. The dove's graceful, serene presence and the love shining in my daughter's eyes filled me with peace.

The night grew colder, and as I floated in and out of consciousness, I fixed my mind on the image of Abigail and her dove. Together, they kept me company throughout the night. Hours later, as the first rays of daybreak appeared, I heard tapping on my window. Relieved to see an emergency rescue team, my stiff lips tried to smile as they hoisted me onto a stretcher and into an ambulance. At the hospital, I was treated for mild frostbite and a head wound before being told I'd have to stay overnight for observation. Anxious to see my family, I propped myself up on the bed pillows and waited impatiently.

Before long, the door opened and my mother burst into the room. "We were so worried about you!" she cried, rushing over to hug me. "I knew you were in trouble! Mothers sense these kinds of things." Her maternal instincts surfaced as she appraised the food tray nearby. "Your tea is cold! I'll be right back."

Seizing the opportunity to have me all to herself, Abigail climbed onto the bed and buried her face in my neck. I scooped her closer. "I've missed you so much," I murmured softly, brushing a silky strand of hair from her face. "And what have you been doing while I've been away?"

"Oh, I forgot!" she exclaimed, jumping out of my arms to grab a large tube of construction paper nearby. "I drew this for you last night when we didn't know where you were. I thought you might've been scared, and I wanted you to feel better."

As if it were a treasure map, I unrolled it and oohed and aahed over the images. "Well, that's our car," I said, pointing to the red square. "And that's me," I laughed, touching my fingertips to a stick person with long hair. "But what am I holding?"

Abigail's eyes brightened as she pushed her fingertip to the small object on the paper. "That's God's spirit," she said excitedly. "I drew it as a dove like I saw in Sunday school." She pressed her soft lips against my cheek and added, "I didn't want you to be alone, Mama, and so I gave you the best friend I could think of."

"Oh, darling," I exclaimed, recalling the white dove that had given me comfort in the darkest of nights. "Your dove was with me." Taking her hand, I marveled at the heavenly bond between mothers and daughters.

"And what are you two looking at?" my mother interrupted, placing a steaming cup of tea on the nightstand. She started to move away, but I grabbed her hand and brought it between Abigail's and mine. It was a remarkable feeling, this incredible connection of three generations.

"We're looking at the love that flows between us," I whispered, kissing the top of my daughter's head as I met my mother's understanding eyes. Returning my gaze to Abigail's picture, I studied the beautiful bird that had, on such a dismal night, connected my daughter's heart with mine.

Years later, that extraordinary event in our mother-daughter relationship became known as the "miracle." The miracle of Abigail's dove.

~Karen Majoris-Garrison
Chicken Soup for the Mother & Daughter Soul

33

Divorce—Cut and Dried

We have two ears and one mouth so that
we can listen twice as much as we speak.
~Epictetus

My divorce was already looming on the horizon by the time I realized my fourteen-year-old firstborn had been carving deep gashes in her milky forearms, using a clean but unforgiving X-ACTO knife. I had been temporarily blinded—my perceptions dulled by my own worries and sixteen-hour workdays.

I truly believed my top priority as a soon-to-be single mother and freelance writer was to boost my solitary income to something above the poverty level, before we (my older daughter, her seven-year-old sister and I) were officially on our own. My older's quest was to escape from emotional bankruptcy through a dramatic expression of her fears and a pain so great it had paralyzed her heart.

Our struggles intersected one quiet Colorado summer evening when I collapsed after midnight on the sofa beside her. My priorities instantly shifted when she lovingly leaned against me, squeezed my hand and forgot to cover the battle scars that now covered her arms.

"I love you, Mommy," she whispered as her fingers laced between mine. I opened my strained eyes, lifted my head from the cushions of the couch where it had landed, raised her fingers to my lips and found myself suddenly mute.

"Baby," I finally managed in little more than a whisper, "what has happened to your arms?" I will never forget the dirty-brown color of dried blood — the angry, silent swelling that flanked the heartbreaking crust.

Her eyes widened, she broke her finger's grip on mine and rushed to pull her long sleeves back over the marks. It was too late. Pandora's box had been opened. The secret would never be secret again.

"Hon?" I said, as I gently nudged the sleeve back and ran my fingers along the wounds. "Did you do this to yourself?"

"You wouldn't understand," she answered. "It's not about suicide or cutting my wrists."

There must have been a goddess of single motherhood watching over me that night, and she must have been astonishingly kind. I'm not sure how, but I somehow found the courage to resist panicking and stepped inside my daughter's troubled mind.

"I will understand," I promised, "if you'll help me. And neither one of us is moving from this sofa until I do."

For the next three hours, we talked and cried together about the terror she had been shouldering alone. She mapped out her feelings with remarkable clarity and wisdom. And I had the good sense to let her talk.

All her life, my daughter had watched two people fight to save a relationship that was never meant to survive. For fourteen years, she'd locked herself away in her room to escape her father's high-volume anger and her mother's esteem-shattering acceptance of the verbal abuse. She wasn't afraid of the thought of her father leaving us. She was afraid I would launch an emotional retreat, and in the end, beg him to stay.

It wasn't such a far-fetched scenario. Years before, her father and I had separated for a seven-month stretch. I'd started college classes to get my teaching degree. He'd found a new girlfriend with kids of her own. But before any divorce papers were filed, his girlfriend had had enough of him. With "for better or worse" echoing through my head, I'd reluctantly submitted when he asked me to come back home. Vanessa's conception guaranteed the temporary success of our reconciliation. But nothing, other than our census standing, had really changed.

"Every time I got my hopes up," my baby tearfully explained that night, "every time I thought we'd finally have a little peace, you guys up and changed your minds." Stress and turmoil silently tore at my teenage daughter, but she didn't know how to tell me. So she went numb as a self-preservation alternative. Her only release from that numbness was the selective carving of her delicate arms. "That momentary sting," she said, "helped me hide from the pain of being afraid."

As the sun came up over the Rocky Mountains, I made her a promise and exacted one from her in return. "This won't be another false start," I swore to her. "It'll be a fresh one—no turning back this time." She believed me, and agreed to talk to me the next time she ached for the feel of the blade.

It's been five years since my daughter and I traded midnight true confessions. Five years since I filed for, and finally got, my divorce. Five years since she has made a cut in her arms. We haven't lived in the lap of luxury, but I've managed to earn enough to pay for the sanctuary my family deserves.

Seven books and twelve hundred articles later, strangers and acquaintances assume my greatest accomplishment has been finding success as a professional freelance writer—supporting two daughters as a single mother. My family knows better: I won the fight of my life the night I was smart enough to listen to my baby. Helping to heal her secret wounds is the success story that will always matter to me most.

~Kelly McLane
Chicken Soup for the Single Parent's Soul

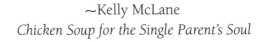

34

A Perfect Skate

*If you paint in your mind a picture of bright and happy expectations,
you put yourself into a condition conducive to your goal.*
~Norman Vincent Peale

She staggered off the practice ice supported by some of her skating-team friends. I hurried over to give Heidi her jacket and to brace her until we could find a seat. At fifteen, she had been living with cancer for a year. We'd learned the news just after returning from Chicago, where she'd won her first gold medal in an international competition.

Then came the tests, the invasive procedures and the surgery. Through it all, what mattered to her most was that she retain her ability to skate. Fortunately, her doctor agreed to let her skate as much as she was able.

Heidi's friend Greg helped me take off her skates. All of the children were initially frightened by Heidi's plight, but gradually pitched in to help keep her safe.

"Is she all right?" Greg asked.

"Yes, she just needs a nice nap before we can get her to the car," I explained.

Happy children swirled around me as Heidi slept away. They all tried to be quiet, but their exuberance for the upcoming Keystone State Games was evident. How I wished those days would return for Heidi.

Heidi had been working hard on her programs and was determined to compete, but now the deadline had passed. I woke her up and we began our journey to the car. "Mom, Coach Barb says I am skating my program well. I want to go to the State Games."

Pain shot through my heart. When I told her the registration deadline had passed, she said her coach could probably still get her in. "Mom," she pleaded. "I don't expect a medal. I just want to go there and be normal for a couple of days. Is that so bad?" A sob escaped her.

"Let's ask the doctor," I said, uncertain.

The next day at her checkup she filled the doctor in on all the details of the State Games.

"I'll tell you what," he responded. "It's okay with me if it is okay with your mom, but you'll have to get permission to miss your radiation treatments."

I added something else to the list: "You have to eat right, sleep right and take good care of yourself."

"I will, I promise!" she responded.

After getting permission from the oncologist and sending in a last-minute registration form, Heidi was set to go to the State Games. Now it was the big night and Heidi was about to alight on the ice for her freestyle routine. I prayed.

The speakers announced her name and I steadied my hand on the camera as she flowed across the ice gracefully, like her old self. Proudly, she took up her stance. Steel Magnolias' theme song filled the arena, and she took off for a full performance.

She picked her toe into the ice and lifted up into a jump. She was so high that a momentary look of fear crossed her face. I cringed, whispering, "Please God, don't let her break anything on the landing."

She landed perfectly, leg out behind her just like the pros. Her face bore a huge smile as if to say, "I did it!" She tore into her next move as the audience went wild. "Go Heidi!" echoed around the arena. She leaned into her ultimate move, the inside-outside eagle, perfectly done.

The stands erupted with joyful noise. None of us could believe it. Another huge jump! She was garnering points for the team. She glided into a lovely spiral, heavy boot held high like a flag of victory. Her cheeks were pink with effort and she was beaming with pride. Heidi had out-skated her best!

She exited victoriously into her coach's arms. Barb grabbed her in a huge hug, crying as they savored this incredible moment. Then her joy turned to shock. Heidi lay lifeless in her arms.

The arena quieted. I ran.

I caught them as Heidi's weight began to overpower Barb. I backed to the bleachers and rested against them. Arms reached to help. I laid her carefully down and felt her neck for a pulse. She had one.

Everyone waited in shock as I checked her over.

The quiet was suddenly shattered by a snore! Bedlam erupted. Applause ripped through the rafters of the frigid arena. Parents of her rivals shared their blankets as Heidi took a well-deserved nap. She was still sound asleep when her teammates ran over to congratulate her. She had earned the gold medal in the freestyle division!

~Nancy E. Myer
Chicken Soup for the Sports Fan's Soul

Planting Day

Gardening requires lots of water—most of it in the form of perspiration.
~Lou Erickson

When I was little, I often helped my mother plant our family's garden. As soon as the chilly winds of Chicago winter gave way to spring, Mom would be outside with a spade, seed packets, gardening gloves and a secret smile that had been hibernating all winter. That smile never seemed to shine as bright as on those first few days in April when she squatted in the mud with tiny seeds in her hands.

I would pull on my grubbiest jeans, choose my shovel with care, and bound across the yard before Mom could say, "You forgot a jacket!" I would kneel by her side for hours, carefully digging holes and cautiously pushing seeds into the earth with my chubby fingers. We spent hour after hour repeating the process, until the formerly snow-smothered area barely knew what hit it!

Unfortunately, I grew up. Somehow, I found better ways to spend the first days of spring, and I threw my annual April morning job into the growing pile of childish, outgrown activities. After all, I was too old to kneel in the dirt all day planting some silly seeds. I came to the conclusion that the shopping mall needed my assistance more than Mom did.

Surprisingly, my mother never said much about my decision until two years ago, the spring I turned fourteen. I was on my way to a friend's house when Mom stopped me.

"Would you please help me with the planting today?" she asked.

"Oh, Mom, I was just getting ready to leave," I pouted. "I'll probably be gone most of the day."

"Well, could you possibly come home a little early and join me in the fresh air?" Mom asked.

I mumbled something along the lines of, "Uh, maybe.... I'll see."

By the time I left the house, Mom was already in the garden. She looked up for a moment as I walked past, and from the corner of my eye I saw a certain pain and sadness in her gaze. At first my heart told me I should stay to help, but as I got farther from home and closer to an exciting day of hanging out with friends, I forgot my impulse.

A few hours later, as the sun started to fall from its place in the warm, spring sky, I decided to leave my friends a bit early and head back home.

Mom usually finishes planting around six, I thought. If I get back soon, I'll still have an hour or so to help her. I felt very noble for my selfless decision. But when I reached home, there were Mom's dirty boots by the door and a small pile of empty seed packets on top of the garbage can. I was too late.

I didn't think much about that day until nearly a year later.

One of my father's good friends suddenly lost his wife to cancer. The doctors hadn't discovered Sara's illness until it was too late. She died shortly after the diagnosis, leaving behind her husband and two small, confused children.

Right away, Mom went south to visit the family and see how the children, David and Rachel, were coping with the sudden loss of their mother. She spent a few hours with little Rachel. When she came home, she told me this story.

When Sara had received her terminal diagnosis, she asked her husband, "What should I leave our children? How do I give them something to remember me by, a symbol of my love for as long as they live?"

Mom learned the answer from Rachel.

"Mommy made me my own garden," Rachel said proudly, as she tugged on Mom's hand and led her outdoors. Sara had decided to plant her children something that would live on long after she was gone.

Although the children had helped with the original planting, it was obvious that most of the work had been patiently completed by their mother. The result was a masterpiece, with so much more among the leaves and petals than simple foliage. A piece of Sara's heart and soul was left in full bloom for her children.

As I listened to my mother tearfully tell Sara's story, I realized the true power of a garden. How had I missed it? Our annual planting was not about kneeling in dirt, throwing in some seeds and hoping for the best. It was about kneeling there together, planting potential life and creating the best memories possible from those moments together. I was so lucky to have a healthy, vibrant, caring mother who was always there for me. As I suddenly realized how badly I missed seeing her soft hands place seeds in mine, many things became clear. I began to understand that the pain I had seen in her eyes that day a year ago had come from missing the little girl who was once at her side.

A few weeks later, I came home to find several bags of seeds on the kitchen table. I knew spring planting was near. The following Sunday, I woke to rays of sunlight streaming through my window. I looked outside to see a figure stooping in the dirt. I threw on the first clothes I could find and ran outside.

The first rays that encircled me were the ones streaming from my mother's smile. The first water our seeds encountered were the teardrops sliding happily from my eyes. We worked together all day and didn't stop until nightfall.

I won't ever miss planting day again.

~Beth Pollack
Chicken Soup for the Gardener's Soul

36

The Prom
That Almost Wasn't

Each day provides its own gifts.
~Martial

My daughter Beth's bright blue eyes sparkled as they caught mine in the mirror at the beauty salon.

"She looks beautiful," said our hairstylist Elaine, who had just put the finishing touches on Beth's up-do style. Beth's smile of pleasure spoke volumes. This remarkably lucky young woman felt like the belle of the ball, which is a fitting way to feel on prom night. But just six short months ago, as doctors fought to save my sixteen-year-old daughter's life, I would have never dreamed she would recover enough to attend her junior prom.

At approximately 10:30 on a November evening, Beth was a passenger in a tiny Dodge Neon, heading to a friend's house to watch a video in celebration of a day off from school. The driver lost control of the car as he sped through some curves. He buried the right front fender in a tree at the edge of the road less than a quarter mile from our home.

At midnight, we received the knock at the door every parent dreads. A deputy sheriff stood on the doorstep. After he ascertained that Beth was our daughter, he told us she had been involved in an accident. As the blood drained from my body and my knees suddenly became too weak to support me, I asked, "How bad is it?"

"It's her legs," he said, "They're bad. They're very bad."

Beth was rushed to the University of Tennessee Medical Center for surgery. The prognosis was grim. She suffered a broken right hand, leg and hip and a fractured left leg and foot. X-rays showed six major breaks and dozens of tiny fissures and cracks in the pelvic region.

Her initial chance for survival was questionable. The orthopedic surgeon, thinking he was just patching her up so we could say our final goodbyes, inserted steel rods above and below the knee in her right leg and three four-inch screws in her hip. An external fixator, a series of metal rods protruding from her hips, kept her crushed pelvic bones in place.

I was not allowed to see Beth after the accident until the regular intensive care unit visiting hours at ten o'clock the next morning, nearly a dozen hours after the accident. Beth spent five critical days in ICU fighting for her life. A collapsed left lung and internal injuries and bleeding caused grave concern. She eventually received six units of blood before she began to stabilize.

Ten short days later, the insurance company deemed her ready to be released. She remained bedridden for nearly two months and was put on a collection of drugs including a blood thinner, Coumadin, to help keep blood clots from forming in her legs, which might lead to heart attack or stroke. Coumadin helps prevent these clots, when taken at the right level. However, too much Coumadin can result in serious internal bleeding.

As her classmates were preparing for Christmas break, Beth was enduring daily blood draws. As they were ringing in the New Year, Beth was weaning herself off pain pills. And as they were pouring over catalogues and magazines full of prom dresses, Beth was retraining her muscles from the waist down.

By the end of January, the rods were removed from Beth's hips and she could begin the journey to walking once again. Jo Scott, our home health physical therapist, gave Beth a list of daily exercises. From the beginning, Beth was determined to succeed. She surpassed Jo's expectations and went from walker to crutches in just a few days. Two weeks later she tossed the crutches and wobbled about on her own.

By May first, Beth was almost back to normal, and she wanted to go to the prom. I was concerned that the evening would be too much for her to handle, but she insisted. As I watched Beth whirl and twirl in prom dress after prom dress, I reveled in a moment I might once have taken for granted.

The accident has changed Beth's perspective and appreciation for life. She is grateful for the little things like being able to take a shower or hold her baby sister. She never fails to wear a seatbelt and chides her friends when they forget to snap their own. Although her gait is different now and she limps when she is tired, Beth's recovery is nothing short of astounding.

This year's prom theme was, appropriately enough, "What Dreams May Come." Thanks to a miracle and her own determination, Beth still has many dreams to fulfill.

As she walked out the door with her date on prom night, I smiled as I told her I loved her. More important than any prom dream, my dream for her recovery had come true.

~Kate Clabough
Chicken Soup for the Mother & Daughter Soul

Help Mom, I Need You!

hatever is the matter with me? I ponder, standing outside on my deck. It's a beautiful evening in early spring, and there's no reasonable explanation for why I've abruptly canceled my plans to go away for the weekend. As I've just explained with some embarrassment to my friends (who have now left for a retreat without me), I simply have a strong feeling that I'm needed at home.

I run through a mental checklist of what might be compelling me to stay. My family is in good health. My older daughter, Lisa, called earlier in the day to wish me a good trip. My younger daughter, Katy, is expecting, but the baby's not due for three weeks. Still, Katy keeps entering my thoughts.

Katy is twenty-two years old and about to be a mother herself, but I sometimes feel as though she's still my baby. Right now things aren't too good between us. A few weeks ago we exchanged angry words after a mix-up about a get-together we'd tried to arrange. "You never have time for me anymore," she said, and I resisted the impulse to say the same. Katy and I had always been close. But lately we just haven't been connecting.

The cool quietness of the night helps calm me. Before going inside I take one last look overhead, staring up at the panorama of stars glittering in the vast darkness. Suddenly, so clear they seem almost audible, words come to mind:

"In everything, by prayer and petition, with thanksgiving, present your requests to God. And the peace of God, which transcends

all understanding, will guard your hearts and minds in Christ Jesus."
(Philippians 4:6–7)

Why did I think of these words now? I'm still wondering even after I go inside. When the phone rings, I reach for the receiver and hear Katy's voice, tight with pain: "Mom, I think I've started labor."

It's ten o'clock when I get to the hospital. Katy is in labor, and she's already in the birthing room, which looks almost like a bedroom with its rocking chair and comfortable recliner. There, too, are Katy's husband, Mike; her big sister, Lisa; and Mike's parents. We're all allowed to stay with Katy throughout the baby's birth.

Katy's IV is started, and a blood pressure cuff is strapped on. The fetal heart monitor is inserted. A machine alongside the bed now sounds with every beat, and a rapid beep, beep, beep fills the room. As Katy's labor becomes more intense, Mike and I take turns as breathing coach. "Katy, focus on the far wall... breathe in... hold it... breathe out...."

At two o'clock in the morning, nurses and technicians come and go, checking machines, monitoring Katy. We joke, trying to keep Katy distracted. We can see from the rise and fall of lines on a screen that the contractions are fiercer and more constant. Katy asks for something for the pain.

By three o'clock in the morning, the anesthetic finally works. While Katy catches brief snatches of rest, I watch the monitor that shows in numerals the beats per minute of the baby's heart—155. The rhythmic beeps lull us. A nurse comes to suggest we all go downstairs to get some coffee. "Nothing much is happening here," she says, smiling at Katy's quiet form.

Our sleepy group straggles toward the door. But as I pass Katy's bed, she says, "Mom, don't leave me."

"Honey, what's wrong?" I send the others on.

"The contractions seem to be different," she says. I squeeze her hand and tell her to rest. "I'll wake you if anything happens," I tease.

I watch the machines. The contractions are less intense but lasting much longer.

And there's another change. Up until now, the digital readout of the baby's heartbeat has remained steady, never varying more than ten beats with each reading: 150... 145... 140.... But now, after each contraction, the beeps are further and further apart... 125... 120... The baby's heartbeat is slowing... 95... 90... 80....

Katy's eyes open wide. "Mom! Something's wrong!"

70... 65....

Two nurses rush into the room. I hold Katy's hand, hoping my grip doesn't indicate my panic.

...40... 30...

The beeps stop. No numbers flash on the screen; it's completely blank.

One long shrill wail fills the room. Suddenly white uniforms are everywhere.

"What's happening?" Katy's voice is jagged with fear as a nurse pulls an oxygen mask from the wall and slips it over Katy's mouth and nose. "Breathe," the nurse says firmly. More people crowd the room.

Tense voices ricochet around us. "Is her doctor in the hospital?" "Who's on call?" "Better set up for C-section." And then I hear words I hope Katy does not. "Tell the doctor to get here fast," someone calls out. "We're losing the baby!"

"Mama, pray! Please pray!" Katy's words are muted but distinct behind the oxygen mask.

I'm frozen with terror; I try to do as Katy says, but it's hard with all these strangers rushing around me. "Katy, Honey, I am praying." I lean closer to reassure her.

"I mean out loud!" Her hands twist frantically in mine.

I'd laugh if I weren't so scared. Katy's been known to roll her eyes when I even talk about praying, much less bow my head to say grace in a restaurant. She's often told me in great embarrassment, "Puh-leese, Mom, don't pray in front of people."

But now she repeats the request. "Pray out loud," she begs. I know I've got to keep her calm. But how to pray, what words to use?

In everything, by prayer and petition, with thanksgiving...

"Thank you, God," I say, "for this baby you've created, this little one we are so anxiously awaiting. Thank you for the hospital and the nurses." My voice starts off weak and unsure, but as more reasons for thanksgiving come to mind, my voice becomes confident and strong.

The piercing alarm fills the room, fills our ears, tries to fill our hearts.

"Louder, Mama!"

Present your requests to God...

"God, we want this baby. But we also want what you want. Help us through this, God, please! Be in the hands and hearts of the good people working here." Katy nods as I pray over the wailing of the alarm.

And the peace of God, which transcends all understanding, will guard your hearts and minds in Christ Jesus.

With each word, I see that Katy is relaxing, that the tension and fear are leaving her body and leaving the baby's body, too. "Thank you, God," Katy murmurs.

The alarm stops. There's complete quiet. And then we all hear it...

...beep... beep... beep....

...30... 40... 45....

The baby's heart beats again.

...70... 75... 80....

No one speaks. Everyone listens to the blessed sound of that tiny heartbeat until it is healthy.

A soft cheer goes up in the room. The doctor pats Katy's arm. "We'll keep an eye on you, but I think you're going to deliver this baby normally. And soon."

Our unsuspecting family appears, bewildered by the crowded room. When I follow the doctor into the hall and ask what happened, he shakes his head. He can't explain what caused the crisis. And he has no idea why it reversed itself. "There are some things we'll never have answers for," he says.

Soon baby Caitlin is born. But since she's been deprived of oxygen, her skin is dark blue-gray. All eyes watch as an oxygen mask is used again, this time on the baby. I hold my breath, then watch in wonder as a pink glow suffuses the tiny body. A cheer goes up in the room once more: The baby is healthy!

A few minutes later, a nurse hands a blanket-wrapped bundle to me. In the early morning light I look long and wonderingly at the exquisite, wide-awake face of my new granddaughter.

"Mom?" Katy stretches her hand toward me. "I'm so glad you were there. I still need you, you know."

"Oh, Katy," I say, "I still need to be needed."

Trusting some inner instinct, I'd been home for Katy's call. And as we trusted in the power of His promises in a time of crisis, God had been there for us.

Ah, me and Katy and Caitlin. Yes, as the years pass, there will be moments when we do not connect.

But then will come the times when we're completely connected in ways that pass all understanding.

~L. Maggie Baxter
Chicken Soup for the Christian Family Soul

A Hug for Your Thoughts

You can't wrap love in a box, but you can wrap a person in a hug.
~Author Unknown

"**M**om, you're always on the computer!" Laura grumbled.
"No, I'm not," I defended.
"Every day I come home from school you're working on the computer."
"Well, at least I'm here for you!"

My daughter, Laura, at twelve years old, was right. Day after day, in my home office, I would stare into space as my hands typed out the thoughts of a presentation or of research completed for an article. It seemed that my work as a writer and speaker cemented my fingers to the keyboard and my mind to valuable ideas. What Laura did not realize was that during her day away, I'd also be doing a load of laundry, answering incoming phone calls, cleaning up dirty dishes, crunching an editor's deadline, sorting the family mail, networking and marketing my speaking service. It was only around three in the afternoon that I'd finally collapse at my desk for a few precious moments of deep thought. Then she'd come in from school.

I prided myself on being available to my children. After all, I am a speaker on child behavior and parenting. But Laura's observation stung my conscience. Her perception of me must have been of a mom who was available but unapproachable. Hardly the image I wanted to project. My relationship with my children is more important than any other career.

"Laura," I called, "come here a minute."

Out of her bedroom, Laura strolled down the hall to my doorway. I had decided to have her alert me when I was obsessed with work. I wanted her to have the power to let me know when she thought I was being aloof.

"So you think I'm preoccupied?" I asked.

"Most of the time," came her honest reply.

After I explained my full schedule and the fact that I chose to work from home to be accessible to her and her sister, I offered Laura this compromise.

"Whenever you feel I'm ignoring you or you need my attention, I want you to hug me," I said. "Just come up and give me a little hug, and that'll be our signal that you need me."

Years later we still have that unspoken sign. I've become much more sensitive to my daughters' comings and goings. And on the days I'm not, Laura gives me a little squeeze to remind me of the real reason I work from home.

~Brenda Nixon
Chicken Soup for the Working Woman's Soul

Climb On

Don't live down to expectations. Go out there and do something remarkable.
~Wendy Wasserstein

A t a workshop recently I was asked to make a list of all the gifts I had received that made a difference in my life. What a task! To sort through my past for the many wonderful gifts of encouragement, of understanding, of real physical or financial assistance, of listening, and of good advice, is to acknowledge the many people who have given me a hand along the way. A gift I received from my daughter Lacy last summer stands out as especially heartfelt.

It was a soft June morning when she called me and said cheerily, "Hi, Mom, you want to go rock climbing?" I longed to go rock climbing. I was just a few months past abdominal surgery for cancer and still regaining my physical strength and emotional equilibrium. I was not sure I could climb a small hill, let alone a big rock. Because I trust her so deeply and because she made it seem fine to go along, I decided to do it.

We ordered picnic lunches and drove to the base of our climbing site. We loaded up with gear — big, impressive-looking blue and purple climbing ropes, harnesses, an assortment of carabiners, special climbers' shoes, helmets, the lunches, water and insect repellent. We hiked up a road and cut into the woods along an overgrown trail. It was hot, and I was working hard — harder than I dreamed I could. I stopped often to catch my breath, but it felt great to be out in the early morning sun, tramping through woods that echoed with birdcalls. I was glad to be alive.

Rose Ledge is a beautiful site deep in the woods and perfect for beginning climbs. The ledge looked awfully high to me, but Lacy and Connie set up the climb with great energy and efficiency. Lacy anchored our ropes to trees above the ledge and dropped them straight down where they landed at my feet. She set up the safety system known as belaying and tested it out. I watched and ate a cookie.

To ready ourselves for climbing we stretched a bit, then did "bouldering" on smaller rocks. This meant clambering around on rocks while Lacy "spotted" me, standing close to break my fall if needed. Bouldering was hard for me and scary, too, even though I was only a few feet off the ground. I did love the feel of the solidness of rock as I wedged a toe here and found a hand-hold there.

I stepped into the big black harness, tightened the waist, and donned a helmet. I was then fastened to Lacy by a rope that could be loosened or tightened as I climbed. Lacy, the belayer, was tied in and anchored at the bottom tree and, because of this system, I could not fall. At least that is the theory, I thought, as I struggled to get my breath.

"Ready to climb, Mom?" Lacy chirped. I wanted to shout out a resounding "Ready!" but what came out was more like the pathetic meow of the cat when he wants his breakfast. "Yeow," I said in a hoarse whisper.

Then came the series of questions and responses between climber and belayer, me and Lacy, to make sure we were communicating and the safety system was working. When it is all secure, the climber says, "Climbing," and the belayer says, "Climb on!"

The first few steps weren't that hard, and I was well off the ground and mighty pleased with myself when I stopped the first time. I was safely wedged into the chimney we had chosen as a first effort. As I climbed higher, the footholds became toeholds, the hand-holds finger-holds, and I was suddenly scared. I stopped.

"I'm scared. I can't go any higher," I called down.

"That's fine, Mom, just rest right there. Remember I've got you," she called back. I took some deep breaths and snuck a look. Oh goodness, I was far from the bottom and nowhere near the top. I wanted to complete that climb so badly I could taste it. "Now what?" I yelled out.

"You're doing great, Mom, just great," Lacy said. I blinked back tears and swallowed hard. Lacy gave me specific instructions and with my heart hammering away, I did just what she said, and before I knew it, I was up further than I ever imagined I could go. Elated by this realization, I scrambled up the last of the climb using feet, knees, elbows, hands, back and sheer determination. I let out a loud "Eeeee haaaa!" when I got to the top. Lacy was laughing and yelling, "You made it, Mom, you did it!"

I was euphoric and giddy with achievement—but wait: I realized with a nasty jolt that I now had to get down again.

There were two ways to go down. I could climb down: hard and slow but safe. Or I could rappel down: glide down while gently bouncing off the wall of the rock. That required a leap of faith because I had to lean back into the harness and let myself go. I had to trust the system we created totally.

It is a heart-stopping thrill to fall backwards into space, let me tell you. After a few mini-falls, I was back on the ground and said loudly and with great confidence, "Off belay!" And Lacy, my beautiful daughter, responded as quietly as a prayer, "Belay off."

Eating lunch, I was famished, exhausted and exhilarated all at once. Through the rest of the warm summer afternoon, I rested and watched Lacy and the others climb. We walked back to the truck in companionable silence as the accomplishments of the day sank in. That day Lacy took such good care of me. She provided for me: lunch, safety, cheer and an opportunity to have what I have always loved best, an adventure. She taught me everything I needed to know about climbing that rock, she provided my physical and emotional safety and she cheered me on. Something deep inside my chest shifted as I experienced a powerful turning of the cosmic coin. Lacy was giving me what I had always worked to give her.

It was months later when I felt another piece of this experience settle into place. At the same workshop, I was asked to discover what the gifts said about me. If the gifts were a kind of mirror, what did they reflect?

This gift reflected a mother who provided safety while encouraging my daughter to climb higher. Since Lacy always has, I must have done my part. Now when either of us faces a difficult challenge we say to the other, "Climbing," and know the response will be, "Climb on."

~Judy Henning
Chicken Soup for the Mother & Daughter Soul

My Turn

Two kinds of gratitude:
The sudden kind we feel for what we take;
the larger kind we feel for what we give.
~Edwin Arlington Robinson

I got lost walking home from kindergarten on a stormy, raining, cold day. I was so scared. A very kind lady was letting her puppy out and saw me crying. I tearfully told her my name and where I lived, which was only a street away, but to a five-year-old it seemed as if I was at the other end of the world. This kind old lady (she must have been at least thirty-nine) took her puppy into the house and called my mother. Mom arrived with a warm sweater and a big umbrella. She gently took my hand, thanked the lady and walked me home. I will never forget the happiness and security I felt when I saw my mother coming to rescue me. It felt so good to be safe and loved.

Now, it is my mom who is lost, in a storm called Alzheimer's. Most of her days are unsettled and cold. I had raindrops, my mom has teardrops. But for her there are no kind ladies to call for help, no warm sweaters, no umbrellas, no hands to lead her home. She will never in this lifetime know the happiness of being found. I take her hand and hold her tightly, but I am frustrated because as hard as I try, I can never lead my mother to a place where she feels safe and loved.

Yet so many times, in the midst of her worst confusion, when she stops her meaningless chatter and says "I love you," her heart is talking to mine. And sometimes when I take her hand and say the

Lord's Prayer, she joins in automatically. These two things are more powerful than a hundred other actions or a million sensible words.

Why do I bother to visit? Friends sometimes ask. Though it breaks my heart, I never look at it as a bother. This very mixed-up person who doesn't know my name is the same gentle lady who once cared for me, comforted me, held me, cleaned me up, cheered me up, and nourished and nursed me through the roughest times. It was difficult for my mom. Knowing how much she loved me, I understand now that her heart must have been broken every time mine was. Before I was able to speak a word, she knew my every need and did all in her power to fulfill it.

Now it's my turn.

~Barbara Jeanne Fisher
Chicken Soup for the Christian Woman's Soul

The Bear

The other day on the radio, I heard a male talk-show host discussing the "awful" plight of Latinas: Their families don't expect them to achieve and don't have goals for their girls to do well in school and go on to college. He believed that all Latino families wanted their girls to start families and be good mothers, aspiring to nothing else. I had to smile—he was right in some ways, but he was also so wrong. He did not understand what our families want for us and why. He did not understand the strength and courage our culture provides for us and how. He did, however, lead me down memory lane to the day when I discovered what he did not know....

She came into my room, gingerly holding a package in her hands, and sat on my bed, shedding quiet tears as I made my way around to her. Walking slowly to where she sat, I kept wondering, What can I say? What can I do? All the time I was thinking, If I am not strong now, I'll never make it. This is my moment of truth. I need to be strong for both of us right now, or I will never get out of here. I will never have a chance to explore my potential.

For the past four years, since my dad had left, I had been looking after my little sister and my mom. She had suddenly been thrust into the role of breadwinner, and I into the role of caretaker. I had cooked, cleaned, babysat, baked goodies for bake sales, helped my little sister with homework and attended school functions. My mother would have preferred that I stay home with her and continue to support her in these roles, but I had made a firm decision to get a college education, and there was no turning back.

Holding back my own tears, I sat down beside her and put my arms around her shoulders. I told her everything would be fine, and that I would always be her daughter. I would still take care of her, but I needed to do this. She said, "I know. I love you, and I'm so proud of you. I know that going to college has been a dream of yours for years. I am going to miss you, but I want you to know that I love you, no matter what, and I understand why you have to go. I am so proud of you."

At that moment, my mom tenderly handed me the package she held so delicately in her hands. I took the gift and opened it slowly, wondering what else she had gotten me after the towels, linens, calculator and dictionary. It was a raggedy, forlorn-looking Paddington Bear. The bear came with an oversized yellow hat, a blue overcoat and a tag that read, "Please Look After This Bear." I burst into tears. My mother looked at me tenderly and said, "Please, look after this bear, take good care of it, and if the bear ever needs anything, let me know." We both knew she was talking about me. We both knew she wanted me to take good care of myself as I ventured forth into unknown territory, as I took steps to become my own person—not by getting married as my mom had done, but by going to the university, as no one else in our family had ever done.

The bear would become a symbol of our bond, of our love and of our growth as mother and daughter. She would frequently call and ask me how "the bear" was doing. I kept the bear on my bed as a constant reminder of the love of a mother who did not understand all that was happening in her daughter's life, but who, in her own way, was trying to be supportive of her ambitious daughter's dreams.

As a Latina, I grew up in a world of very different expectations. I was expected to be the stereotype the radio talk-show host was speaking about: I was supposed to be a good wife and mother someday, the keeper of family traditions, the holder of the beliefs and values that were an integral part of our family heritage and culture. I was expected to learn how to cook and to support my husband's efforts to care for the family. No one expected me to want something else for myself.

I, on the other hand, had different expectations. I had dreams that went beyond what my family, my community and my culture had in mind for their daughters. I wanted to get a college education and have a career.

Reconciling dreams with cultural and familial expectations can be very difficult. When we decide to pursue a different path, it is a break with tradition, belief and values. Our culture does not always expect women to go out and seek their place in the world. It can be especially hard for our mothers because they may see our breaking the mold as a comparison of a life not lived, opportunities not taken, dreams not fulfilled. We, as Latinas, need to be careful that we do not reject the way of life our mothers chose—and instead, honor and respect them for the women they chose to be, for the foundation they laid for us to build our dreams upon.

Yes, it took me a while to appreciate all my mom has done for me and the sacrifices she has made, but I know she had the courage to do what she did because she, like me, is a strong Latina—a Latina who has taken all that is good about her life and her culture and channeled that energy into loving and supporting her family.

I still have my Paddington Bear gracing my bedroom. It is a constant reminder to me of a mother's love that has given me roots and given me wings. Roots that anchored me throughout all of life's challenges. Wings that allowed me to soar and to freely dream of becoming the woman I could become.

My mother's support taught me that our cultural legacy gives us the courage to become the individuals we were meant to be and to inspire others to do the same.

The man talking on the radio that day about the "poor Latinas?" He obviously never met me or my mother!

~Zulmara Cline
Chicken Soup for the Latino Soul

Marathon Women

It is time for us to stand and cheer for the doer, the achiever,
the one who recognizes the challenge and does something about it.
~Vince Lombardi

On an ordinary afternoon in March, Eliza, my sixteen-year-old daughter, plopped her backpack at my feet, waved a brochure so close it grazed my nose and made a declaration. "I'm signing up for the Marine Corps Marathon. I'll be running with a group that raises money for AIDS and trains Sunday mornings at seven."

"Seven A.M.—are you crazy?" Then, pausing for less time than it takes to say "PowerBar," I added, "Tell you what, I'll sign up with you." It was as though, for just this microsecond, I had morphed into Jane Fonda.

Now alone, I began to confront different questions. Was I doing this for myself or for Eliza? Or to bolster my athletic image with friends and acquaintances? Was I willing to risk injury and, in turn, all the skiing and swing dancing that filled the void left by my divorce? Wasn't there a simpler bonding opportunity with Eliza? And an easier way to meet guys? Would I ever find a sports bra that worked? And why would I give up six months of Sunday mornings to arrive at my weekly training sessions earlier than the newspaper arrived on my doorstep? Surely not because running 26.2 miles with thousands of other Type As had always been my dream. More likely, my interest could have been called curiosity.

Nonetheless, I attended an orientation meeting with Eliza where we signed up and exchanged motives with other hopefuls. A trim secretary, seated beside me, told the group, "My best friend is dying from AIDS. He can't run, so I'm going to do it for him." Ashamed of my egocentric motivation, I sheepishly introduced myself and expressed my desire to regain a sense of focus in my life. When Eliza announced that she looked forward to training with her mom and raising money for AIDS, I felt exonerated.

At our first weekly training session, we were assigned partners and placed in pace groups. These were the people with whom we would work out as well as run the actual marathon. Eliza's tight-abs pack lined up near the front; despite our neon CoolMax costumes, my partner, Rayford, and I found ourselves in the rear among the less hurried. In the weeks that followed, the pain of placing one foot in front of the other was eased, ironically, by Rayford's sagas of his partner's death from AIDS and living with his own HIV. After we got through a twelve-mile Sunday run by exchanging the ordeals of Rayford's coming out and the final year of my marriage, we agreed on "single in the seventies" as our topic for the upcoming three-hour, fourteen-mile run.

If I were still married, I would have bristled at the idea of striding the equivalent of halfway from Washington to Baltimore (or if you compute all the training miles, round trip to Scarsdale). Isn't it striking how a major life change, like divorce, can transform you into the opposite of who you thought you were? Yet, dim recollections suggested that the marathoner was who I originally was. It seemed that marriage had molded me, temporarily, into someone far more sedentary.

Sometimes I imagined Eliza and myself as two intersecting rings. I worried that I was treading on her exclusive territory when I asked her, "Would you mind if I try to keep up with your group on next week's six-mile maintenance run? It might be my only chance to jog with you before the distance increases."

Even before she answered, her response was evident in her bright eyes, lit up the way they did on the trail when her group, in their homestretch, passed me as I was still huffing my way to the halfway mark, and her fellow speed-mates cheered, "Go, Liza's mom."

As Eliza and I planned a party for the fundraising component of our marathon, she asked, "Mom, how can I take credit for half the donations? They'll be mostly from your friends." I told her that so many of my friends were the parents of her friends and that we were in this together—a partnership. We not only jointly crafted invitations and baked brownies, but we also explained to our guests what raising money for drug therapies that offered hope to people with HIV/AIDS meant to us. I reminded Eliza that, without her, this expansion of my world would never have occurred.

As the training distances mounted, I began to believe that I could actually make it to the finish line. New queries surfaced. Would Eliza wait at the finish line on marathon day until I completed the course? Wasn't it backward—shouldn't the mother be the one to soak up her little girl's I-did-it grin as she crossed the finish line? Or was this one of those role reversals dealt to us by the passing years? On my birthday, Eliza hauled out a cake she had baked and shouted, "Yay!" when I extinguished the candles in one blow.

And on marathon day, there I was sailing by on my merry-go-round as I cried, "Look at me!" Eliza jumped and waved and cheered my victory—hers, mine, ours.

~Susan Fishman Orlins
Chicken Soup to Inspire a Woman's Soul

Chapter 5

Like Mother, Like Daughter

Gratitude

*Each day offers us the gift of being a special occasion
if we can simply learn that as well as giving,
it is blessed to receive with grace and a grateful heart.*
~Sarah Ban Breathnach

Your Friend, Mommy

I gave birth to Whitney in the spring of my teenage years. From the outside, this could have looked like a logistical nightmare. Indeed, sometimes it was. Diaper changes interrupted studying, and she had to be put to bed before I went off to my school dances. I was filling out elementary-school registration forms for her while trying to meet college financial-aid applications for myself. Now that she's fifteen, it feels like she has always been a part of my life. We've shared important moments. She was there when I learned how to drive, graduated high school and got accepted to college — Harvard, no less! We've been doing our homework together for years.

Whitney and I used to go over her homework in the evenings. We were often so tired (and irritable) by the time we sat down that these sessions could be tense — sometimes ending in tears or bruised emotions. Our evening meetings often came at the close of long days; days that Whitney and I had likely spent starved for each other's affection. Otherwise, we shared rushed exchanges: Do you need lunch money? Yes. Don't miss the bus! I won't. Grandma will be here when you come home. Okay. I have a class tonight and I'll come in to say good night when I come in. All right. Did you eat? Not yet. I love you. I love you, too.

When we sat down, our hearts ached with questions that we didn't ask: Are you as famished for my attention as I am for yours? Am I special to you? Are you okay? Am I doing okay? Are you happy that I am yours, and you are mine? Are we going to make it? We made it by the skin of our teeth today, but can we pull it off tomorrow, next week... next month, next year? We looked for answers to these unspoken questions in every touch, glance and remark. We scrutinized each other's tone of voice and facial expressions for affirmation. A curt response or innocent correction could be mistaken for disapproval. I knew I had to be careful not to communicate anything that could be taken the wrong way. I tried to exude excitement. Most of the time, I fell short, holding exhaustion at bay just long enough to muscle some neutrality.

One evening, Whitney was finishing a homework assignment in which she was instructed to draw a grid and place the people that she knew into the correct categories: friends, family, neighbors and so on. I checked it over for mistakes. Everything was in order, except that she had drawn a picture of me in the "friends" box.

"Whitney," I said, "this picture of me is supposed to be in the 'family' category."

She looked at me, her big brown eyes wide and charitable. "You're my friend, too," she said. She was not defensive or offended. She spoke as if she were reminding me of an eternal truth that I had only momentarily forgotten—the same way she would remind me that two plus two equals four.

"Oh," I said quietly. I was embarrassed, but delighted to be reminded of all of the special roles that we filled in each other's lives.

That evening I went to bed assured of the answers to our unuttered questions. Yes, you are special to me. No, I wouldn't want to belong to anyone else in the world. Absolutely, we are going to make it. We are okay.

~Patricia J. Lesesne
Chicken Soup for the Single Parent's Soul

It Runs in the Family

He who trims himself to suit everyone will soon whittle himself away.
~Raymond Hull

My childhood had its ups and downs but included my momma, Karen, who was so supportive that I was destined to succeed in life.

She never missed any of my school events, poetry contests, honor roll assemblies, student government elections or the countless football and basketball games spanning six years of cheerleading. When I graduated from college, I was selected to give the commencement address. Just like old times, my mother sat in a chair in my dorm room and listened to my speech over and over again.

That reminded me of a time when I used to be embarrassed by my mother. She always laughed just a little too loud. She never dressed the way I wanted her to dress. She had very few outfits that weren't gold or red, and you'd be hard pressed to find something in her closet without a sequin sewn on it. I respected my mother for her talents, but I just wanted her to be a little more like other mothers and a lot less crazy.

When I entered a statewide speech contest, I prayed for my mother to magically transform into the normal mother everyone else seemed to have. The whole time I gave my speech she moved her lips as if she were coaching me. Instead of feeling grateful for her involvement, I worried other people would think she was talking to herself.

It felt impossible to pass for normal when our craziness was as obvious as the frilly Easter-looking dress I had to wear. By the time I made it to the finals, I had given my mother strict conditions. First, even though we couldn't afford it, I demanded a blue suit, like the other girls. I instructed her not to mouth the words to my speech. Finally, I warned, under no circumstances should she jump up and down and make whooping noises if I won. This wasn't a Dunbar High School pep rally; it was the suburban Optimist Club speech contest, and we had to look the part.

When I took to the stage, one of ten finalists remaining of the thousands of girls in the competition, I looked around the room. There was only one other brown face that looked like mine. Momma's. The opinion of the other contestants, the crowd and the judges became increasingly less important to me.

As I delivered my presentation, possibly one of the most flawless performances of my fourteen years on Earth, I realized my mother was sitting in her seat with her face turned toward the door rather than the stage—obeying my strict directives. I had thought that if she didn't look at me, she wouldn't be tempted to do any of those crazy things that distracted me.

I realized now that the only way she knew all the words to my speech was because she had obviously memorized it, too—just to show her support for me. I knew then that I had no desire to win without my mother seeing it and celebrating in whatever way she chose to.

Near the end of my speech, I stepped from behind the podium, walked down the stage and onto the main floor. I wanted Momma's attention. My mother sat still in her contorted position gripping the side of the white linen tablecloth, desperately trying to do what I had asked her to do: Be someone else. She never moved. I finished with a dramatic close, but she never looked up. While the rest of the crowd rose to their feet in a standing ovation, Momma was still. When they handed me the plaque and the scholarship money, Momma allowed herself to simply smile.

Without our traditional "cutting up" and "act a fool" celebration, my victory felt empty. In that moment, with my future looking bright,

I realized you can't enjoy where you are going if you deny where you are from.

I let her know from that moment on she could whoop and holler and be herself. I wouldn't want her any other way. After all, she was my momma, and if she was crazy, then call me crazy, too.

~Jarralynne Agee
Chicken Soup for the African American Soul

My Mother's Cure

To break the spell of a long, cold Minnesota winter, my mother and I pored over seed catalogs making plans for a garden. "Maybe we should plant tomatoes," my mother suggested. "Grandma had good luck with tomatoes. Wish I could remember what she said about growing tomatoes. Hmm. Maybe it will come to me."

"I hope we have better luck with tomatoes than we did last year with flowers," I grumbled. Ever since I had turned fifteen in the fall, I seemed to grumble about everything.

"Oh, come on, Jeanie. Cheer up. We'll have lots of fun in our tomato garden. It'll be a real mother-daughter project. Two by two, we'll see them through, from seeds to soup," my mother said, adding a little soft-shoe step to her words.

When the precious seeds came to our house, my mother sowed them in what she called a "baby" flat. When they grew too big for that flat, she transplanted them into bigger flats. "Sixty plants!" she exclaimed. "Why, we've got our work cut out for us this summer, that's for sure."

"How many tomatoes do you think we'll get from each plant?" I asked, looking dubiously at the spindly little things.

"Well, if we had a bigger plot, we'd have hundreds. But the yard is too small for that. We'll have to stake them. That way, we'll decrease the number of tomatoes per plant. It will mean we'll have to trim some 'kiddos' from each mother plant."

"Oh, Mom!" I wailed. "That sounds horrible!"

"Oh, don't be silly, Jeanie," Mom said, with a touch of impatience.

"Honestly, you teenagers are all alike. The merest little thing and you go into hysterics. A summer of good, hard work will be the cure for what ails you. As soon as there's no longer any danger of frost, we'll get these plants outside."

It was barely daylight one Saturday morning when my mother yanked me out of bed. As she tossed me a pair of overalls and a trowel, she said, "We haven't a minute to lose. Weatherman says we are in for rain by mid-morning. Let's get those plants in so they can soak up that nice spring rain."

I kept up a constant stream of complaints as I worked along with my mother. She brushed them all aside with a song she said Grandma always sang as they gardened together. "Just wish I could remember what she said, though, about growing tomatoes. Might still come to me as we go along here, two by two, from seeds to soup."

My mother was relentless in her "cure" for whatever it was that ailed me that summer. I had barely recovered from my planting experience when she informed me that it was time to hoe and weed our garden plot. If we weren't hoeing and weeding, we were warding off cutworms by wrapping the bases of the plants with paper. The more I griped about all the hard work, the louder my mother sang about the joys of working together.

As the summer slipped away, out came the canning equipment. We spent a long, boring weekend boiling and rinsing each item with great care.

"We'll have to labor away on Labor Day," Mom said. "I wouldn't want to waste even one tomato. We'll have tomato juice, some we'll can whole and some we'll boil down for soup. And I have the recipe for Grandma's chili. I sure wish I could remember what it was she said about growing tomatoes. Still hasn't come to me. Oh, say, Jeanie, run down the street, will you, and get Mrs. Nelson's Mason jars? She has a sack set aside for me."

I barely recognized the boy who opened the Nelsons' backdoor. Could that really be Eddie, the Nelsons' grandson? Where was the gangly, awkward Eddie of last summer? I was so stunned by his movie-star good looks I felt a peppy tune building up inside me. When I stumbled down the steps, Eddie offered to carry the sack of jars and walk me home. When my mother saw him, she was as surprised as I had been. She stammered out something about fixing iced tea.

"Are you here for the Labor Day weekend?" she asked, when I was unable to break the silence.

"Uh—well, no. I mean, yes," Eddie blushed. "I'm going to the academy this year, and I'm here early for football practice. I'll be living with my grandparents while I go to school."

"Isn't that wonderful!" my mother glowed.

"Yeah, it's great," Eddie said. "We're having a team picnic on Labor Day. Uh—hmm—uh, say, Jean, maybe you'd like to come with me—I mean, if you're free Labor Day," Eddie concluded, looking directly at me.

I looked around at the kitchen counters heaped high with tomatoes and canning equipment, gazed with great pain at the sack of Mason jars, and dared not meet my mother's eye. I had been by her side all summer. She had met my gripes and sass with as much love and care as she had lavished on her tomatoes. She had wanted us to be a mother-daughter team, seeing this project through from seeds to soup. But I hoped she would realize how much I wanted to go to that picnic. At the same time, I hated to think of her working alone in our kitchen, humming and singing her little tunes to herself.

My mother took off her glasses and wiped them slowly on a corner of her apron. Surveying the kitchen counters, she seemed to be looking far beyond the tomatoes and canning equipment. Perhaps that is why she said softly, "I remember now what Grandma said about growing tomatoes. She said, 'Children and tomatoes grow much too quickly. But at least you can preserve tomatoes when they blossom.'" In a stronger voice, my mother added, "Of course, Jean may go to the picnic. I'm sure you two will have a wonderful time."

I was so happy I couldn't speak a word, so I couldn't thank my mother until after Eddie left. I was smiling—beaming—for the first time in months. I kissed my mother, and I kissed every tomato within reach. Then I thanked my lucky stars I had a mother who knew how to raise tomatoes—and a daughter.

~Jean Jeffrey Gietzen
Chicken Soup for the Gardener's Soul

She Came Back
Bearing Gifts

The best things in life are unexpected—because there were no expectations.
~Eli Khamarov, Surviving on Planet Reebok

My daughter, Carey, was never really like other children. She began talking in sentences by the time she was a year old. She was extremely inquisitive and always too mature for her age. She excelled scholastically and showed signs of musical talent at an early age. She was inducted into our state's program for gifted and talented children and was invited to be a violinist in the local Youth Symphony. Awards for outstanding achievement in academics and music lined the bookcase in her bedroom. Her stepfather and I couldn't have been more proud.

Then, slowly and dramatically, everything changed. Carey's appearance changed. She started running around with a new group of "friends." She dropped out of the symphony and sports. Truancy notices and reports of her absences from school became commonplace. She became sullen, withdrawn, belligerent and, at times, violent. She scoffed at any form of discipline, crept out of the house in the middle of the night, and often stayed out all night. She ran away from home three times. Carey had discovered drugs.

I fretted, worried, and spent many sleepless nights anticipating a call from local police telling me she was in jail or, worse yet, dead. I lamented over the things I must have done wrong in raising this child and wondered what had become of the moral and emotional foundation I thought I had provided her. Little did I know that this was just the beginning of the end of my dream of a "normal" family with a perfect life.

Over the next two years, my primary goal was to "fix" Carey. I asked a police friend to "scare" some sense into her. I arranged a private "tour" for her of the juvenile detention center. I put her into private counseling. Last, but not least, we moved away from the city, away from the bad influences. Carey loves horses, so we bought three, one for each of us, thinking that if we shared her interest as a family her problems would get better. It was a good plan and it did work... for a while. Before long, it all started again.

Just when I thought things couldn't get any worse, my husband confessed that he was seeing someone. We separated on Memorial Day weekend. I'm not sure how I made it through the first few months. I was scared and lost. I couldn't sleep, forgot to eat, worked twelve-hour days between two hours' driving time, and did my best to keep up with three horses, two dogs, fifteen cats, three acres of yard work and normal household chores. As you might guess, Carey's contribution was, at best, minimal. I felt hopeless.

Then came Christmas. I had always loved Christmas, a time that would bring back sweet memories of childhood surprises, family truces and special traditions. But this year there was nothing to celebrate, no reason to even drag out the Christmas decorations.

On Christmas Eve, I worked until noon. If I could have, I probably would have worked right through to the New Year. The hour drive seemed longer as I imagined my cold, empty house... very much like my heart. I pulled into the drive, reluctantly got out of the car, obligingly petted the dogs and grudgingly walked toward the back door. Suddenly a sweet aroma wafted toward me, beckoning me forward. As I opened the door, a potpourri of tantalizing scents enveloped me. I first identified the smell of food... not ordinary, quick-fix food, but festive, only-on-holiday food. Then I recognized the sweet smell of scented holiday candles. If my nose was merely delighted, my eyes were in awe! This house I was entering had been transformed from the drafty, colorless old farmhouse I had left behind that morning into a warm and glowing Christmas fantasy, a joy to all my senses! Soft Christmas music playing on the stereo relocated from Carey's upstairs bedroom gently competed for my attention to the holiday décor as I floated through each neatly groomed room. When I reached the living room, Carey was sitting in her holiday finery, complete with an apron and a childlike smile I remembered from long ago but hadn't seen in several years. She said, "Sit down and relax. Christmas dinner will be ready soon."

I'm not sure what I said to her then to let her know how much I appreciated what she had done, but no words could have adequately described the way I felt. I just sat and allowed the sights, sounds and smells to fill my senses... and my heart. Over Cornish game hens stuffed with cranberry-orange dressing, homemade sweet potatoes (not from a can), rice pilaf and creamy chocolate pudding, we laughed as we talked of Christmases past.

Lying in bed that night, I thanked God for giving me my daughter. The daughter whom I thought I had lost had just blessed me with the most wonderful gift I have ever received: a much-needed reminder of the true spirit of Christmas... love and hope.

~Luann Warner
Chicken Soup for Every Mom's Soul

The Reunion

My kids knew something was up the minute I took a phone call during dinner and failed to return for three hours. After twenty-five years of wondering and praying, that long awaited call finally came. To be frank, I can barely even remember what we said. How do you fit twenty-five years of unanswered questions into one conversation? Having learned that she lived less than twenty-five minutes from my home, we made immediate plans to reunite, the sooner the better. I emerged from the phone call with a very heady feeling and a date to meet her the next evening.

My husband knew about Nicole from our first date. I had a very well-developed sense of what I wanted in a life-mate. I knew I would spend the rest of my life with him and felt the need to share with him the story of Nicole. I told him with the hope that she would eventually rejoin my life. I wanted him to know that she would also be joining his.

I had gotten pregnant at the age of sixteen, after having been the victim of what is now called date rape. Nicole's biological father was nineteen at the time, and I broke up with him immediately after he forced himself on me. My family fortuitously moved shortly thereafter. Having had sporadic menstrual cycles, I wasn't concerned with the missed periods. I must have attributed the baby's kicking to gas. Being a healthy teenager, I carried her entirely inside, never showing until a month and a half before her birth, and then only slightly.

It was Christmas Eve, after an argument with my mom, when she looked at me in a very serious manner and asked if I was pregnant. I was indignant and vehemently denied the possibility. It did give me plenty of food for thought, and a week later, I asked her to take me to the doctor. I'll never forget her face as she was putting on her mascara, and I casually asked the question. She had forgotten about the Christmas Eve argument. It was one of the hardest things I've ever had to do, mustering up enough courage to stop the denial and face the facts.

Upon learning that I was indeed pregnant and due within thirty to forty-five days, my parents rallied around me and assured me that they would support whatever decision I made. They also made certain that I understood the ramifications of each of my potential choices. It wasn't a hard decision to make, since I really had no bond yet with the baby. I chose to place the baby for adoption.

In those days, if the baby was to be placed for adoption, the mother was not allowed to see the child after delivery. Neither was any other family member, but the hospital staff didn't know my mom. She managed to sneak into the nursery every day of my stay and get as many looks at Nicole as she could steal. As we were leaving the hospital, my mom casually reminded my dad that this would be his last opportunity to take a look at Nicole. He had not joined my mom on any of her stealthy trips to the nursery. The social worker was scheduled to pick Nicole up from the nursery that day. Dad unlocked the doors of the car, got us all settled, was about to drive off, then said, "Wait, I'll be right back." We waited, and on his return he simply said, "Kathy, she's beautiful."

I believe it was the hand of God ensuring I never had the opportunity to emotionally bond with the baby growing inside of me. When Nicole was two weeks old, we met at the Social Services office, where I was to spend time with her in a contrived living room setting. This meeting was to ensure that I still wanted to give her up for adoption. They brought her to me and left me there, alone with her, for fifteen minutes. That was a long fifteen minutes. I was a very young woman and terribly frightened I might drop her. I do remember thinking she was the most beautiful thing I'd ever seen, but I knew I couldn't keep her.

We finalized the paperwork, the adoption process was initiated, and as far as we knew, she went to a family in Richmond, Virginia. I returned to school, finished out the year, and we moved at the end of the year. I went on to graduate from college and gained a commission as a naval officer. It was there that I met my husband. We married three months after meeting each other, nineteen years ago.

We went on to have two children of our own, and thanks to the Naval Reserves, I am now a retired reserve commander. Throughout the years, not a single day went by that I didn't think about Nicole, and pray that she had a good, happy and healthy life. On her eighteenth birthday, I put a letter in her adoption file which detailed how to contact me in the event she ever came looking. My husband and parents were very supportive of this.

When Nicole decided to search for me, my letter made it very easy. The long-awaited phone call had finally come, and my husband shared with me the excitement of the prospect of finally meeting my daughter. The day of the reunion, we sat our boys down and explained the situation. They were wonderfully supportive about it, and asked some frank questions, which we answered very honestly. Excited at the prospect of actually having a sister, they wished me well, gave me big kisses and sent me on my way to my reunion.

Nicole and I met outside the church after my bell choir rehearsal. I will never forget watching her climb out of her Mazda RX-7 and just keep going up, up, up. She was tall, she was blond and she was gorgeous. We very slowly hugged each other with the gentleness afforded only the most precious, fragile treasures in your life. The rest of the evening was spent in a cozy booth at a restaurant down the street. The waitress was observant enough to realize that something very special was going on, and she prudently left us alone to try to catch up on a lifetime.

That night, Nicole told me that if she were to be limited to saying only one thing, she would thank me from the bottom of her heart. "Thank you for having me, for giving me up, and for welcoming me back into your life so warmly and openly." We sat there and compared our hands, feet, the same laugh, the same way we hold our mouths, all the answers to Nicole's questions of "Where did I get that?" This continues to be a resounding thread through our lives— "Oh, that would explain where I got that."

After twenty-five years, I felt as though a tremendous weight had been lifted, and I remember feeling as though there was simply nothing that could beat the joy I felt at finally knowing she was safe, healthy and had grown up with a very loving family. We went on to spend time together each week. She got to know her new brothers, and she very bravely accompanied me to many outings with our friends, getting to know all the people who are special in my life, as I met all those who were special in hers.

My husband took particular pleasure in our reunion since Nicole is almost a mirror image of what I looked like at her age. He loves to go out with us, feeling as though he has the best of both worlds, me at my current age, and me at the age we got married. Even now, more than two years after the reunion, he marvels at the fact that we have the same mouth, smile and laugh.

I don't know if I can ever adequately express the gratitude I owe to her parents for having given her such a wonderful upbringing. They are two very special people, and I am deeply indebted to them. They welcomed me and my family into their lives with the same open arms that welcomed Nicole. The card her mom gave me for Mother's Day that year said it all: "I truly believe children are gifts from God, on loan, for us to raise to become independent and assets to society. Ever since we adopted Nicole, you have been in my thoughts—each February 17, but especially on every Mother's Day. So, Happy Mother's Day, not only have you found a daughter, but a best friend." And to her, I also say thank you.

~Kathy N. Jublou
Chicken Soup for the Mother & Daughter Soul

A Peace Corps Mama

Get over the idea that only children should spend their time in study.
Be a student so long as you still have something to learn,
and this will mean all your life.
~Henry L. Doherty

I went to visit my daughter, Deidre, who spent two years with the Peace Corps in Cameroon from 1994 until 1996. I wrote this poem while I was waiting for the plane to take off from Africa and return home.

I taught my daughter to walk
And she showed me how to walk in the dark
I taught my daughter how to talk
And she spoke for me in French and Bamoun
I taught my daughter to eat with utensils
And she showed me how to eat with my fingers
I taught my daughter how to bathe
And she showed me how to take a bucket bath
I taught my daughter how to vacuum a carpet
And she showed me how to squeegee cement
I taught my daughter first-world greed
She showed me third-world need
I taught my daughter how to love her family
She showed me how to embrace the world.

~Cheryl Reece Myers
Chicken Soup for the Traveler's Soul

Cinderella

y mother committed suicide when I was thirteen, four years after my father died. So my sister Alyce, a battered spouse and mother of two, became my guardian and the only mother I would really know. Within two years, we fled to Los Angeles to escape from her abusive husband.

One day in our second year in L.A. as I thumbed through college catalogues, Alyce asked, "What are you doing about the prom?"

I shrugged. "Who would I go with?"

"We'll see about that." She gave me a June Cleaver smile. "Every girl needs to go to her prom."

I felt more an outcast not being asked to the prom than I had on my first day in the L.A. high school. That day I was noticed because I was a farm girl who looked like one of the Beverly Hillbillies. And as a teenage girl, getting good grades didn't get many points, so I, with my straight As, was out of luck finding a prom date. I hid behind a proud smile and told Alyce, "The prom is nothing special."

I held up the stack of schoolbooks I was carrying. "I'd rather study. You know how important getting a college scholarship is to me."

Alyce ruffled my hair. "You're going to the prom."

The rest of that semester I studied extra hard to be sure I got a scholarship. Alyce, on the other hand, apparently was beating the bushes for my prom date. One day she came home from work and announced, "I've found him."

"Who?"

"Your prom date." Alyce's face was lighted by a smile that sprawled from ear to ear.

"What? You can't be serious. I have no intention of going to some dumb prom with a guy you bribed."

"I didn't bribe anyone. He's a colleague's son."

"I can't believe you're doing this. I'm not going."

Then she produced a gold satin tea-length dress that I could only imagine Princess Grace wearing. The dress had cap sleeves, a scoop neck and a bodice that would hug my torso. The full skirt gracefully flared from the waist, which was accented with a matching gold satin sash. "What's that?" I pointed at the gown.

"Your prom dress. That is if you like it."

It was beautiful, and after a lifetime of inheriting hand-me-downs, the thought of wearing my first truly elegant dress almost melted the horror of being escorted to the prom by a store-bought guy.

"Try it on." Alyce pushed the dress towards me. I didn't take it.

"Go ahead. Just see how it looks."

I knew what she was up to. She believed once I had the dress on, I would change my mind. She was right. I was caught off guard and should have remembered her stubbornness once she had her mind set on something. Yet standing there with that gorgeous dress held in front of my face, I temporarily forgot my sister was an expert in obstinent persistence.

I knew better than to fight Alyce's determination so I grabbed the dress from her and retreated to my bedroom to try it on. As I slipped the dress over my head and down my body, I shuddered with delight at the luxurious softness of the satin. I closed my eyes and caressed the gown's silky bodice and skirt. Then I twirled around so I could listen to the rustle of the new material.

When I came back to the living room to model the dress, Alyce pulled out matching high-heel satin pumps and bag. I shook my head in disbelief. When she held up the new white wool coat, I surrendered.

"You've thought of everything," I said.

"Almost. I've got to make an appointment to get your hair and nails done. You're going to stun them at this ball."

"Hmmm," I said and escaped to my room with my bounty. I sat on my bed fingering each item laid out before me and dreamed about the prom. But then I thought: What if I hate my date? I yelled out to my sister, "What's my date's name?"

"Troy Marvel."

"Ah, the marvelous Troy," I chuckled, wondering if she had invented the name, just as perfect as the dress. Later that evening, I discovered Troy was a student at UCLA and he drove an MG. Not only did I have a date, but he was an older man, a college man.

On the day of the prom Alyce kept her promise and dragged me to Michael's Salon to get my hair and nails done. "I'll have to work a miracle," Michael said as he rubbed his hand in my hair. "It's so fine and no body."

Michael scrubbed my hair with a fragrant shampoo that made my head tingle. I began to feel the transformation taking place from a charwoman to Cinderella. While I sat under the hair dryer, a manicurist turned my hands — raw cuticles, shaggy nails and all — into ones that I'd only seen the likes of in magazines.

As I admired my new pearl nail polish, a woman in a pink lab coat approached me carrying a suitcase and grabbed my newly perfect right hand. "My name is Bobbie," she said and pulled me toward a bar stool in front of a mirror. "Sit," she said, pointing to the stool. I did as I was told. She placed the suitcase on a shelf beneath the mirror that faced me. She opened the case and produced layers of colorful makeup.

"Oh no," I screeched and scowled at Alyce. "It's bad enough I'm going through this date thing, but this?" I pointed to the container.

"This won't be painful," Bobbie laughed. "Besides you need a little color." Bobbie winked.

I groaned but gave in when Alyce hovered nearby.

When Bobbie finished her task, I didn't recognize the girl in the mirror. Michael had created a soft, yet sophisticated upsweep hairstyle and Bobbie's magic gave my skin a glow which looked completely natural. I had never imagined looking like this.

"It's not bad," I said, tilting my head from side to side. Secretly

I felt like a swan rather than the ugly duckling I thought I was. For once, I didn't stick my tongue out at the image staring back from the mirror.

Promptly at seven that night, Alyce and I heard a knock at the door. I wanted to bolt from the room, but Alyce was too quick. She flung the door wide and produced Troy, a drop-dead handsome twenty-one-year-old with black curly hair and perfect white teeth. "What a dream boat," I mumbled to myself.

Troy handed me a corsage of white baby roses held together by gold satin ribbons that matched my dress. Then in one fluid motion he helped me on with my coat, took my arm and led me out the door. I was charmed.

Troy's MG sped into the school parking lot. He walked around the car to open my door as I sat like a queen waiting for him. Several students stopped to see who he was. He reached his hand toward me and helped me out of the car seat. I tried to remember Alyce's lesson about swinging both legs out at the same time. You could hear the gasps from the group when I rose out of the car and they recognized me.

Troy and I strolled into the gym, transformed for this night into a Hawaiian resort complete with miniature waterfalls, fountains sculpted like fish, potted palm trees, flaming torches and non-alcoholic punch served in coconuts. A hush filled the room, and with everyone staring at us, Troy circled his right arm around my back to dance. Then, as though someone had ordered an attack, the same girls who had ignored me for the past two years surrounded us and greeted me, their new best friend.

Prince Charming had rescued me and completed the metamorphosis begun by my sister. For one night I was a swan, Cinderella touched by her fairy godmother—and it was wonderful. Yet like all fantasies, that one came to an abrupt end. All too soon I was home again, pulling off the beautiful dress and stepping out of the matching shoes.

When Troy discovered I wasn't the glamorous woman manufactured by Alyce, Michael and Bobbie, he moved on. Unlike the real

Cinderella story, Alyce wasn't a wicked stepmother, and the glass slipper didn't fit my foot. Yet that one evening will forever be special to me, because I learned about the love of a sister—my mother—and to what lengths she would go to make my life magical.

~Tekla Dennison Miller
Chicken Soup for the Mother & Daughter Soul

The Most Precious Gift

You give but little when you give of your possessions.
It is when you give of yourself that you truly give.
~Kahlil Gibran, The Prophet

'll never forget that warm summer day in July 1965, when my mother unexpectedly died of a still unexplained illness at the young age of thirty-six. Later that afternoon, a police officer stopped by to ask my father's permission for the hospital to use my mother's aortic valve and the corneas from her eyes. I was absolutely stunned. The doctors want to dissect Mom and give her away to other people, I thought as I ran into the house in tears.

At fourteen, I could not understand why anyone would take apart a person I loved. To top it off, my father told them, "Yes."

"How can you let them do that to her?" I screamed at him. "My mom came into this world in one piece and that is how she should go out."

"Linda," he said quietly, putting his arm around me, "the greatest gift you can give is a part of yourself. Your mother and I decided long ago that if we can make a difference in just one person's life after we die, then our death will have meaning." He went on to explain they had both decided to be organ donors.

The lesson my father taught me that day became one of the most important in my life.

Years passed. I married and had a family of my own. In 1980, my father became seriously ill with emphysema and moved in with

He cheerfully told me that when he died, he wanted me to donate whatever was in good condition, especially his eyes. "Sight is one of the greatest gifts a person can give," he said, noting how wonderful it would be if a child could be helped to see, and draw horses the way my daughter Wendy did.

She had been drawing horses all her life, winning award after award. "Just imagine how proud another parent would feel if her daughter could draw like Wendy," Dad said. "Think how proud you would feel knowing that my eyes were making it possible."

I told Wendy what her grandpa had said, and, with tears in her eyes, she went into her grandpa's room and gave him a big hug.

She was only fourteen years old—the same age at which I was introduced to the donor program. What a difference!

My father died April 11, 1986, and we donated his eyes as he had wanted. Three days later Wendy said, "Mom, I'm so proud of you for what you did for Grandpa."

"That makes you proud?" I asked.

"You bet! Have you ever thought what it would be like not to see? When I die, I want my eyes donated just like Grandpa."

At that moment, I realized that my father gave much more than his eyes. What he left behind sparkled in my daughter's eyes—pride.

What I couldn't know that day, as I held Wendy in my arms, was that only two weeks later I would be once again signing papers for the donor program.

My lovely, talented Wendy was killed when a truck hit her and the horse she was riding along the roadside. As I signed the papers, her words echoed over and over: "You bet! Have you ever thought what it would be like not to see?"

Three weeks after Wendy's death, I received a letter from the eye bank.

Dear Mr. and Mrs. Rivers,

We want you to know that the corneal transplantation was successful and now two people who were blind have regained their sight. They represent a living memorial to your daughter—a person who cared enough about life to share its beauties.

If somewhere a recipient discovers a new love for horses and sits down to sketch one out, I think I'll know who the donor was. A blond-haired, blue-eyed girl will still be drawing.

~Linda Rivers
Chicken Soup for the Father's Soul

Happy Birthday, Baby

A mother is the truest friend we have, when trials heavy and sudden, fall upon us; when adversity takes the place of prosperity; when friends who rejoice with us in our sunshine desert us; when trouble thickens around us, still will she cling to us, and endeavor by her kind precepts and counsels to dissipate the clouds of darkness, and cause peace to return to our hearts.
~Washington Irving

It took me a while to realize what day it was. I awoke to gray skies and the chance of snow in the forecast for Wednesday, January twenty-eighth. My birthday. I was thirty-five. I turned away from the clock radio and wished I'd taken the day off from work. I wanted to stay in bed and snuggle up to my self-pity about being alone — yet again — on this significant day. My most recent attempt at romance had crashed and burned two weeks earlier, and the wounds were still fresh. It hadn't been a long relationship, and it wasn't even that much of a relationship, but it had refueled my hopes and dreams about having someone to come home to. As I lay in bed, I remembered blowing out last year's candles and wishing for the man of my dreams — sure that my luck would change this year. "What the hell is it gonna take?" I asked my walls, angry and terrified at the same time. When the phone rang, I expected to hear warm wishes from my parents or brothers. Instead, it was a man that I once cried over, calling to say hi and completely forgetting my birthday. My sister-in-law called next, updating me on her happy life with my brother, and putting my two-year-old niece on the phone to sing to me. I hung up, fed my cat, and tried to remember what I loved about the glamorous single life when I was twenty-something.

Adding to the gloom was the fact that I no longer liked my job as a news reporter. I was dragging myself into the radio station every day, trying to figure out where else I belonged and what else I should be doing. Today would be bearable, I thought, because they'd probably have a party for me at work, or maybe my recent ex would do the unexpected and send flowers. I was also looking forward to interviewing a favorite jazz musician whose saxophone and sense of humor were typically delightful. Little did I know that he'd be cranky from a recent root canal, and so uncooperative that I wanted to shout, "Screw you and your attitude—I shouldn't even be here today!" To add insult to injury, my co-workers forgot my birthday, and I went home in a snit, empty-handed, slipping in the snow and cursing myself for wearing boots with heels and no tread.

A dinner party with a great circle of women was the bright spot in my day, as my friends made me laugh and look on the bright side of my latest romantic disaster. But after they left, the sadness returned. I didn't want to be alone at the end of the day, I didn't want to be alone at age thirty-five, and I didn't know where my life was going. My parents had left me a birthday message, and I was glad that I had missed the call, because I didn't want to talk to them when I felt like such a miserable failure as a daughter and as a woman. I questioned my choices in life, and wondered just what I had passed up marriage and motherhood for. What was so great about my independent life?

I poured myself a glass of wine and sat down to seek comfort from birthday cards that I'd grabbed from the mailbox after work. One envelope reached out to me with the familiar, feminine script of my mother, whose handwriting echoed my grandmother's. I pulled out a pink card that read, "The only thing better than having a delightful daughter is watching her become a beautiful woman." Inside, were these unexpected words.

As I write, it's snowing outside—just like the day you were born, thirty-five years ago. I'll never forget the moment they placed you in my arms, and I knew what I was meant to do with my life. I was so thrilled to have a baby girl—it was a dream come true! Through the years, you continue to be a delight to me—so sweet and thoughtful, and smart and talented. I am so grateful for our friendship, and I admire your courage and adventurous spirit. You are a warm and beautiful woman, Kim Childs, and you are my best friend. Know that I wish you a wonderful year ahead—filled with everything you desire and deserve! I love you, xxoo Mom.

My teardrops hit the paper as I read those powerful words of love. I cried for the deep connection I had to this woman who considered me a gift, a success and an inspiration. Her message stirred my soul and breathed new life into me. I knew, as I lay down to sleep that night, that I was treasured, and that my life made a difference and brought joy to someone I cherished. It was my mother's second-greatest birthday gift to me—thirty-five years after the first.

~Kim Childs
Chicken Soup for the Mother & Daughter Soul

Never Enough

Sometimes I know the words to say,
Give thanks for all you've done,
But then they fly up and away,
As quickly as they come.
How could I possibly thank you enough,
The one who makes me whole,
The one to whom I owe my life,
The forming of my soul.
The one who tucked me in at night,
The one who stopped my crying,
The one who was the expert,
At picking up when I was lying.
The one who saw me off to school,
And spent sad days alone,
Yet magically produced a smile,
As soon as I came home.
The one who makes such sacrifices,
To always put me first,
Who lets me test my broken wings,
In spite of how it hurts.
Who paints the world a rainbow,
When it's filled with broken dreams,
Who explains it all so clearly,
When nothing's what it seems.
Are there really any words for this?
I find this question tough...

Anything I want to say,
Just doesn't seem enough.
What way is there to thank you,
For your heart, your sweat, your tears,
For ten thousand little things you've done,
For oh-so-many years.
For changing with me as I changed,
Accepting all my flaws,
Not loving 'cause you had to,
But loving "just because."
For never giving up on me,
When your wits had reached their end,
For always being proud of me,
For being my best friend.
And so I come to realize,
The only way to say,
The only thank you that's enough,
Is clear in just one way.
Look at me before you,
See what I've become,
Do you see yourself in me?
The job that you have done?
All your hopes and all your dreams,
The strength that no one sees,
A transfer over many years,
Your best was passed to me.
Thank you for the gifts you give,
For everything you do,
But thank you, Mommy, most of all,
For making dreams come true.
Love,
Your Daughter

~Laurie Kalb
Chicken Soup for the Teenage Soul II

An Angel in Disguise

Patience and perseverance have a magical effect
before which difficulties disappear and obstacles vanish.
~John Quincy Adams

"I wouldn't be your daughter if you paid me!" I vehemently declared to my new stepmother, in response to her introducing me as her daughter to a man fixing our windows. That was one of the many conflicts we had throughout my high school years. In my rebellious youth, my insecurity compelled me to lash out, to hurt people before they hurt me.

Imagine a divorced woman, living in Colorado with two small children, ages three and five, who meets, falls in love with, and decides to marry a man who lives in New Mexico. To do so, she must sell her home, give up the teaching job that she loves, and go to court against her ex-husband, in order to be allowed to move her children out of the state. After all this, she is confronted with two unruly teenagers, my brother and me, who are convinced she is the enemy and the source of all their problems. When she secures a job as a history teacher at their high school, they inform friends and students that she is a "bitch." They pick on her children with a relentless cruelty. They embarrass her, insult her and ignore her. How does she respond?

With pure, unconditional love. Out of instinct, Mary Jo exercised tough love long before the term was mainstream. She laid down the rules. Dinner was at 6:30 P.M. I had to call by 6:00 if I wouldn't be there. In addition to family dinners, there would be family nights and family vacations.

I was used to being independent, basically coming and going as I pleased. Mary Jo wanted to know what my schedule was and who my friends were. The minimal rule was to say "Hello" when I came home and "Goodbye" before going anywhere. I tried to avoid even this, sneaking in the house, up to my room with friends. She would appear instantly, "Hi, I'm Mary Jo, Alice's stepmother. What's your name?"

When she tried to talk to me, I yelled and walked away. When she tried to hug me, I pushed her away. She said, "I know you don't like it, but I'm going to hug you anyway." She wrote me letters and signed them, "I love you! Mary Jo." I tore them up and threw them in the garbage where she could see them. The next letter said, "I know you're going to tear this up. I love you, anyway! Mary Jo."

On my sixteenth birthday, Mary Jo and I got into an argument because I was picking on her daughter. I was sent to my room. I called my friends to meet me on the corner and climbed out the window. I got home around 6:00 that evening, afraid to go in the house. As I pushed the door open and stepped in, I heard, "Surprise!" Six of my girlfriends were sitting around the table, which was full of food and presents. Mary Jo had planned the party and cooked for me. She treated me like a princess in front of my friends. I felt so special, yet so guilty. When the party was over, Mary Jo said, "Happy birthday. I love you. You're grounded."

One day I was walking past my dad and Mary Jo's bedroom. I heard her crying. I don't remember what she was saying, but it was about me and how she never knew how tough it all would be. To say I stopped acting out or that we never fought again would be an exaggeration, but listening to her pain invited me one step closer to her.

Most of my anger and hurt was about my father, his past actions and the walls we had built between us over the years. Mary Jo was often caught in the middle. Over time, I came to love and respect her. Since the day my father had introduced her, I thought she was beautiful. I used to sincerely question, "What do you see in him?" She would tell me all the good things about my father I was desperately trying to forget in an effort to hate him. I asked that question and heard the answer so much that I began to see the good that she saw in him. I began to take the love and acceptance that Mary Jo had poured into me and practice it on my father. After a while, there was a bridge where there used to be a wall.

When I was in trouble, Mary Jo dealt with my behavior directly. She told me what I had done wrong and what the punishment was. She didn't make a big production. She made it clear what she would and would not tolerate. In the midst of it all, she built my self-esteem by saying things like, "You're better than that" and "I expect more from someone like you." After hearing, "You're always doing things like this" and "Are you going to be a permanent problem?" for years, I walked away from Mary Jo's lectures feeling two inches taller.

More important than how she dealt with my unruly behavior was that she taught me positive alternatives and introduced me to things I could feel good about. To an outsider, playing cards, cooking and family dinners may be casual events, but these events were like shots of joy and self-worth to me. They were medicine for a sickness that could have lasted a lifetime.

One of the strongest medicines I have ever tasted is running. That, too, was a gift from Mary Jo. She ran a ten-mile race the day she married my father. I had never run before, but I figured if she could do it so could I. I walked almost as much as I ran. However, I have run, and won, many races since that day. Mary Jo and I have run through mountains and neighborhoods together. In high school, I ran track and cross-country. I acted as if I didn't care if Mary Jo came to my races or not, as well as ignoring her when she did. Sometimes I wouldn't even tell her if I had one, but she'd find out through the school. Before I'd start, I'd scan the crowd. When I saw her face, though I told no one, comfort surged through my body.

To say Mary Jo made a positive difference in my life is an understatement. She made a pivotal difference in my life. She served as a role model, a mother and a friend. She taught me what it means to be a family and created events that make up some of my most cherished memories. She made every holiday a celebration. She passed down the gift of running, which has given me strength, peace, privacy, a place to cry, to pray, to evolve. She taught me the manners that have allowed me to excel in business and in life.

Above it all, Mary Jo taught me about love. She showed me that love cures; love softens; love sees beneath the tough exterior; love changes people; love is the creator of metamorphosis. Today, I am proud for Mary Jo to call me her daughter, and I am privileged to call her my friend.

~Alice Lundy Blum
Chicken Soup for the Mother & Daughter Soul

Happy Returns

A daughter is a gift of love.
~Author Unknown

"Happy birthday, Jane!"

Inwardly, I groaned. Couldn't our too-efficient receptionist have forgotten to consult her calendar just this once?

"Thanks, Carol." I tried to inject enthusiasm into my tone as I zoomed into my office. The less said about this momentous occasion, the better.

However, by leaning forward at her desk, Carol could look through the open doorway right toward my desk. She did this, beaming a huge smile at me. "Lordy, lordy, look who's forty! Planning a big celebration tonight?"

"Nah. Just family."

My mother would probably bring over a cake, and my sole hope for the day was that it would be her heavenly chocolate, full of fruit and nuts and spices. My daughter, Kathy, had the night off from the movie theater where she worked part-time — "shoveling popcorn," as she put it — and my son, Stewart, would have finished his paper route long before I got home. We would sit down together to something quick and simple, maybe the tacos the kids liked. No romantic candlelit dinners for this birthday girl.

Carol's smile widened, if that was possible. "It's nice with just family."

Faker that I was, I agreed. Then I grabbed my coffee mug and scurried off. Unfortunately, to get to the kitchen, I had to pass through the art department. One of the designers looked up and chortled, "Over the hill now, huh, Jane?"

"Rub it in, Bill," I grumbled. Still on the sunny side of thirty, Bill just grinned.

Another designer, Dottie, was a little more perceptive, and with good reason. At about forty-five, she was even more shopworn than I was.

"You know what the French say, don't you?" She peered up at me slyly through her auburn bangs. "They don't think a woman is even worth noticing till she's forty."

I grimaced. "I don't know any Frenchmen."

She just gave me a throaty chuckle and went back to her work. I filled my coffee mug and skulked back to my office. My desk was turned so that my back was to the raw January day outside, but I seemed more than capable of making my own gloom.

Bill was right; I was over the hill. And I hadn't exactly reached much of a pinnacle on the way, either. As I slurped coffee, I summarized in my head: I had achieved no real career, just a low-paying job as a small-time copywriter. I had salted away no savings. I had provided my children with none of the things they assured me all their friends had: VCR, microwave, answering machine, vacations. Worst of all, for one who had spent her childhood playing Cinderella, I had failed—both in my marriage and during the three years since it had ended—to find true love.

Even so, the minutes were ticking away, as quickly as they had for four decades, and the billing sheet in front of me was waiting for entries. So I applied myself to the task of writing a brochure for seed corn.

Seated as I was just five or six feet from the receptionist's desk, I had learned to tune out the opening of the front door, especially when I was under such enchantment as "yield per acre." Therefore, I was a little startled when I heard an unfamiliar voice speak my name in a questioning tone.

I looked up. "Yes?" A man was standing in my doorway holding some sort of huge, shapeless mass covered in tissue paper.

"Flowers for you."

He stepped forward, deposited what he claimed to be flowers on the corner of my desk and disappeared.

Carol took his place in the doorway and demanded, "Did somebody send you flowers?"

"I guess so," I replied, dazed.

"Some secret admirer you forgot to tell me about?"

I tried a shaky laugh. "I doubt that."

"Well, aren't you going to look at them?"

"Well... yeah." As I ripped away the tissue, I wondered if Carol could possibly be right. Had I somehow impressed one of the few men who had taken me out? My rational side butted in to remind me that wasn't likely. Maybe the people in the office or a kind client had taken pity on me.

The bouquet that emerged from the tissue paper was an enormous sheaf of spring flowers: irises, daisies, carnations—quite a contrast with the scene outside my window. I was stunned.

"Well, see who they're from," practical Carol ordered.

I fumbled for the card. The tiny envelope bore my name in the unfamiliar handwriting of someone at a florist shop. I pulled out the card.

"Dear Mom." I smiled as I recognized the self-conscious, curlicue letters I had watched develop for a dozen years. "Today, life begins—right? Love, Me."

My eyes stung. Of course. Who else could it have been but Kathy? Kathy, who had lent me her favorite top because she thought I had nothing suitable to wear to a party. Who had once found me sitting alone in the dark and whispered, "Mom, what's wrong?" Who had offered to split weekend nights out with me so someone would always be home with Stewart.

I reached out and started touching petals. Each festive pastel made a memory spring forth, and I thought with tender dismay that my hardworking daughter could ill afford such an extravagant gesture.

Dottie appeared next to Carol. "Oooh, flowers! Who from?"

I blinked against my tears and said proudly, "My daughter."

"Aaaw," Carol cooed. "That's so sweet."

I could tell it was more of an effort for Dottie. "That's very nice."

My only answer was the radiant smile a woman is supposed to wear on her birthday. I just couldn't hide the fact that I had found true love.

~Jane Robertson
Chicken Soup for the Single Parent's Soul

55

The Mother Who Matters

Gratitude is not only the greatest of virtues, but the parent of all the others.
~ Cicero

I have eyes that are said to be "cow brown," and my long blond hair is my best feature. My nose is a little too big; my face is oval shaped. I am not overweight, but I'm not skinny either. The only way to describe my height is "vertically challenged."

I'm relatively happy with my appearance, but where did I get it? Do I share the same features as some unknown stranger? Oftentimes, while walking down the street, I try to pick out that stranger, imagining that one of the women I pass could possibly be my biological mother.

I never met my birth mother. I was adopted the moment I was born, and I was taken into a wonderful family. For a long time I wondered what life would be like with my birth mother. Would I still be the same? Where would I live? Would I be happier? Who would my friends be?

I was never dissatisfied with my life; I just never stopped wondering what it would be like to have been raised by my biological mother. And then one day, I was babysitting with a friend, and I came across a poem on the nursery wall. It compared adoption to a seed that was planted by one person and then taken care of by another. The second person had watered the seed and made it grow to be tall and beautiful. I found that it compared perfectly to my situation.

I realized that my mom had made me who I am today, no matter what either of us looks like. And I started to notice that we had the same silly personality, the same outlook on life, and the same way of treating people, along with some other things. She curled my hair for my first dance. She was there for my first heartbreak. She held my hand every time I got a shot at the doctors. She'd been smiling in the crowd for my first school play. She'd been there for everything that ever mattered, and what could compare to that? She's my mom.

Sometimes when we're out somewhere, people comment on how much we look alike, and we turn to each other and laugh, forgetting until that moment that it wasn't she who carried me in her womb for nine months.

Though I may not know why I look the way I do, I know why I am who I am. The mom I have now is the best one I ever could have hoped for, not only because she holds a tremendous amount of unconditional love, but because she has shaped who I am today, my qualities and characteristics. She is the one who made me beautiful!

~Kristy White
Chicken Soup for the Teenage Soul III

Chapter 6

Like Mother, Like Daughter

Saying Goodbye

Man never made any material as resilient as the human spirit.
~Bern Williams

I'm Okay, Mom and Dad

Never part without loving words to think of during your absence. It may be that you will not meet again in this life.
~Jean Paul Richter

When I returned home from the funeral of a church member, my grown daughter, Jenny, asked me about the service. I had been very moved by a story the priest told about a dragonfly, so I shared it with Jen.

A group of water bugs was talking one day about how they saw other water bugs climb up a lily pad and disappear from sight. They wondered where the other bugs could have gone. They promised one another that if one of them ever went up the lily pad and disappeared, it would come back and tell the others where it had gone.

About a week later one of the water bugs climbed up the lily pad and emerged on the other side. As it sat there, it transformed into a dragonfly. Its body took on an iridescent sheen, and four beautiful wings sprouted from its back. The dragonfly flapped its wings and took off in flight, doing loops and spins through the sunlit sky. In the midst of its joyful flight, it remembered the promise it had made to return and tell the other bugs where it had gone. So the dragonfly swooped down to the surface of the water and tried to reenter the water, but try as it would, it could not return.

The dragonfly said to itself, Well, I tried to keep my promise, but even if I did return, the others wouldn't recognize me in my new glorious body. I guess they will just have to wait until they climb the lily pad to find out where I have gone and what I have become.

When I had finished relating the short story, my daughter said, with tears running down her cheeks, "Mom, that's really beautiful!" I agreed, and we talked for a while about it.

Two days later, early Sunday morning, July 9, 1995, Jenny came into my room, waking me to say goodbye before leaving for work at a resort on Lake Okoboji. I hugged and kissed her and told her I would see her that night when I joined her for a week's vacation at the lake. I asked her if she had eaten breakfast and if she was wide awake, as we had been out late the night before. I knew she was tired.

"Yes, Mom, I'll see you later!"

Several hours later, our worst nightmare began. Jenny had been involved in a head-on collision and was flown to Sioux Falls, South Dakota. Thoughts crowded in on me: Why hadn't I fixed her breakfast? Did I tell her I loved her? If I'd kept her with me a few minutes longer, would things have turned out differently? Why hadn't I hugged her a little longer? Why hadn't I kept her home with me that summer instead of letting her work at the lake? Why? Why? Why?

We flew to Sioux Falls and arrived at noon. Our Jen was hurt mortally, and at ten o'clock that night, she died. If God had given me a choice, I would have traded places with her in a second. Jenny had so much to give this world. She was so bright, beautiful and loving.

On Friday of that week, my husband and I drove to the lake to see family, and we stopped to see where the accident had occurred. I don't remember a lot, but I know I was hysterical trying to figure out what had happened and why.

Leaving the scene of the accident, I asked my husband to take me to a greenhouse, as I needed to be around beautiful flowers. I just couldn't face anyone yet.

Walking to the back of the hothouse, I heard the fluttering of wings as if a bird or hummingbird was hitting the top of the roof. I was looking at a beautiful rose when a beautiful, large dragonfly landed within arm's length of me. I stood there looking at this lovely creature, and I cried. My husband walked in. I looked at him and said, "Jenny is telling us that she's okay." We stood and looked at the lovely dragonfly for a long time, and as we walked out of the hothouse, the dragonfly remained on the rose.

A couple of weeks later, my husband came running into the house telling me to come outside quickly. When I walked out our door, I could not believe what I saw. There were hundreds of dragonflies flying in front of our house and between ours and the neighbor's. I have never seen that many dragonflies at once in town, and the strangest thing about it was that they were only by our house.

There is no way these two experiences were just coincidences. They were more than that. They were messages from Jen.

Each time I see a dragonfly, beautiful memories of my daughter kiss my grieving heart.

~Lark Whittemore Ricklefs
Chicken Soup for the Grieving Soul

57

To See You

The best conversations with mothers always take place in silence,
when only the heart speaks.
~Carrie Latet

Many say their most painful moments are saying goodbye to those they love. After watching Cheryl, my daughter-in-law, through the six long months her mother suffered toward death, I think the most painful moments can be in the waiting to say goodbye.

Cheryl made the two-hour trip over and over to be with her mother. They spent the long afternoons praying, soothing, comforting and retelling their shared memories.

As her mother's pain intensified and more medication was needed to ease her into sedation, Cheryl sat for hours of silent vigil by her mother's bed.

Each time she kissed her mother before leaving, her mother would tear up and say, "I'm sorry you drove so far and sat for so long, and I didn't even wake up to talk with you."

Cheryl would tell her not to worry, it didn't matter; still her mother felt she had let her down and apologized at each goodbye until the day Cheryl found a way to give her mother the same reassurance her mother had given to her so many times.

"Mom, do you remember when I made the high school basketball team?" Cheryl's mother nodded. "You'd drive so far and sit for so long, and I never even left the bench to play. You waited for me after every game and each time I felt bad and apologized to you for wasting your time." Cheryl gently took her mother's hand.

"Do you remember what you would say to me?"

"I would say I didn't come to see you play, I came to see you."

"And you meant those words, didn't you?"

"Yes, I really did."

"Well, now I say the same words to you. I didn't come to see you talk, I came to see you."

Her mother understood and smiled as she floated back into sleep.

Their afternoons together passed quietly into days, weeks and months. Their love filled the spaces between their words. To the last day they ministered to each other in the stillness, love given and received just by seeing each other.

A love so strong that, even in this deepened silence that followed their last goodbye, Cheryl can still hear her mother's love.

~Cynthia M. Hamond
Chicken Soup for Every Mom's Soul

58

A Name in the Sand

Perhaps they are not the stars,
but rather openings in heaven where the love of our lost ones pours through
and shines down upon us to let us know they are happy.
~Inspired by an Eskimo Legend

I sit on the rocky edge of a boulder, letting my feet dangle in the stillness of the water, and gaze out at the rippling waves crawling into shore like an ancient sea turtle. A salty mist hangs above the water, and I can feel it gently kissing my face. I lick my lips and can taste the familiar presence of salt from the ocean water. Above my head seagulls circle, searching the shallow, clear water for food and calling out to one another. And in my hand rests....

The sound of a hospital bed being rolled down the hallway outside my mother's hospital room brought me out of my daydreams. The ocean was gone and all that was left was a bare hospital room, its only decorations consisting of flowers, cards and seashells carefully arranged on a table next to my mother's bed.

My mother was diagnosed with cancer about a year ago, a year full of months spent in various hospitals, radiation therapy, doses of chemotherapy and other methods to try to kill the cancer eating away at her life. But the tumors keep growing and spreading, and all the treatments have done is weaken her already frail body. The disease is now in its final course and, although nobody has told me, I know my mother won't be coming home this time.

I tried to change my thoughts, and they once again returned to my daydreams. Everything seemed so clear and so real, the sound of the waves, the taste of salt, the seagulls, and the... what was in my hand? I glanced down at my hands and realized I was holding my mother's favorite shell. I placed it against my ear, and the sound of the ocean sent cherished memories crashing into my mind.

Every year, my mother, my father and I would spend our summer vacations in a little cabin down by the ocean. As a little girl, I would explore this stretch of sand with my parents. Walking hand-in-hand, they would swing me high into the air as we ran to meet the incoming surf. And it was there, in those gentle waves, where my parents first taught me how to swim. I would wear my favorite navy blue-and-white striped swimsuit, and my father's strong arms would support me, while my mother's gentle hands would guide me through the water. After many mouthfuls of swallowed salty ocean water I could swim by myself, while my parents stood close by, proudly and anxiously watching over me. And it was in those grains of sand, not on a piece of paper that could be saved and displayed on a refrigerator, that I first painstakingly wrote my name.

My family's fondest memories weren't captured on film and put in a photo album, but were captured in the sand, wind and water of the ocean. Last summer was the final time my family would ever go to the ocean all together. This summer was nearly over and had been filled with memories of various hospitals, failed treatments, false hopes, despair, sorrow and tears.

I glanced over at my mother lying in her hospital bed, peacefully asleep after the doctor had given her some medicine for her pain. I wanted to cry out to God, "Why, why my mother? How can I live without her to help me through my life? Don't take her away from my father and me!" My tears and sobs began to fade away, as the dripping of my mother's IV hypnotized me into a restless sleep.

• • •

"Ashes to ashes, and dust to dust," droned the pastor, while my father and I spread my mother's ashes over the ocean water. Some of them fell into the water and dissolved, while others were caught in the wind and carried away. This was my mother's final wish—to be in the place she loved the most, where all her favorite memories live on.

As the funeral concluded and people began to drift away saying words of comfort to my father and me, I stayed behind to say my final farewell to Mother. I carried her favorite shell that brought her so much comfort while she was in the hospital and unable to hear the sounds of the ocean. I put it to my ear and the sound of the ocean seemed almost muted. I looked into the shell and was surprised to find a piece of paper stuck inside of it. I pulled the paper out and read its words:

To my daughter, I will always love you and be with you.
A name in the sand will never last,
The waves come rolling into shore high and fast.
And wash the lines away,
But not the memories we shared that day
Where we have trod this sandy shore,
Our traces we left there will be no more.
But, wherever we are,
The memories will never be far.
Although I may not be with you,
Know that my love for you will always be true.
Those memories will last forever,
And in them we shall always be together.
Hold them close to your heart,
And know that from your side I will never part.

As I crossed the beach, I stooped and wrote my mother's name in the sand. I continued onward, turning only to cast one last lingering look behind, and the waves had already begun to wash my lines away.

~Elizabeth Stumbo
Chicken Soup for the Teenage Soul III

59

Angel Escort

I peeked anxiously into the living room where my grandmother was dozing in a morphine-induced euphoria, apparently free from pain, and lulled by the soothing scratchiness of carols on the radio. It had been three weeks since the Hospice Foundation released her to my care. At the age of ninety-two, she developed cancer of the gallbladder. The oncologist gave her less than a month to live, and discharged her to my home in Fishkill, New York, to die.

She sat in the overstuffed recliner that appeared more like a cloud with my son's pale blue blanket draped across the broad arms of the chair. Her skin was so white it was blue, disappearing into the color of the soft, woolen folds.

"How has she been?" I asked, strangling with concern.

My husband continued to stir his bubbling tomato sauce, tasting puddles of it from the wooden spoon, and shaking spices into the pot accordingly.

"She's fine. Terry has been driving me nuts, though. I know it's tough for you to deal with that son of ours right now, but...."

I slumped into a kitchen chair, amid the damp, crumpled bags and rolling oranges.

"Were you able to get the 'good' kind of Parmesan?"

"Yes. The man at the deli counter grated it fresh," I assured him as I walked into the living room.

Gingerly pulling my son's wooden rocking chair close to Mum, I stroked the coolness of her gnarled and freckled hand. The lights of the Christmas tree refracted through the thin whiteness of her hair, lending an unearthly glow. She appeared as if she belonged atop the tree instead of beside it. Mum opened her eyes with the slow deliberateness of an ancient sea turtle. Her eyes were clouded from cataracts, watery with wisdom.

"You're home, dear. I was getting worried. Are the roads bad?"

"No, Mum. It's that big, fat 'cartoon' snow that doesn't stick to the roads," I explained licking salty tears from my upper lip.

"Christmas Eve snow. Remember how you used to think it was magic?"

"I still do...."

She reached up and touched the droplets in my hair, lightly brushing the bangs from my eyes. Looking past my head, Mum strained with her fingers outstretched.

"I see a blue light behind you, and little gold bells in your hair...." Her voice weakly trailed off, and then her face widened with a look of realization.

I listened, almost as an intruder. She was on the other end of a conversation that I could not hear.

"I will always love you, dear. Nothing can ever change that. And I will always be with you, even forever. Promise me, you won't be afraid...."

"I promise, Mum," and I kissed the inside of her wrist as I replaced her hand in her lap.

But I was afraid. I didn't know how I would get through the rest of my life without the strength of this tiny woman. Mum, as I always called her, had raised me from infancy, whenever my mother's frequent and episodic manic-depression interrupted her maternal tasks.

My grandmother was an oasis of sanity and calm, and she faced all of life's adversities with quiet dignity. I could no longer pretend to be brave for her, or anyone else. I stopped praying for a miracle to save her, and asked God to show me a way to get through the loneliness I would know when she was gone.

"Who's having shrimp?" was my husband's signal that the traditional Christmas Eve feast was about to begin, whether I was ready for it or not. He came out of the kitchen, unfolding my grandmother's walker, and motioned for me to get our son.

The first angel arrived Christmas afternoon.

I was watching my son play obliviously with his new toys, when Mum began to shriek. When I reached her, she was huddled in a corner of the bed, her eyes glowing like a cat hit with light.

"Elissa, you have to save me! I'm dying!"

She clawed my forearms and pleaded for me to deny the sudden reality, all the while staring at the blank bedroom wall as if a ghost stood before it.

I held her quivering shoulders—that had become a human hanger for her nightgown—firmly to my chest until I felt her relax against me.

Slowly, her countenance softened and her eyes shone with the familiar recognition of an old friend. She smiled and resigned herself to me as I placed her limp frame onto her mountain of pillows.

Days suffused to nights without my noticing, as Mum slipped into a purgatory world, and the hospice nurse informed me that my grandmother was "actively dying."

I was understandably alarmed when she began speaking to deceased relatives and friends as if they were standing behind me. In the week or more that passed, though, I accepted it as naturally as I did drawing water up a 50-cc syringe to drop onto her cracking tongue. One by one they came, all of her lost loved ones. I especially remember the smile on her face when her brother, my great-uncle, joined the angel visitors. I could almost see the brightly colored medals shining on his chest as Mum's eyes welcomed him home from the war.

"How 'bout this little girl here, Bill? Isn't your niece taking good care of me?" and I sensed the end was near from the warm pride in her voice that was present whenever her younger son was near. I caught myself praying for God to just let her go to him. Even the experienced hospice nurse could not explain why my grandmother was hanging on.

Twelve mornings had passed since Christmas, and I looked at my church calendar that notated the Epiphany.

"You have to eat something," my husband reproached as he removed my untouched plate of eggs.

"I don't know how much longer I can go on like this! I can hardly tell the real-life callers from the unearthly ones! I'll end up like my mother if I don't get some rest."

"It won't be long, now, honey," Steve reassured me with a shoulder squeeze. "I didn't want to upset you, but I heard Mum talking to your father before you woke up. I knew it was him when she mentioned the 'flashlight.'"

My father was the official family escort who owned every kind of flashlight on the market. Mum and I had buried him with his favorite, a high-tech contraption that appeared as if it belonged on top of an ambulance. We joked that he would come for us with it, one day.

"Of course, who else would she go with?" and I walked down the hallway to the bedroom, steadying myself on the paneled walls. I offered my farewell, at last, cradling Mum's stiffening hands to my cheek, and assuring her that it was time to leave me.

I never saw the angel escort. Nor was I aware of the exact moment of Mum's passing. But, as I looked out the window at the circling snow, I felt the cool, connective threads of unending love, and the strength to go on without her.

~Elissa Hadley Conklin
Chicken Soup for the Mother & Daughter Soul

60

Joan's Bouquet

To live in hearts we leave behind is not to die.
~Thomas Campbell

e hurried to our gleaming limousine parked at the curb outside the church. Smiling, cheering and blowing bubbles of congratulations, guests lined the sidewalk. It was a sunny July afternoon — our wedding day.

Mark and I waved our goodbyes, while the big car headed for the reception. I turned my attention to my wedding bouquet of delicate pink and ivory roses and thought of the printed words on the program: "The bride's bouquet is dedicated in loving memory of her mother, Joan Miller."

My throat tightened again. I took a breath of the roses' scent and then smiled at Mark.

"On to the party!" he called to the driver.

After a festive reception featuring a prime rib buffet and dancing, I felt the need to spend a private moment with my father.

"Thanks for everything, Dad. It was more than wonderful!" I gave him a lingering hug.

Mark and I slipped into the white limousine to leave. He wrapped his arm around my shoulder and pulled me close. Pastel balloons crowded my side of the seat, but I didn't mind. The young driver started for our destination, forgetting about our special stop. Mark spoke up to redirect him.

"Oh, yeah, you wanted to make a stop. Just tell me where to go." Mark gave him the location.

"It's a cemetery," I said softly. There was silence in the car. "My mom is buried there."

"I bet you don't get many requests like this," Mark chimed in.

"No, sure don't," the driver replied, glancing through his rearview mirror. "But I understand. I lost my mother when I was thirteen."

At the cemetery, I clutched Mark's hand. How could my heart be filled with so much happiness and so much emptiness at the same time?

There we were—me, a bride in long white gown, and Mark, a groom in handsome black tuxedo—strolling on the sun-scorched grass, gazing at tombstone after tombstone, caressed by the summer evening air.

One hand held my husband's and the other gripped my bouquet. My chin quivered as we neared my mother's gravesite. We stood prayerfully above it in the dusk. Then, without saying a word, I bent and tenderly laid my bridal flowers on her headstone. Lightly, lingeringly, I stroked the carved letters of my mother's name.

I just had to come here on this special day, Mom, I thought. How you would have rejoiced at our wedding. The guests, the smiles, our joy.

Mark held me to his chest while, together, we read the etched scripture my mother had chosen for her marker: "I know that my Redeemer lives." (Job 19:25) Next to those words lay the elegant bouquet that symbolized the most important day of my life.

~Julie Messbarger as told to Charlotte Adelsperger
Chicken Soup for the Bride's Soul

Thirsty

"I'm thirsty," my little girl, Becky, shouted many nights when she couldn't get to sleep. Like all good mothers, I got up and accompanied her to the refrigerator to get her something to drink. Together we sat down at the kitchen table over a glass of water. We talked about the things that were important to her. Since everyone else in the house was fast asleep, those few minutes served as quality time together.

Sometimes we laughed, while at other times we shed a few tears. The conversations always ended with great big bear hugs and, as soon as the glass was empty, a good-night kiss. Then Becky contentedly skipped off to bed while I quietly slipped back into my bed and thanked God for the blessing of my little girl and for our quiet moment.

The years went by very quickly. Before I knew it, Becky was a teenager. We shopped together and watched a few movies, but unfortunately our time together was often short. She was busy playing in the high school band and twirling flags when she wasn't studying. I missed having her home during the day and always looked forward to her return each night. Those were the times that I became thirsty for her. But luckily, many nights, still over a glass of water, she shared her adolescent concerns with me. I discovered that she wasn't always seeking my motherly advice. She simply needed me to listen to her. And so our quiet moments continued, on and off, even through her teen years.

I realized that my life was about to change drastically after Becky finished high school. My twin sons were already living on their own. Becky was our last child. I was very proud of her and knew that she needed to gain a sense of independence, even though her absence would leave a great void in my life. The first few days after she moved out, I couldn't bear to go into her room. Finally, when I opened the door about a week later, I saw her face on everything. The familiar squeak of her door made me cry. I could still smell the heavenly scents of her perfumes and powder. Her empty room left an even bigger vacancy in my heart. I discovered how much I missed our nightly discussions. I truly thirsted for her now that she was gone.

Three weeks after she moved away from home, I had to laugh as I was reminded of the many nights from the past. Shortly before midnight, right after I went to bed, I heard the back door open.

"I'm thirsty," Becky shouted, as she came inside. I jumped up from my bed, went into the kitchen, and together, just like old times, I got her something to drink. We sat down and shared the humorous events of her day. Again, she did the talking while I listened intently.

Just before she left, she gave me another big old bear hug. I went back to bed, laughed again about her stories, and this time thanked God for the blessing of my grown daughter. Even though our lives are very different now, I'm convinced that our quiet moments and midnight bear hugs made certain that the love between us will never grow old.

And after momentarily fearing that our private late-night ritual ended when she moved, I now believe Becky will come home thirsty many more times in the future, especially when she needs a bear hug to get her through the night.

~Nancy B. Gibbs
Chicken Soup for the Mother & Daughter Soul

The Red Sweater

If I had a single flower for every time I think about you,
I could walk forever in my garden.
~Claudia Ghandi

Time didn't ease the pain of losing my mother. Each day brought new sorrow since her death over a year ago; often I found myself fighting back unexpected tears.

Mom died just before the Christmas season the year before, after a short battle with cancer. At the age of seventy-two, she had been well prepared for her death, but I was not.

All her life, Mom was there for me; although now a grown woman, I still needed my senior parent for advice and comfort. We were the best of friends, and over the years, we shared, laughed and cried together.

I often found myself wearing her red sweater, holding it to my cheeks, drinking in its aroma. It had been Mom's favourite, and it was faded and worn from years of use. I claimed the sweater after her death. It held so many memories, and now I drew comfort from them.

Mom came from West Arichat, a tiny Acadian fishing village on Cape Breton Island, Nova Scotia. Of both French and Indian background, she had a gentle, soft touch. To cope with my grief, I began imagining my aged parent reaching out to comfort me. Her tanned hands, worn and shriveled from age and work, had cradled babies, cared for a large family, and brought life to plants and flowers. I would imagine her wearing the red sweater, her hand reaching out and covering mine, and then she would whisper a memory in my ear.

I'd smile, remembering.

Mom lost both her cultures when she married my father, a white man, and moved from her island to live on his. When she arrived in isolated and rural Cardigan on Prince Edward Island at the age of eighteen, she began to learn English. Sadly, her knowledge of both French and her native Chinook began to fade away.

One of my favourite memories is the native powwows we attended on Panmure Island. Part of Prince Edward Island, Panmure Island is an old Mi'kmaq gathering place. First Nations people from all over North America travelled there to participate in the powwows. It was an opportunity for Mom to mingle with the First Nations people, wear her native shirt, dance in the sacred circle and socialize. She loved going to those powwows and proudly identified with her ancient roots, which had been silenced for so many years. I remember her telling an elder once, "I'm Indian, too." Although she had moved into the white man's world when she married, she never lost her Chinook heritage of strong native spirituality, deep respect for the land, and love for the outdoors—all of which she passed on to me and my eight brothers and sisters.

During the last powwow we attended, a few months before she became ill, I heard the Great Spirit whisper in my ear that it would be the last time we would travel to the powwows together. It was.

Now, her image travels with me in the car or visits when I feel grief and pain. She always wears the red sweater and for an instant, our hands join. Death has not separated us.

Sometimes the momentary images are so strong I find myself reaching out my hand to her imaginary one. It is as if she is always there, always with me, watching over me.

One day I sat waiting for my turn to have my hair done in the beauty parlour. I was exhausted from working, and I became frustrated with the wait. Then I noticed a small child watching me. She and her mom were holding hands while they stood at the counter.

They moved to the area where I was sitting, so I moved over one chair to give them room to sit down.

The little girl looked around, then said to me, "Where did the woman go that was sitting beside you?" Surprised at her question, because no one had been sitting next to me, I asked her who she was asking about. "The woman wearing the red sweater," she quipped. "She was holding your hand, just like my mommy and me."

My fatigue and frustration were suddenly gone as a warm glow washed over me. Smiling, I realized my mom never left me. She really is only a shadow away.

~Stella Shepard
Chicken Soup for the Canadian Soul

Tough Love

Growing up wasn't easy for my oldest daughter. Michelle was different, somehow. Despite her cherub's beauty and gentle soul, she stood apart from her peers, and they felt the difference.

Her high school years came and went without much mention of friends except for her small "group." Michelle stayed within their protective shell until they all gradually moved on or moved away, off to start their own lives. Only Michelle was left behind. I watched, trying to help yet not interfere, as she struggled to find new friends.

In her desperation to belong at any cost, Michelle found "friends" who were not friends at all. It was then that she tried drugs for the first time. The drugs made Michelle feel different, powerful. Then, they took her.

I lost my daughter that first year. It was as if she became possessed and lost her soul. Inside, she did not exist. Over the next year, Michelle stormed in and out of our lives. She was gone for days at a time. I later learned she lived, by choice, in her car with Jim, a go-nowhere drug addict. He hit her and pushed her and burned her with cigarettes. Yet she stayed with him, with the night life, with the drugs. When she was gone, I ached to see her, but I dreaded the times she did come home. Then, our house rang with shouts and tears, pleading and accusation. And after a few days, Michelle would be gone again.

That New Year's Eve, I sat alone on my sofa, wondering what the new year would bring. Thinking of the disaster that engulfed our dear daughter, I felt as if I were dying. I knew I had to make some changes.

Searching for hope, I cast back in my mind, seeking other times and other events that had brought me happiness. What were the happiest times in my life? I asked myself. What past loveliness could help carry me through the ugliness of today?

Memories rose to the surface, images of myself as a little girl in springtime. I recalled moments with warm mud between my toes, afternoons lying in the high grass, the smells of spring that gave my soul a joy I hadn't felt since my youth.

How could I relive those moments? Perhaps, I thought, the answer was right in my backyard. If my soul felt like dying, perhaps I needed to make something else grow.

At first, I thought I'd taken on too much; our dark, barren yard had little to offer in the way of inspiration. But then I recalled a saying: "Yard by yard, it's too hard; inch by inch, it's a cinch." I promised myself to go inch by inch in creating some beauty in our family's broken world.

We cut down trees and brush. I shoveled topsoil and pulled weeds and planted bulbs. As I worked in my new garden, I tried to focus on light and hope. I became quiet and at peace with God, my garden and myself. The healing began; the garden became my sanctuary from the sorrow and pain in my home.

I watched that first spring come. I'd pluck snails in my nightgown at 6:00 A.M. after a sleepless night spent praying that Michelle was safe and warm somewhere—though I knew she wasn't. Michelle roamed alone. But I survived, one day at a time. I learned to garden and I learned to pray.

The calm and clarity I found in the garden gave me the strength to finally take a stand against Michelle. For a year, we had always been there for her, waiting to welcome her back, providing money and a home, only to have her leave again, refueled for another round of drugs and abuse. "Inch by inch" wasn't enough now. I had to do something bigger. I told my daughter not to come home anymore.

"I have a key to the house. I'll come back whenever I want," Michelle retorted angrily.

I reached deep inside for the strength to reply.

"I'll change the locks," I said in a trembling voice. "I can't watch while you kill yourself."

The "tough love" broke through. Truly alone, Michelle suddenly started crying like a lost child.

"All I want is to be happy," she sobbed.

In my garden, I had prayed many times for Michelle's sobriety. In that moment, with the faith I had found in my garden, I caught a glimpse of her soul struggling back to us.

Soon after, Michelle was accepted into a women's recovery home. I went to my sanctuary and got down on my knees. I thanked God for the hope of answered prayers.

Later that week, I found a bare-root rosebush at a nursery. Its name was "Betty Boop," Michelle's pet name. I went to visit Michelle in the recovery house and told her about "her" rosebush.

"When you come home from the recovery house, the rosebush will be blooming," I said. "It's like you—simply beautiful."

Michelle's recovery was not easy, but she made it. She, too, learned to put her faith in the old saying, "Yard by yard, it's too hard; inch by inch, it's a cinch." Today, Michelle has hope for a future. She has met a wonderful young man, and they are engaged to be married. They are so in love, and Michelle is blooming at last, just like the "Betty Boop" in my garden. That garden truly saved us both, for it gave me the strength to stand up to my daughter and give her what she really needed: not just love, but tough love.

~Mary Harrison Hart
Chicken Soup for the Gardener's Soul

Anticipating the Empty Nest

It's always been my feeling that
God lends you your children until they're about eighteen years old.
If you haven't made your points with them by then, it's too late.
~Betty Ford

Tomorrow is about to arrive. My first child is preparing to leave for college, and the family unit will change forever. This is not a surprise to me, and yet, I am deeply surprised by how quickly this day is speeding toward us. I'm not quite finished with her. I feel betrayed by time.

This is a happy and healthy step in the expected, and hoped for, chain of milestones. She is eager and ready to leave, but I am not nearly ready to let her go. I need to make a few more cupcakes with her, read and recite from *Goodnight Moon*, and maybe create one more fruit basket from Play-Doh. I want to tell her, "Wait a minute!" and have her stand still. And in that time I would hurry to fill her head with the things about life that I am afraid I forgot to tell her. But standing still, she would impatiently reply, "Yes, Mom, I know. You've told me." And she would be right; but I can't help feeling that I forgot something.

Seventeen years ago, as I stood over her crib watching her breathe, I wrote a letter to my four-day-old infant. It said, "These are the days when doorknobs are unreachable, the summer is long, and tomorrow takes forever to arrive." In this letter, I told her of the plans and dreams I had for the two of us. I promised her tea parties in winter and tents in the spring. We would do art projects and make surprises for her daddy. And I promised her experience. We would examine sand and flowers and rocks and snowflakes. We would smell the grass, the ocean and burning wood. I would have the gift of learning about our world once again, as she absorbed it for the first time.

We experienced so much more than I promised on that night long ago. We endured many of life's painful interruptions. When the continuity of our plans had to pause to accommodate sorrow, we grew from the shared hurt and the coping. I never promised her that all of our experiences would be happy, just that her father and I would be there with unquestioning support.

When this tomorrow is actually here, I will keep the final promise I made to my baby daughter. In the letter I told her, "I will guide you as safely as I can to the threshold of adulthood; and there, I will let you go... for the days quickly pass when doorknobs are unreachable, summers are long, and tomorrow takes forever to arrive."

As I prepare to let her go, I reflect upon her first day of nursery school, when I, like countless mothers before me, said goodbye to a tearful child and went back to look in the school window a few minutes later. I needed to know if she was still crying. I believe that in September, when I leave this child at her college dorm, she will slip down to the parking lot and find me there, crying.

Seventeen years ago I watched her breathe. Tomorrow I will watch her fly.

~Bonnie Feuer
Chicken Soup for Every Mom's Soul

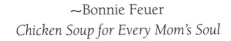

A Rose for Mother

S ometimes, when sorrow is deep and the healing balm of time moves too slowly, a grieving heart may look for consolation in something more tangible. When I lost my mother, the comfort I sought depended on the survival of a single rose. Nothing could have prepared me for the answer I received.

My husband and I are avid rose growers. When we joined a local rose society, we became involved in rose competitions where hundreds of blooms of every color and variety are judged for trophies. Growing show roses takes a great deal of time and energy, but the garden was our haven where we gladly retreated into a world of sunshine and beauty.

My mother also loved our yard, and each time she came to our home, she would soon disappear into the garden. I often teased her about wanting to visit with the roses more than with us. She had been struggling with progressive kidney failure, and the garden was where she went to recover after her exhausting dialysis treatments. When she was strong enough, she would roam through the pathways inspecting and clipping her way around the bushes, since it was her self-appointed mission to fill the house with beautiful bouquets. Eventually, when she became too ill to walk through the garden, she was content to sit in the shade surrounded by the flowers and birds. By the end of summer she had grown very frail, and with a heavy heart I knew this would be her last summer in the garden.

An unpredictable complication sent her into a coma, and she

suddenly passed away two days before Christmas. After the funeral, I went into the garden hoping to find some comfort in the place she had loved so much. I was searching for a sense of her spirit among the roses, but the garden was in its dormant stage and the barrenness matched the emptiness I felt in my heart.

The following day, some friends from church brought us a new rosebush in her memory. They had selected one called Dainty Bess, a beautiful five-petal rose in cotton-candy pink with dark red stamens and a soft, sweet smell. It would be a lovely reminder of Mother. We planted the rosebush near the place where she had spent so many peaceful hours, and for me the bush became a symbol of her ongoing spirit. I spent the winter months pampering the little plant, urging it to survive and grow strong.

The cold rains finally stopped, and an early spring transformed our yard into a riot of fragrant color. Mother would have loved it, and I missed sharing her joy and enthusiasm for the garden.

Dainty Bess was thriving, covered with bright green leaves and, to our surprise, five long-stemmed buds. When the first delicate bloom opened, my spirits soared for the first time in months.

Our first rose show was five days away, and I became determined to enter a Dainty Bess bloom in memory of my mother's life, believing this would finally put an end to my grieving. Unusually warm weather had quickly opened three of the five buds, so I cut the last two and placed them in the refrigerator to slow the blooming process. The day before the show, I tried to force them open by putting them in warm water. The first bud refused to open and simply bowed its head, but the second one was perfect. I placed it back in the refrigerator and prayed it would survive. Later that day, a nagging fear of losing the rose sent me out to the garden hoping to find another Dainty Bess hiding among the leaves, but there was no sign of a bud anywhere.

The next morning I opened up the refrigerator to find a bare stem in the vase and five pink petals lying on the shelf! I burst into tears. Losing the rose suddenly brought back all the memories of losing my mother. My husband gave me a comforting hug. "We'll enter a Dainty Bess at the next show," he said soothingly. But I could hear the disappointment in his voice.

With heavy hearts, we went into the garden to check the rest of the rosebushes for last minute blooms before leaving for the show. Barely glancing at the Dainty Bess bush as I walked by, a small splash of color caught my eye. My gasp of surprise brought Rich rushing over to see what was wrong, and together we stared in disbelief at a single long-stemmed, tightly folded bud in the center of the bush. Faith had taught me to believe in miracles, but this was beyond all understanding. Almost afraid to touch it, I finally cut the stem. In stunned silence, we drove to the show.

When we arrived at the exhibit hall, the bud had barely begun to unfurl. I polished the leaves, then cupped my hands over the bloom and gave it several warm puffs of my breath to encourage it to open. I knew the rose would be disqualified if the petals weren't fully opened by the time it was judged.

After I had done all I could, I stood back and looked at the little rose. Its beauty was breathtaking. Its half-opened petals reaching upward reminded me that I had been blessed with an extraordinary act of compassion. Then I realized that my competitive spirit had momentarily blinded me to the real reason for showing this rose—not for the prize or the glory of winning, but to honor my mother's life. The rose was perfect just the way it was, and the judge's opinion was no longer relevant. With a grateful heart and a sense of reverence, I placed the rose on the display table and walked away, free at last from sorrow's grip.

When the judging was completed, we rushed over to retrieve our special rose. It had disappeared from the table! Seeing our confusion, a friend came over and asked if we had looked on the trophy table. There it was—opened to perfection, draped with a blue ribbon and standing next to a large silver trophy that said "Best Single-Petal Rose in Show." It was a beautiful and unexpected tribute to my mother.

A few days later, I pressed the rose, hoping to keep it forever as proof that miracles do happen. But when I checked it just one week later, it had disintegrated into a fine powder that scattered into the air as I unfolded the paper around it. The rose had come into my life to console my aching heart, then vanished as mysteriously as it had appeared once its work was done.

~Maria E. Sears
Chicken Soup for the Grieving Soul

Leaving Home

Where we love is home,
Home that our feet may leave, but not our hearts.
~Oliver Wendell Holmes, Sr., Homesick in Heaven

"I'm not going to cry," I told my husband, Chuck, as we left the parent orientation session held several months before our daughter would attend college in the fall.

Maybe those other mothers were going to cry after dropping off their kids at the dorm, but not me. I looked around the auditorium at the other mothers, wondering which ones were going to be crybabies. I thought, I won't clutch a box of tissues when the time comes to say goodbye to Sarah. I'm from sturdier stock than that. Why snivel and sob just because my little girl is growing up?

We'd spent the afternoon listening to parents of upperclassmen talk about how our lives were going to change when our children left home for college. One seasoned mother warned that we would cry all the way home.

I elbowed Chuck. "That's ridiculous," I said. "Why are they making such a big deal out of this?" Being a mother has always been important to me, but — for crying out loud — it isn't the only thing! I have a job, I have friends, I have a life!

Sarah and I spent the summer sniping at each other. I hated the way she talked about how she couldn't wait to leave — as if her life at home with us had been some kind of hostage standoff. She hated the way I nagged her about cleaning up her room and putting her dishes in the sink, the way I grumbled when I needed to use the phone and she was tying up the line, the way I questioned her whereabouts when she went out with her friends. After all, she was eighteen. She didn't need to check in with her mom every five minutes.

In August, I ran into my friend, Pat, at the library. Pat remembered the weeks before her daughter left home for college the previous year.

"We fought all summer long," she said. "I think it was our way of getting used to the idea of living apart. When you're arguing all the time and angry, then you don't feel so bad about her leaving."

"And," I responded thoughtfully, "she doesn't feel so bad about leaving when she's mad at Mom."

On moving day, we helped her unpack and store her belongings in the dorm room. I tucked the extra-long twin sheets onto Sarah's mattress while Chuck assembled a storage shelf for her closet. After lunch, we said goodbye, hugged at the curb, and then Chuck and I drove away.

The woman at the parent orientation session was wrong, I thought. This isn't so bad.

Two days later I walked by her bedroom. The door was open, her bed was made and all the clutter of her childhood, of her teenage years, was missing. Suddenly, it dawned on me: She's gone.

Later, as I was vacuuming in the living room, I thought I heard someone say, "Mom," and I turned off the vacuum cleaner to listen for footsteps coming through the door, to answer a child's call. Then I realized I was alone in the house. Sarah was gone, and nothing would ever be the same.

I longed to hear her voice. I wanted to know what she was doing. I wanted her to sit on the edge of my bed at night like she used to and tell me about her day, her classes, her teachers, her friends, the boys she liked, the boys who liked her....

"What's wrong?" Chuck asked when he came home. I was chopping vegetables for stir-fry. He peered into my face. "Are you crying?"

"It's just the onions," I sniffed as a tear snaked down my cheek.

After dinner I said, "Let's call her. Maybe she's expecting us to call."

"It's only been two days," Chuck said. "Let's give her at least a week to settle in."

He was right, of course. I didn't want to turn into some kind of Stalker Mom. I remembered what it was like to be eighteen and away from home for the first time. She was meeting new friends, learning new ideas, forming new bonds. I had to give her the space—the distance—she needed.

Then the phone rang.

"Hi, Mom," Sarah said. "Could you send me some pictures to put on my bulletin board? And a few stuffed animals?"

She wanted her teddy bear. She wanted a photo of her father and me—and one of her younger brother. She loved being at school, but she missed us, too. And then she started telling me about her day, her classes, her teachers, her friends, the boys she liked, the boys who liked her....

~Beth Copeland Vargo
Chicken Soup for the Mother's Soul 2

Like Mother, Like Daughter

Through the Generations

*Life affords no greater responsibility, no greater privilege,
than the raising of the next generation.
~C. Everett Koop*

67

Lessons on Napkins

In a child's lunch basket, a mother's thoughts.
~Japanese Proverb

In 1974, my mother was a junior at an all-girls Catholic college in New York. She was an excellent student and wanted to be a special education teacher. But her dreams of becoming a teacher were interrupted by an unexpected child: her own. My mother became pregnant with me during her junior year of college and left school to marry my father. Yet even though my mother left the field of education formally, she did not leave it entirely.

When I was born my mother immediately made learning an integral and fun part of my life. Everything we did was a positive learning interaction, whether we were baking cookies or spending the day at the library. I never watched television, not because I was not allowed to, but because it was more fun writing stories with my mom. There was never a lot of money in our home, but with all of the books, laughter and hugs, it was a scarcity I never felt.

When I finally entered a school classroom at age five, I was excited, but terrified. That first day of kindergarten I quietly sat at my desk during snack time and opened my Miss Piggy lunch box. Inside the lunch box I found a note from my mother written on a napkin. The note said that she loved me, that she was proud of me and that I was the best kindergartner in the world! Because of that napkin note I made it through my first day of kindergarten... and many more school days to follow.

There have been many napkin notes since the first one. There were napkin notes in elementary school when I was struggling with math, telling me to "Hang in there, kiddo! You can do it! Don't forget what a great writer you are!" There were napkin notes in junior high school when I was the "new girl" with frizzy hair and pimples, telling me to "Be friendly. Don't be scared. Anyone would be lucky to have you as her friend!" In high school, when my basketball team was the first team in our school's history to play in a state championship, there were napkin notes telling me, "There is no 'I' in team. You have gotten this far because you know how to share." And, there were even napkin notes sent to me in college and graduate school, far away from my mother's physical touch. Despite the tumultuous changes of college — changing majors, changing boyfriends, changing the way I looked at the world — my one constant was my mother's encouragement, support and teachings, echoed in years of love, commitment and napkin notes.

My nineteen-year-old sister is now a college sophomore. Somewhere in her dorm room, amid her varsity basketball uniform and her nursing books, she has a box of well-read napkin notes hidden, but accessible. At home, my sixteen-year-old sister and nine-year-old brother also have their own private stashes of napkin notes. When they read them I know they feel the same warm surge of confidence that I felt all through my school years.

For Christmas this year, my mother received a book bag, a daily planner, notebooks and a full-tuition college scholarship. These gifts reflected an impending change in her life. After a twenty-five-year hiatus, my forty-four-year-old mother was finally going back to school to earn her degree in teaching. And although I was immensely proud of my mother for following her dreams, I wanted her to know that she didn't need a degree to make her a stellar teacher.

So I also gave her a Christmas gift for school: a lunch bag filled with her favorite foods. She laughed as she opened the lunch bag and took out cans of tuna fish and V-8. Then she pulled out a napkin with writing on it.

As she opened up her "You can do it!" napkin note from me, tears began running down her face. When her eyes met mine, I saw she understood my unspoken message: My mother is—and has always been—a teacher.

~Caurie Anne Miner
Chicken Soup for the Mother's Soul 2

68

The Gift of Memory

We all grow up with the weight of history on us.
Our ancestors dwell in the attics of our brains as they do in the
spiraling chains of knowledge hidden in every cell of our bodies.
~Shirley Abbott

It was Amy's idea from the start. Our middle daughter, now a thirty-something TV producer, kept raising the notion of video-taping her grandmother, chronicling her life and memories in order to preserve them.

And I kept resisting.

"Mom... Mom won't want to," I argued. "She'll be uncomfortable," I told Amy, projecting, perhaps, my own feelings about video cameras.

Amy would have none of it. And because she and her grand-mother have always had a connection that is as mighty as it is inde-finable, Amy ultimately prevailed.

So, on a recent weekend, Amy arrived at my mother's city apart-ment carrying a sophisticated video camera and a grand plan for recording the life and times of her beloved grandmother. The gift of my mother's life on tape, I came to realize, would be invaluable to us. As a middle-aged daughter, I began to realize how finite our time together is — and how precious.

The "star" of the show was initially most concerned about feed-ing Amy and those few of us who were to be observers of this mile-stone: my sister, my husband and me.

After we had been stuffed with bagels and fruit and cookies, a small, beautiful lady with shining green eyes faced the camera and began. Nobody had told Mom what to do or say because, in some ways, the format had to be hers.

And after Amy asked the first broad questions, my ninety-one-year-old mother was off and running.

There we sat listening to the story of a woman born to immigrant parents—a woman who had lived the first years of her life behind the family grocery store on a gritty city street—who would go on to see granddaughters graduate from Ivy League schools.

We heard what it was like for her to witness her own mother giving birth to the flamboyant younger sister who would then take center stage in the family's life. We listened as my mother described the father she loved so much, a frail man for whom my own oldest daughter is named. Joseph Goldberg was gone before I had a chance to know him well, and has remained a somewhat shadowy figure in my memory bank. But sitting in my mother's apartment that Saturday afternoon, listening to her talk about him, my grandfather suddenly came alive for me. It was moving—and marvelous.

As the camera rolled, what it tracked was a deeply personal chronicle of what life was like when the twentieth century itself was young, and when just being born in this country was considered a gift. But not an unqualified one.

The story of how my mother faced rampant anti-Semitism on her first job search, when the name "Goldberg" was clearly not an asset, was profoundly disturbing. I'd never known that to get her first job, my mother had assumed a name she invented because it seemed safe. "Gould," she reasoned at eighteen, was surely less telling than Goldberg. And as Lillian Gould, she was on her way.

How my parents met, their first official date, the richly textured tale of my mother buying her wedding dress and feeling, in her words, "like a princess" because a dashing lawyer had asked her to be his wife: priceless.

As Amy let the camera do its work, the stories kept coming. It was as if my mother had been given this astounding gift she couldn't let go of as she reflected and processed a long, full, richly-textured life.

I know there were moments when she forgot the camera was there, and they, of course, were the best moments of all. That camera rolled for hours, pausing only when we "young ones" worried about Mom's stamina and insisted on periodic breaks. But Mom—Mom could have gone on and on, remembering the magnificent and mundane moments of her life: her first job, the birth of her daughters, the war years, the sweetness of walking into her first home as a mother.

She could talk of my late father with humor, with candor and only occasionally with what my sister and I recognized as "revisionist history." He was a wonderful, brilliant, complicated, difficult, impractical man—and the video camera now holds that rich and complex marital history for all time.

Her becoming a grandmother, and then, miracle of all miracles, a great-grandmother—all recorded on that marvelous piece of modern technology.

Only when darkness began to fall, and other obligations beckoned, did Amy shut off the video camera. Only then did we pause to realize what a treasure it held, and how right Amy had been all along.

A life—a history—a part of us—has been preserved for all time. We have a true treasure in that deceptively simple-looking cassette. And as we summoned up the energy to return to the tensions of the present, we realized that there was no way to thank my mother for this astounding gift of memory.

There are only feeble ways to try.

~Sally Friedman
Chicken Soup to Inspire a Woman's Soul

Yellow Irises

A s a mother of five, Mom had little time during the day to be out in the garden with her beloved rhododendrons or planting bulbs. But a loyal gardener always finds a way. As soon as we were tucked away in bed, she'd grab her garden tools and car keys and go outside into the night. Starting up the car, Mom shined the headlights onto a section of the garden. In peace and quiet at last, she'd settle into a gentle rhythm of weeding—a rhythm she hoped would soothe her nerves after another busy day.

With five kids comes a lot of energy, and my parents found relief in Washington State's trail system. Packing the car with lunches and a mess of kids, off we went to the mountains. The moment the car stopped at the trailhead, the doors flew open and we bounded up the path with my parents following in the rear.

Along the trail, I looked for unusual plants, ones I didn't think Mom would recognize. Whenever I came across an oddball, I would proudly present her with a sample. Thus challenged, she'd open her wild plants guide and together we'd flip through the chapters, looking for a match. Years later, I came across the battered book and discovered dried wafers of leaves and flowers still pressed between the pages.

On days the weather kept us indoors, sometimes we would flip through fine art catalogs or visit museums and art galleries. One day, a beautiful museum catalog arrived in the mail. Mom and I leafed through it, marking pages of our favorite flower paintings.

"Look!" I gasped, pointing to a Japanese print. Mom had seen it, too. It was a beautiful landscape. Tall green grass seemed to ripple in the breeze and clouds dotted the blue sky. A small hut, perhaps the family home, sat near a well-tended flower garden.

"We'll get that one," she smiled. And we filled out the order form.

During my senior year in high school, I took a forestry course. The end of the semester loomed, but thanks to Mom, I didn't have to take the final exam. The student who brought in and correctly identified the greatest number of native plants was exempt from the Big Test. The night before class, Mom and I toured the yard collecting samples and packed them in a cardboard box. The next day, I (we) won hands down.

Mom's creativity and love for children was reflected in everything she did, from setting the dining room table with craft projects as an alternative to TV, to making houses from grass and cattail reeds.

Life was not all fun and games, though. Sometimes, things weren't quite right with Mom. Sometimes she did things we didn't understand. She tired easily. She missed appointments and went on strange eating binges.

One night, my sister and I heard a commotion from outside our bedroom. We opened the door just enough to see two men wearing white coats carrying our mother away on a stretcher. As soon as they disappeared, we ran to find Dad.

"What's wrong with Mommy?" we cried.

"She's not feeling well," Dad said, his voice trembling. "Mommy's going to a special hospital for a couple of months."

From that point on, the family had to deal with the fact of Mom's mental illness. It was often hard for us to understand; doctors back then were still struggling with how to treat manic depression and schizophrenia.

The years went by, and we kids grew up and moved away. My parents divorced. Mom struggled with alcoholism, severe depression and loneliness. Unable to hold down a job, she ended up in low-income housing in downtown Seattle. Undaunted by living in the middle of the city, Mom was determined to be near flowers and green things, so each spring and summer she rode the city bus to and from her community garden plot.

Eventually I moved to Alaska, but Mom and I stayed in close touch, our letters and phone conversations laced with "garden speak."

"Someone's stealing my tomatoes," Mom once lamented. "What should I do?"

"Plant more!" I said, laughing. "You'll really make them happy!"

Then one autumn, Mom was diagnosed with pancreatic cancer. The doctors gave her a few months to live. Mom suffered immeasurable physical pain, but for reasons unknown to her doctors, she was suddenly free of the mental illness that had plagued her most of her adult life. It was as if all of the darkness just lifted and was gone. For the first time in many years, Mom was "there" more than she'd ever been, allowing us to share whole conversations, walks and meals together. I made several visits from my home in Alaska.

On a midsummer morning, I was out in my garden when my sister and older brother called to say that Mom was refusing any sort of care, food or water. She was fading fast. They promised to stay in close touch from her hospital room.

I wanted to be alone, so I returned to the garden. After a few hours, I picked a large bouquet of yellow irises and carried them into the house. The phone was ringing. It was my sister. Mom was slipping in and out of consciousness and hadn't responded in several hours.

My sister held the phone up to Mom's ear so I could talk to her. The yellow irises beside me misted into a golden haze as I held back tears.

Speaking slowly and deliberately, I told her that every time I'm in the garden I think of her. I told her I was grateful for all she had taught me.

"I will always love you, Mom."

She was so weak, she could only whisper.

"Thanks, honey." Those were her last words. Mom died that evening.

The next morning, I was going through a box of family papers and photographs, searching for memories of Mom. As I gently pulled back a handful of faded newspaper clippings, my heart stopped. There was the Japanese print Mom and I had picked from the catalog over thirty years before. The sunlit garden scene was as lovely and tranquil as ever. And in the foreground was a large clump of yellow irises.

~Marion Owen
Chicken Soup for the Gardener's Soul

70

It's a Date!

A daughter is a little girl who grows up to be a friend.
~Author Unknown

"Should I meet him there Saturday night?" she asked.

"Of course not. You know the family rule," I said. The cold pork chops hissed against the sizzling skillet. "Your date must always..."

"It's not a date," she interrupted.

"...come right to the door," I chanted without missing a beat. We had rehearsed this very conversation before. A slight pause followed. "Where is he taking you?"

"Out for supper and maybe somewhere afterwards." Panic peppered her voice. "A whole evening together—alone. What will we talk about?"

"Knowing you, you'll talk about anything and everything. Since when have you been at a loss for words, anyway?" I joked, handing her a short stack of stoneware salad plates.

"But this is different. I hardly know Tom."

Brushing aside crisp kitchen curtains, I peered into the deepening dusk. A gentle rain blurred the boundaries, skewing the scene like a photograph out of focus. "Well, there's always the weather. Better yet, get him to talk about himself. Ask your boyfriend...."

"He's not my boyfriend."

"...about his interests. And, by the end of the date...."

"It's not a date!"

"...you'll know each other better and probably have lots to say," I encouraged. After all, I was experienced with this mother-daughter thing. I had raised four teenagers—all at one time—in the not-so-distant past. Could this be much different?

"Well—if you're sure." She paused. "It's just that..."

"Yes?" I coaxed, a little impatient with her hesitancy, my mind racing ahead to the details of dinner.

But the voice that answered had slowed, softened and deepened.

"Do you realize how long it's been?" Her words hung there, suspended, unsupported in the sudden silence. Reaching across me to the stove, she flipped the pork chops and turned down the heat. "...how long it's been," she cleared her throat, "since I've dated, I mean? Fifty-five years! With your dad gone so long now, I think... maybe... well... maybe it's time. Why, Carol, I was seventeen the last time I went on a date."

I turned—once again a daughter—and winked. "Oh, but Mom... it's not a date!"

~Carol McAdoo Rehme
Chicken Soup for Every Mom's Soul

71

Pantyhose Hair

hen I was six, I donned my mother's pantyhose and wore them... on my head. They were my very own long, luxuriant pantyhose hair. What necessitated my resorting to this was the fact that my mother kept cutting my hair into one of those "cute little pixie cuts." I got expert at layering several pairs, so that I could braid and style my many-legged pantyhose hair. I was never allowed to wear my beautiful hosiery hair out in public, but at home I gloried in it. I promised myself, with all of the fierce determination of my six-year-old self, that if I ever had a little girl, I would never, ever cut my little girl's hair.

So, when I found out at thirty-two years of age that I was pregnant with a little girl, I felt two things. First, I felt an absolute feathertickle of joy all throughout my body. Second, I was suffused with a fierce maternal protection toward my little girl's unseen tresses.

Imagine with what joy I looked forward to my little girl's Rapunzel-like ringlets. All of my thwarted longings for flowing tresses, all of my impeded desires for an enviable mane would be made right, accounted for, sublimated by my own daughter's inviolate strands. I went into a veritable frenzy of buying hair accessories. Hair bows, hair bands, hair clips, hair scrunchies, little hair bows that attached by Velcro, I bought them all. I bought every color of the rainbow and every pattern that I could find. My little girl actually had more hair accessories than she could ever hope to wear, unless of course I adorned her head with four or five at a time, which I did not consider out of the question or in any way extreme.

I was only mildly discouraged when Jasmine Rain was born with very little hair—just a light vanilla fuzz. I took to proudly adorning her fuzzy little head with those headbands for newborns that look like garter belts (despite the rude discouragement I received from one of my brothers-in-law to the effect that I was squeezing her little brain and the fact that he would surreptitiously remove them when I wasn't looking—as if I wouldn't notice—and the fact that he kept trying to convert my husband to his "no headband" philosophy).

I received hope from nature. Kittens, puppies, bunnies, all are born hairless. All of these, in no time, sport thick, luxurious growths. I wasn't worried. I waited patiently through the first, second and third months. Of course I was always brushing and lavishing unstinting attention on the little bit of encouragement that was there in the form of blond dandelion fluff.

Then in the fourth month there was still no hair. I started to worry. I read every article I could get my hands on regarding hair growth and developmental expectations. I quizzed friends and coworkers about their experiences and stared forlornly at the heads of all the thickly haired babies that seemed to accost my stricken eyes everywhere I went. What was I doing wrong?

The ribbons, bows and assorted hopefuls sat dusty on her closet shelf—a sad testament to my optimistic expectations of just a short time ago. I was horrified to hear the same words uttered in regard to my Jazzy that had so mortified me as a child ("What a cute little boy!") always offered in the heartiest and most jovial of manners. But still I maintained my hope. Every little tuft of growth was greeted with excited enthusiasm and happy pleasure.

Finally, when Jazzy turned two, I was rewarded for my patience and faith. Jazzy's hair began to grow (whether it was just time for it to grow or whether the naked-with-a-carved-wooden-mask-ceremo-nial-hair-growing dance I did accomplished it, I just don't know). Whatever the reason, it was now my supreme pleasure to contemplate the appropriate adorning of Jazzy's hair.

Unfortunately, contemplate it is all I've been able to do. Would you believe that every time I try to put her hair in pigtails Jazzy squeals a high-pitched scream and will absolutely not allow me to do it? Would you believe that every headband that I put lovingly on her head is yanked off immediately in the most annoyed manner? Can you credit the fact that now that her hair is at the right length to finally utilize her extensive hair fashion wardrobe that she vehemently refuses to do so?

I've read that asserting her opinions and preferences is the first step on the road to her developing independence. I've read that it shows a healthy level of self-confidence and incipient autonomy. I'm trying to look on the bright side and I am happy that she has a very opinionated little mind of her own. But still, it has been a bit disillusioning for me. And frankly I'm starting to worry that Jazzy will be the exact opposite of me and hate long hair and feel like I forced it on her and end up shaving her head just to get back at me. I hope by the time she is old enough to do that, I will be peacefully accepting of her in whatever guise she chooses to coif herself. Maybe I'll have shaved my head by then too—in utter frustration!

At least, for now, I have my own long hair to console me. And one other thing, Jazzy does, sometimes, allow a stylish hat.

~Annette Marie Hyder
Chicken Soup for the Mother & Daughter Soul

Sandwich Generation

Motherhood is being available to your children whenever they need you,
no matter what their age or their need.
~Major Doris Pengilly

I am a member of the "sandwich generation." I'm forty-two, my children are fifteen and twelve, and I visit my eighty-two-year-old debilitated mother three to four times a week.

Widowed, she lives alone in her condo six miles from my home. She no longer drives and is dependent on others for transportation and social activities. I get very bogged down running two households. I'm either taking her to my home for a visit, to the grocery store or for a haircut, or I'm driving her around with me on my errands just to get her out of the house. She appreciates very much every small thing I do for her and tries hard to understand my busy schedule.

One particularly hot Texas day in July, I was driving my daughter from one errand to another when I realized I was running behind—again—and needed to call Mom and tell her I would be late picking her up. As I sped down the road, I called her on my cell speakerphone. I told her we were coming by to get her but that we were behind schedule. Her Irish lilt filled the car. "I'll be ready whenever you come." Then we ended our conversation with our daily, "I love you. See you soon."

As I hung up, my precious twelve-year-old said, "I was just imagining that I was you and that my daughter was sitting next to me in the car and we were talking to you, the grandma, on the phone." I was stunned. My prayers were being answered. As hard as it is sometimes, with all the running and juggling schedules, I am modeling something for my children after all, teaching them that nothing matters more in this world than the time we spend with those closest to us.

Yes, I may very well be old, one day, and all alone. I hope my daughter will then say, "I love you. See you soon."

~Tricia Short
Chicken Soup for the Grandma's Soul

Of Satin and Ceremonies

Memories are stitched with love.
~Author Unknown

She slips the wedding gown from its padded hanger and fingers the flowing length of pearly satin. She smoothes its streaming folds, lifts its cascading train, tests its lush weight.

Her two daughters had always shared. They shared Barbies and boyfriends, messy bedrooms and midnight secrets, cramp complaints and crowded closets, and—finally—a confining college apartment. They even shared the same choices of shoes and clothes. So it came as no surprise when her girls expressed an identical taste in bridal attire: simple, yet elegant. And this gown was both. Luxuriant and luminous.

A gown to share.

And much too lovely to be packed away forever.

A single shaft of sunlight haloes the fabric with the patina of platinum. It looks fresh and radiant. Radiant the way each of her daughters, in turn, had looked in the custom-designed, custom-made gown. First the older, then, later—rescuing it from the garment bag hanging in a dark closet—the younger. Draped in ivory dreams, brides full of promise and brimming with hope, they had stood next to their husbands in solemn ceremonies sealing upon them blessings and new names. Celebrating their futures.

But that was then. Cleaned and bagged, the dress was once more relegated to a corner in the closet. Until now.

One of the girls was asking about the gown. But the dress

belongs to each girl... and yet to both. What else can she do but divide it? What better opportunity for them to share it once again? After all, there's a lavish expanse of the rich fabric—as well as a good reason now.

Spreading the skirt wide, she picks up her sewing scissors in one hand and opens a seam from bodice to hem. And another seam. And yet another. She separates the thread attaching the bustle, removes the train, and snips off the row of covered buttons.

She smiles as she smoothes the pieces. It's time to transform the milky satin into different gowns for a different generation. The old gives birth to the new; it deserves a future. From sections of the bridal skirt and train, she will fashion and custom-make infant christening gowns. One for each of her daughters to own.

A legacy to share. Gifts from mother to daughters to grandchildren and beyond.

Of course, the gowns will be simple, yet elegant, and fasten with the small, salvaged buttons. Talcum soft, the lustrous satin will soon swaddle precious granddaughters (and, perhaps someday, grandsons) held by their fathers during solemn ceremonies—sealing upon them blessings and new names. Grandbabies full of promise and brimming with hope.

She fingers the fabric and straightens the separate sections. She will fashion christening gowns to pass down and bond succeeding generations. Cherished heirloom gowns to celebrate and share the future... with the same passion as the past.

~Carol McAdoo Rehme
Chicken Soup for the Soul Celebrates Grandmothers

I Never Saw
My Mother Do a Sit-Up

The dress was a full-length sheath the color of sweetened condensed milk, its simplicity the perfect canvas for the hemline's hand-painted flowers. Wearing it, I was a fashion success and I basked in the symphony of compliments it garnered.

But fitting into the dress year after year was difficult, for although shapeless by design, I had to stay in shape to wear it. Despite daily exercise, sometime between birthdays fifty-one and fifty-two, my metabolism slipped into a coma and my svelte figure, along with my derriere, disappeared. Although I'd noticed my pants were snug at the waist and baggy in back, it was my husband who questioned the geographic relocation of my rear. "Where'd your butt go?" was his eloquent query.

To reveal my buttocks' travel plan, I tried on the dress. With my head and arms through the appropriate openings, the barometer by which I judged weight gain followed gravity and flowed southward. But unlike in previous migrations, the dress stopped its journey midway. Gently tugging on one side, then the other, I eased the fabric down my hips and over my thighs. Then I looked in the closet mirror. From waist to knees, the dress clung to what appeared to be a lunar landscape made of dough. I'd found my butt.

Determined to wear the dress to an upcoming family celebration, I immediately began starving and sweating calories.

For several weeks, I worked out with a variety of video partners and a thigh gizmo (the purchase about which I was so embarrassed, I set the box and its packaging in the alley by a neighbor's trash can). I nibbled foods befitting the rodent culture and stuck my nose in the Oreo package to sniff dessert. I was miserable but determined to fit into that dress.

It was during a crunch session with Miss Abs of Steel that I suddenly recalled I'd never seen my mother do a sit-up. It wasn't as if she hadn't had side rolls and a tummy bulge. My mother had managed her flab by wearing a girdle.

I remembered sitting cross-legged on my parents' quilted bedspread and watching as Mama prepared for a special evening out with Daddy. Stepping into her All-in-One, she'd grip the sides and pull upward, while at the same time doing the most wonderful dance... a performance that involved much shimmying and shoving and squishing and shaking until everything loose between her knees and armpits was encased in latex. With her firmly curvy, hourglass figure, she'd looked like Sophia Loren. Sophia Loren!

Grabbing the dress, I headed to the mall to buy myself a girdle. I soon learned that yesterday's shapewear is today's control undergarment. With names like Thigh Trimmer, Minimizer, Smoothie, Belly Buster, Body Reformer, Invisible Shaper and Slim-O-Matic, it wasn't difficult to envision their purpose — a quick lump-and-bump fix.

I tried on the shapewear and like my mother, I danced my looseness into the slimming casing of each. When 100-percent squished, I slipped on the dress and watched in the department store mirror as it glided over a spandex highway and journeyed to my ankles. Preening, I appraised my silhouette, now a smooth and slinky curve. For the price of $27.00, the lunar landscape was gone, and I'd reincarnated the figure of my inner babe, who in the dim dressing room, surprisingly resembled Sophia Loren.

I don't dress my inner babe every day, but when fitting her into a pretty dress means "lifting the fallen," it's spandex, not sit-ups I now turn to.

I am, after all, my mother's daughter.

~EllynAnne Geisel
Chicken Soup to Inspire a Woman's Soul

Sweet Sixteen

I remember my mother's prayers and they have always followed me. They have clung to me all my life.
~Abraham Lincoln

"**H**urry and get dressed, Shelly." Mom's overly cheerful voice penetrated the closed door to my room. "The sun's shining. Let's go riding!"

Mom knew I was on the phone with my boyfriend. The last thing I wanted to do on that Sunday afternoon was go horseback riding with my mother. Yet, I dared not argue back, not after our blowup the night before. I'm sixteen years old! I seethed. Why can't she just stay out of my life?

Sometimes, I hated my mother. I desperately wanted her to give me space. She sponsored my cheerleader squad. She came to every one of my volleyball and softball games. She even taught at my school. Wherever I went, there she was. As if that weren't bad enough, she was always ordering me around. When I was little, I liked it when Mom was protective and when she got involved in my activities. But now I wanted more independence, a chance to make my own mistakes.

Truth is, in spite of Mom's constant surveillance, I managed to break most of the rules at our private Christian school. And the more I rebelled, the more Mom clamped down. The more she clamped down, the more I rebelled.

Take the night before, when we had the blowup. Okay, so I was a few minutes late coming in. Well, maybe it was more like an hour late. Anyway, just as I expected, Mom followed me into my room. "Where were you all this time, Shelly? I worry about you when you're late. Anything could have happened! Why didn't you call me?" On and on and on.

As usual, Mom threw in a little scripture for good measure, as if she didn't drill me on memory verses at our breakfast table every morning! "Remember, Shelly," she'd said that night, "the Bible says, 'Children, obey your parents.... If you honor your father and mother, yours will be a long life, full of blessing.'" Then, she added, "Shelly, your life just shortened by one day!"

"Mom!" I yelled. "Will you just leave me alone?" When she finally left, I slammed the door behind her.

Today she was pretending nothing had happened, trying to make us look like the ideal, loving family of her dreams. Meanwhile, after hanging up the phone, I was sitting there thinking, What is all this horseback-riding business? Mom isn't even a horse person! She just wants to know what I'm doing every minute.

Halfheartedly I pulled on my riding boots, then went over to the dresser. Reaching for a comb, my hand brushed against the necklace Mom had given me for my last birthday. I'd better wear this or she'll ask where it is. Reluctantly, I fastened the silver chain around my neck and straightened the pendant—the silver outline of a heart with its message, in script, suspended inside: "Sweet Sixteen."

By the time I got to the barn, Dad had already saddled our horse, Miss CharDeck—we usually called her Charcey—and Mom was swinging into the saddle. "Mom, what are you doing?" I shrieked. "You've never ridden Charcey before! She's a big horse." I cannot believe this woman! I thought. She'll do anything to be part of my life. And I just want her out of it!

While Dad was bridling the Arabian, Babe, Mom discovered her stirrups were too long. Before Dad could turn around to adjust them, Charcey charged away at full gallop.

Scared and inexperienced, Mom probably reacted by doing all the wrong things. Whatever the reason, Charcey was out of control. I had never seen that horse run so fast, her mane and tail flying in the wind. It was as though she had to show off what a quarter horse is bred to do: win short-distance races. With every stride of her powerful haunches, she gained speed.

I watched, horrified, as Charcey's hooves beat at the earth, faster and faster like something possessed, a thousand pounds of straining muscle thundering across the pasture. With lightning speed, Charcey reached a corner of the pasture fence—a place of decision. Should she jump? No. Too high with a ditch on the other side. Other choice? Make a ninety-degree turn. Charcey turned. Mom flew high into the air, crashed through a barbed wire fence and landed on the sun-parched ground.

Then nothing, except for Charcey's hoofbeats as she tore back to the barn.

Dear God! No! No! This can't be happening! I sprinted across the pasture, outrunning Dad on the Arabian. "Mom! Mom!" Please, God, don't let her be dead! I didn't mean it, God. I don't really want her out of my life! Please!

The barbed wire was holding her in an almost kneeling position. Her right wrist and hand dangled the wrong way, her neck and head were turned as if broken, and blood oozed from gashes on her back. Is she breathing? Please, God, she thinks I don't love her. "Mom?"

After what seemed an eternity, I heard a moan, then a weak, "I'm okay, Shelly."

"Mom! I didn't mean to be hurtful. I love you, Mom." Ever-so-carefully, I began untangling her hair from the barbed wire, barely able to see through my tears. "Oh, Mama, I'm so sorry. I'm so sorry."

"I know, Shelly," Mom somehow managed, while I made one last tug on her now-shredded pink sweater and freed her from the wire.

"We've got to get you to the hospital," Dad said, jumping back astride Babe and turning her toward the barn. "I'll call an ambulance."

"No," Mom said, and because she was a nurse, we listened. "You can carry me in the van."

It wasn't easy, but we did it. Dad barreled down the highway. Meanwhile, I did what Mom had taught me—I quoted scripture, the first one that popped into my head. "Rejoice in the Lord always," I said, close to her ear. "And again I say rejoice." For once, I must have done the right thing, because Mom, through all her pain, started quoting scripture, too, one verse after another, all the way to the hospital.

Mom spent most of the next three months in a wheelchair, and during that time the two of us did a lot of talking. "Mom," I told her, "I know I act a lot like Charcey did that day of the accident. I just want to charge through life without being held back, not missing anything."

"Yes, Shelly, and I always want to be in control, to make sure things go right. To protect you from getting hurt."

We decided because we were very different, we'd probably always clash over one thing or another. We agreed on something else, too. That we loved each other, no matter what.

Still, I felt a need to do something more to make things right. One day at school I asked permission to speak at our chapel service. Standing on stage at the microphone, I took a deep breath and started. To the other students, to the faculty and especially to Mom, who sat in the back of the room in her wheelchair, I said, "I want to apologize for all the mistakes I've made this year, mistakes that have hurt others. Worst of all, they have hurt my mom."

I told them how hateful I had been to my mother, how I had yelled at her to stay out of my life. Then I told them about Mom's accident, about how, at the thought of losing her, I realized she is my very best friend, and that she only wants the best for me. "Please, you guys," I begged my fellow students, "tell your mother you love her. Don't wait until it's too late, like I almost did."

I looked back at Mom who was beaming, while dabbing at her eyes with a tissue. "Mom," I said, voice quivering, "I ask you to forgive me. I ask God to forgive me."

As if on cue, one of Mom's Bible verses popped into my head. "If we confess our sins, he is faithful and just to forgive us our sins." Thank you, God, for believing in me, even when I disappoint you over and over.

Just like Mom! I realized in a flash of insight. Instinctively, I reached up and caressed the silver pendant at my neck. My fingers traced the intricate lettering, "Sweet Sixteen." Sixteen? Yes. Sweet? Hardly! But I will try, Mom. I smiled through my tears. I will try.

Leaving the platform, I became aware of a new-for-me feeling, one that said, It's okay, Shelly, to let your mom into your life.

Even when you're sweet sixteen.

~Shelly Teems Johnson as told to Gloria Cassity Stargel
Chicken Soup for the Christian Teenage Soul

Two Grannies in the Kitchen

It was time for Pat to redecorate the bedroom. She'd put it off for years, always using the money for something else—Tom's college tuition, Cathy's nursing school, Jim's diving classes, Mike's trip to Mexico.

But now the children were grown, and it was her turn. First, Pat and her husband, Al, bought a century-old black-walnut bedroom set at an auction. The seven-feet-tall headboard, ornate dresser and matching chest of drawers were splendid, especially after they painted the room bright white to show off the beautiful dark wood furniture.

Next, Pat hired a decorator, who designed the most magnificent blue and white draperies. Thick pale-blue carpet picked up tones from the multi-colored sunburst quilt. The pillows, pictures, knick-knack shelf—everything was perfect. Now that their parenting years were ending, it was time now to enjoy life and each other.

Camelot lasted two months.

In May, Al's eighty-seven-year-old mother, Mabel, came to live with them. She'd moved into a lovely nursing home a month earlier, but each time they visited, Mabel lamented, "I can't stand this place! There's no kitchen! How do they expect me to entertain my friends? I'll come live with you. At least you have a kitchen."

It wasn't a problem for Pat to take Mabel in. As a full-time nurse, Pat knew Mabel's medication needed to be better regulated, and she could do that easily if they lived together. Plus, Mabel had driven the five-and-a-half hours to their home in Milwaukee many times over the years to stay with their children when Al and Pat took trips together, and for weeks at a time when each of the four children was born. Mabel had been Pat's support system, caring for her children, mending their clothes, cooking their meals. She was always there when Pat needed her.

Now, Mabel needed them.

The only room large enough for Grandma's treasured pieces of furniture that she insisted come with her was the newly decorated master bedroom. The elegant walnut bedroom set was moved into the small room down the hall, the room with the race car wallpaper.

When Grandma arrived, she made it clear that the kitchen was her domain. By the time Pat arrived home from work at 4:30, the potatoes were boiled, and a lettuce and mayonnaise salad was cooling in the refrigerator.

"Supper's ready, except for the meat. Didn't know what you had planned," was Grandma Mabel's daily greeting. Pat started hiding the potatoes.

That summer was one of ups and downs while they learned to adjust to Grandma Mabel's fierce independence, her memory failures ("I already took my pills!"), her old-fashioned way of cooking and dominance of the kitchen, her increasing urinary problems and her threats whenever the slightest thing upset her ("I'll get my own apartment!").

In the meantime, problems started developing with Pat's mother, Olive, also in her eighties, who lived alone in a small farmhouse just fourteen miles from where Mabel had lived. First, Olive developed Parkinson's disease, then she fell and broke her hand. A small nursing home was her next home, but, like Grandma Mabel, she hated it.

"There's no life in this place! I'm all cooped in. I just can't stand not doing anything."

Pat and Al realized that both Mabel and Olive belonged in their home. After all, they'd known each other and compared Mother's Day and birthday gifts for twenty-five years. They'd talked on the phone regularly—Mabel from her elegant city home, Olive from her farmhouse. Mabel was forgetful but in pretty good shape, physically. Olive was mentally sharp but confined to a wheelchair. Each one could do for the other what the other couldn't do for herself.

So, just five months after Pat and Al had redecorated their master bedroom, they had two grannies in their kitchen. Since Al and Pat both left for work early, they hired a woman to help get both grandmas up, dressed and ready to go to a day care for the elderly, where they were treated to a full day of physical and occupational therapy, aerobics and continuing education classes.

When Olive's little house finally sold, she insisted they move more of her things into Pat and Al's home — chests of drawers, books, tables, pictures and ancient mementos of her life on the farm.

Grandma Mabel followed suit by demanding that her treasured collection, all two hundred pieces, of Haviland china be brought in so she could "entertain her friends properly." Soon, Pat had delicate pink and white china all over her house.

Other problems appeared as the months ticked by. Both Olive and Mabel developed arthritis. Sometimes, the pain made them cranky. Pat's mother, especially, often became depressed and manipulative. "I'm pitiful and such a bother. I'm no good anymore." Al would give her a hug of reassurance, yet, Olive would say, "I don't know how you can stand it with me here."

Grandma Mabel lost control of her bladder but refused to wear the necessary protection. She'd wet her clothes, then hide them under the bed or hang them back in the closet, hoping they'd dry by morning so she could wear them again.

Pat felt like a young mother with mounds of laundry. Only, she wasn't young. She was tired. Sometimes friction developed between her and Al. She'd come home from work, tired from a long day in the pediatrics ward, and both grannies would be floundering about in their small kitchen. When Pat finally shooed them both out of her way, Al would come on the scene with "Let Mom do it. She's just trying to help." Cooking had always been Pat's favorite household duty, and now it seemed she was doomed to a life of meat and boiled potato dinners.

Pat wanted it to work. And, with a great deal of organization and patience, it usually did. But sometimes when she was really down, the nursing home seemed mighty tempting. Pat prayed. She remembered the days when both grandmas were saving her life when she had four preschoolers.

One night when the frustrations mounted, Pat retreated to the race car wallpapered bedroom and sat with her head in her hands. Then, from the room next door, Pat heard Mabel reading her Bible to Olive. Mabel was a staunch Methodist; Olive a strict Roman Catholic. Here they were, the city mouse and the country mouse, sharing the one thing they had in common.

Mabel read her favorite verse, John 3:16: "For God loved the world so much that he gave his only Son, so that anyone who believes in him shall not perish but have eternal life."

Pat smiled and whispered to herself, "If these two exasperating, wonderful old women can have such hope for life eternal, then I can certainly have hope for today, tomorrow and next week." She stared at the race cars for a while, and promised herself once and for all that she would never send them back to nursing homes. That promise was hard to keep. About a year later, Olive had a severe stroke and died. Two months after that, Mabel died peacefully too.

The weekend after the second funeral, Al and Pat moved their antique walnut bedroom set back into the master bedroom. On the shelf by the bed, there's a picture of Grandma Mabel and Grandma Olive sitting together, holding hands.

"Somehow," Pat said to her husband as they stepped back to admire it, "this room feels much better now than it did before we had to move out of it. I feel better, too. Growing old doesn't seem too scary anymore."

~Patricia Lorenz
Chicken Soup for the Caregiver's Soul

Chapter 8

Like Mother, Like Daughter

Like Grandmother, Like Mother, Like Granddaughter

Just about the time a woman thinks her work is done,
she becomes a grandmother.
~E.H. Dreschnack

Sticky Memories

I t was a warm summer day and my kids were driving me crazy. They were licking popsicles while traipsing back and forth between the patio and our family room. With each trip, they left behind a sticky display of fingerprints on our large, sliding glass door.

"Watch what you are dong! Keep your fingers off the glass!" I yelled at them.

Granted, our sliding door was a real bear. The track had warped from the weight of the heavy glass. The only way to get the door open was to grab the handle with one hand, prop your foot against the wall for leverage, and pull with all your might. At three years old, my daughter Kelly had very little might. She tried to open the door by running her fingers across the glass. Perhaps she thought she had magic powers, who knows?

Her older brother, Derrick, was a bit stronger, but even he soon tired of the effort. When he wanted to be let back in, he would pound on the door with his fists. My mother was visiting on this one particular day, and noted my temper flaring.

"Don't be so hard on them," she admonished. "Some day you will miss those little fingerprints on the glass."

"Oh right," I replied, as I headed for the closet where I kept the window cleaner.

"Well, your grandmother sure was fond of your fingerprints on her French door windows," my mom said, as she opened the door for her granddaughter.

"What are you talking about? Grandmother was a fastidious housekeeper. She wouldn't even let us play in her living room. We were relegated to the guest room or the attic!" Not that my sister and I minded our restrictions. The attic was filled with trunks full of treasures—long evening gowns for dress up, and old teddy bears and wooden soldiers. Best of all, we could spy on unsuspecting adults by peering through the attic fan's grating.

We only saw my mother's family for a few months each summer. They lived in Arkansas and we called California our home. Those summers were a magical time of picnicking at the lake and chasing lightning bugs with our cousins.

Now, as hard as I tried, I could not dredge up a single memory related to fingerprints on my grandmother's French doors. I remembered the doors well. They stood in the formal dining room and after supper we exited through them to rejoin our friends at play.

"I would offer to clean the windows," my mother continued. "But Mother wouldn't let me. Those little fingerprints are all I have to remind me of the girls when they leave," she would say.

If there were tears at the time of our departure, we never saw them. It was only after hearing my mother's story that I realized the intensity of my grandmother's love. Only now, as a mother, could I comprehend her longing to hold on to a little piece of us.

It's been years since that summer day when I fumed over my children's fingerprints. Derrick and Kelly are grown now. French doors that open easily to the touch have replaced that troublesome, sliding door.

"Nana, come outside and watch me shoot baskets," Aaron yells from the patio as he pounds on the doors to get my attention.

On the other side of the French doors, Trevor toddles on chubby legs. As he presses his face against the glass to get a better glimpse of his big brother, I swoop him into my arms. Noting the tiny fingerprints left behind, I try not to weep.

My son and his wife have decided to trade their California residency for Colorado. They are packing up their house across town, and in two weeks they will be gone. I know the boys will love their new Rocky Mountain home — so many lakes to picnic by and lots of cousins to join in the chase for fireflies.

We will keep in touch, of course. They will come back to visit. And until then, I have fingerprints to cherish.

~Mary Ann Cook
Chicken Soup for the Soul Celebrates Grandmothers

78

The True Lesson of Homework

*A Grandmother is a little bit parent, a little bit teacher
and a little bit best friend.*
~G.W. Curtis

She is a study in consternation. Hannah's brow is furrowed; she is squinting and biting her lower lip, sure signs of anxiety in this granddaughter.

The woeful mood is due to a second-grade scourge known as "homework."

Hannah has begged to play outside on this glorious day, but I am under strict orders from her mother that she must first attack her assignments. And as the babysitter-in-residence, I am pledged to follow instructions.

Never mind that I, a former teacher, have decidedly mixed feelings about the importance of missing a golden afternoon when the sun is winking off the back patio, the trees are dancing in a lovely breeze and nature herself is celebrating spring.

Hannah's work sheets are spread out in front of her. It's been a while since I've seen what second grade homework looks like, so I sit near Hannah, careful not to disturb her, but fascinated by watching this child I love so much as she attacks word configurations on a printed page.

Her teacher wants Hannah to transpose some letters to make new words. Hannah is working on set number three — and has been at this for nearly twenty minutes. She had sailed through the first two sets—the easy ones, she'd assured me—but this third set was the killer.

So we sit together, a grandmother and a grandchild, and neither of us speaks. Once, Hannah throws down her pencil in frustration. Another time, I think I see the start of a tear in her chocolate-brown eyes.

"Let's take a break," I attempt. I even offer to make her favorite apple/raisin treat, one that usually gets Hannah racing off to the kitchen with me. But this earnest child is resolute. "If I finish," she reasons aloud, "I can go outside and play with Julia and Trevor." And to make matters worse, we can hear their shouts and occasional laughter through the open window.

Minutes later, Hannah has symbolically climbed to the language arts mountaintop. The word work sheets are finished. Now only two pages of addition stand between Hannah and the great outdoors.

Once again, all goes swimmingly at the beginning of Hannah's math homework. The computations come so easily that she's lulled into eight-year-old cockiness. "These are SIMPLE!" she exults, almost offended, it would seem, at the lack of challenge.

But on the second math worksheet, toward the bottom of the page, Hannah collides with a tough set. And she has her comeuppance. No matter how she struggles, the instructions—and thus the solutions—elude her.

I feel a meltdown coming.

It's nearly five in the evening. Hannah has been up since six-thirty in the morning. She's put in a full day in school, including a play rehearsal that both delighted and drained her. Her little brother is on a playdate, and he doesn't have homework because Zay is, after all, only in prekindergarten.

The injustice of it all finally gets those tears spilling. "I HATE homework," Hannah sobs. And she means it.

This time, I ignore my pledges to her mother. I make an executive decision that my granddaughter and I are going outside to catch the last—and hopefully best—of this gift of a day.

For the next hour, I watch Hannah as she celebrates liberation. She runs and leaps and then climbs to the top of the jungle gym that is in the yard. I snap a photo of her as she performs feats of daring up there that still make me gasp.

Her cheeks are flushed, her hair is wild, and I wish that utter abandon and unbridled joy could last forever.

When my daughter comes home, Hannah is momentarily stricken. "I didn't finish my math sheets," she confesses at once.

I hold my breath. I watch my daughter as she looks at Hannah, at me, and at the day that is surrendering to dusk.

And Jill says the very thing I might have written in a script for her:

"You can finish your homework later," my daughter tells hers. "Play some more!"

And on a glorious spring day, I silently bless my daughter for her wisdom.

~Sally Friedman
Chicken Soup for the Grandma's Soul

Becoming a Grandma

It's such a grand thing to be a mother of a mother—
that's why the world calls her grandmother.
~Unknown

After three days of labor, my daughter Déjà had her first child, a beautiful seven-pound four-ounce girl. I was amazed to observe that the instant she saw her new baby, the pain of childbirth was immediately replaced by the bliss of motherhood.

In those first few heart-stopping minutes of becoming a grandmother, one particular moment stands out for me. A moment set apart from everything else that was happening by the sudden depth of our connection—daughter, mother and grandmother.

My beautiful daughter turned to me, her eyes shining with a light I had never seen there before. "Mom," she said, "now I know how much you love me."

~Robin Lim
Chicken Soup for the Mother's Soul 2

Crinkles and Crow's Feet

Grandmas are just antique little girls.
~G.W. Curtis

I gasped in horror as I stared at the picture on my driver's license. "Who is that old woman?" I cried, clapping my hand over my eyes. What happened to the slender blond girl who used to be there? I peeked out between my fingers. With just the barest hint of a smile curving her lips, the unfamiliar face gazed steadily back at me. There were crow's feet crinkling out from her eyes, and multiple strands of gray streaking through her hair. Though I didn't recognize her face, my name marched boldly across the bottom of the license. I shuddered and tucked the offensive piece of plastic into my pocketbook.

For the next few days I walked around in a state of mild shock. Physically, I didn't feel a bit older. In fact, I felt as chipper and cheerful as always. But I hadn't seen a picture of myself in a long time and the license photo was a rude awakening. The only good thing about it, I told myself, was that nobody else who saw it seemed to be shocked by my mature appearance. Maybe I was the only one surprised by the fact that age had snuck up behind me and unkindly retouched my looks.

I fought to get past the nagging plastic reminder that I would never be smooth-faced or blithely young again. But no matter how I struggled, I found myself swinging between bouts of depression because I looked so old, and feeling proud that I had thus far survived all the curves life had thrown my way. Then, while browsing through the newspaper one day, I spotted something that snagged my attention. Shocked, I pulled the paper closer and squinted at the grainy black and white photograph of a former classmate.

I added up how long it had been since we graduated from high school. Frowning in disbelief, I counted again. How could it be possible that thirty years had zipped by? I studied his face. Though he had aged well, there was no doubt that he hadn't seen eighteen in a very long time. With a sigh, I realized that all the people I remembered as being young and baby-faced were now older and life-worn. And besides that, many were grandparents. I consoled myself with the fact that at least I wasn't that far gone.

Then the telephone rang. It was my daughter, calling from work. "Are you sitting down?" she asked.

"Yes," I said. An uneasy knot of something twisted in my stomach. In my experience, conversations that started like this never brought good news.

"I'm pregnant!" she blurted out.

Instantly, a myriad of emotions washed over me—shock, fear, concern for my insulin-dependent daughter, and a blinding, bright burst of extreme joy. Laura's voice sounded from the receiver. "Mom? Are you happy?"

"Oh, yes!" I replied.

Suddenly, the idea of being a grandmother seemed pretty wonderful as I fell totally and completely in love with that baby. My hands itched to start crocheting and before the week was out, a blanket, two pairs of tiny booties, and a soft little cap emerged from my flying crochet hooks. With a heart full of prayers for the health and safety of my daughter and her unborn baby, I spent my days planning the fun things I would do with the new little one, and my nights worrying myself sick thinking about all the things that could go wrong.

Finally the tense months of waiting were over and on one of the coldest, nastiest days of the year, Bailey made his grand entrance. At nearly ten pounds he was the largest newborn I had ever seen. And he was perfect!

Later, as I proudly displayed his picture, a few friends and relatives teased me about my updated status. "Old grandma," one of them snickered.

"You're just jealous," I retorted. Yes, I was a grandma, and darned happy about it. And I treasured every moment spent cuddling that sweet little bundle.

One day while visiting, I gave Bailey a loud smooch on the cheek and he rewarded me with a toothless grin. As he stared up into my face, he squinted his eyes and giggled.

"Look, Mom!" cried Laura. "When he laughs, his eyes crinkle up like yours do."

What? My eyes crinkle when I laugh? I sat back in amazement. Suddenly it dawned on me that my crow's feet had emerged from years of smiles and laughter. And if Bailey crinkled his eyes when he smiled, that meant that someday he'd have crow's feet, too. I burst into peals of joyful laughter, not caring how many lines spread across my face. Somehow, crinkles and crow's feet never sounded so good.

~Anne Culbreath Watkins
Chicken Soup for the Soul Celebrates Grandmothers

81

Travels with Grandma

If nothing is going well, call your grandmother.
~Italian Proverb

My daughters, Linda and Leslie, never called my mother anything but Honie. Mother announced early on that she was much too young to be a grandmother, and Honie was the closest derivative of her name Helen, so Honie she was to all of us.

Honie was an inveterate traveler, and fortunately for us, she derived great pleasure from taking us on her journeys. Although Linda was fifteen and Leslie was twelve and I was thirty-five, Honie always referred to the three of us as "her girls" and treated us as if we were all the same age. And on her trips, since she was well read and very knowledgeable about everywhere her travels took us, we all acted childlike. No matter what the country, every morning Honie would determine our destination and our destiny for the day, and we would follow like dutiful little ducklings wherever she led. For one so small (she was barely five feet tall) she was a born leader and not to be deterred in whatever she determined to achieve.

Her notion of speaking a foreign language was to speak English very slowly, very loudly and act out the words as one might in the game of charades. We would stand aside as she went through her convolutions, and although we might risk a whispered "Is it bigger than a breadbox?" we generally shut up and let her elicit whatever answers she could with her dramatic efforts.

Our first Sunday in Lisbon, she approached a Portuguese gentleman on the street, pulled on his sleeve, pointed to the heavens, then folded her hands in supplication and said, "God—pray, God—pray?" The gentleman looked at her quizzically, and then as the light dawned, responded, "You want a church, lady?"

Honie beamed in pleasure as he pointed out the nearest church and went on his way. She had already mastered Portuguese. We rolled our eyes in despair and followed her into the church, not sure whether to pray for indulgence or beg for forgiveness.

In our week's stay at the Avenida Palace, there was scarcely a morning that she did not have a request for the front desk, and to their credit, they were always tolerant and usually accommodating.

One morning as we rode down to the lobby in the big iron elevator, Honie was doing her usual "tch, tch," as she decried the fact that European hotels "never, ever, ever supplied wash-cloths" and announced that she would just stop by the front desk to request three for the next morning. Approaching the desk clerk, she said slowly and distinctly, "Excuse me, but we... don't have... any...." and folding her hand into a ball, she vigorously scrubbed her cheek.

"Soap?" he asked.

She shook her head in irritation. "No, no, washcloths."

"Ah," he nodded knowingly. "I will see to it, señora."

Mission accomplished, we were off to Nazare for a day of explor-ing. The next morning she informed us once again that she needed to stop at the front desk.

Timorously, we followed and waited while she informed the clerk that we were out of Kleenex in our bathroom. This request included placing her hand over her nose, saying "achoo" several times and wiping her nose. Now it was the clerk's turn to roll his eyes, but he acknowledged her request and we were on our way.

The next morning we were halfway across the lobby and almost out the door when Honie stopped us. "Just a minute, girls. I need to tell the desk clerk that we're out of toilet paper."

The picture of how she might dramatize that request was more than any of us could face. We were out the door in a flash, leaving

Honie to face the clerk on her own. There is a limit to what even the most dutiful ducklings will endure.

~Phyllis W. Zeno
Chicken Soup for the Grandma's Soul

82

"What's in a Name?"

A child needs a grandparent, anybody's grandparent,
to grow a little more securely into an unfamiliar world.
~Charles and Ann Morse

I am a grandma by default. Excuse me, I need to rephrase — I am a step-grandma by default.

Let me try again; I am part of a grand-parenting unit that I entered upon by means of a second marriage to my formerly widowed boyfriend.

If your reaction to this statement is that I am a slave to semantics, then you most likely are not involved in a blended family. For those of us who are, we know that semantics is either the path of diplomacy or the route to familial brouhaha.

When I began dating Bob, his middle child was expecting her first child, Bob's first grandchild. Jill and her husband lived far away, across the country. I first met Jill and her beautiful baby girl when they came home for a visit. Kelly was only three months old. By the time Bob and I married two years later, Kelly was beginning to talk. She called me Patty.

Shortly after our wedding, a second grandchild, Ryan, came along. If one baby could steal your heart, two held your entire mind, body and soul captive.

Still, I was more than a little hesitant to insert myself into the role of grandma when I had no claim to the name. My heart longed to smother these gorgeous children in my woefully undersized bosom, which ironically reflected my credentials as a grandparent.

I took my concerns to my husband, asking him how I should engage the grandchildren without overstepping. I did not want to assume a role that rightly was reserved for another. Nor did I want to be separated from the love or the involvement of each stage of their growth because I was not a charter member of the family. I definitely did not want to be viewed as disinterested when in fact I was deeply invested.

I told Bob I yearned for the luxury of casual acceptance; the kind where you can lavish blatant, biased praise over the smallest achievements without looking like you're pandering, and the right to step in with aged advice of years and experience without appearing like a know-it-all blowhard. I coveted the safety net of ownership.

Bob's wisdom came in the form of a parable. He told me a lovely story about his paternal step-grandfather, Guy. Bob's dad lost his father when he was only fourteen years old. His mother, Gigi, married Guy a few years later. Bob's eyes glisten with child-like anticipation when he speaks of Guy and Gigi. Gigi and Guy owned an ice cream store. (Who among us would not wish for our grandparents to own an ice cream store?)

Beyond spooning dollops of ice cream into Bob's eager mouth, Guy took Bob fishing. Guy baited and hooked not only the fish, but young Bob, too. Guy reeled Bob in with his kind, gentle, and loving spirit. They laughed, joked, and did "guy" things. The only name Guy ever held was Guy, but Bob's heart hears grandpa thirty years after Guy's death.

Bob's story was very comforting to me. I know that gaining acceptance as a new step-grandparent can take time. I can wait. In the meantime my love pours out into their open willing spirits in spurts, sometimes gushing forth, other times more measured, but always wholesome and pure.

Then when the time comes, and in my best grandma fashion — as all good grandmas do — I will relate a multitude of family stories to Kelly and Jill and the nameless wonders of future step-grandchildren and grandchildren. My wish is that all the "grands" will be cousins-in-arms gathered around the sprightly little old woman (me) while she weaves her tales.

And the first story I will tell will be this: One day not too long ago, in a city far away, four-year-old Kelly was happily chatting to her mom when her mother mentioned something about Grandpa. Kelly asked for clarification; my grandpa with grandma, or my grandpa with my Patty?

At this point in the story telling I will pause to ask, "How do you like that? I am Kelly's Patty!" I will shout these words with tremendous animation by flinging my arms wide open as if to embrace the world, throwing my head back, giggling in delight, kicking my bare feet into the air and wiggling my toes. I will proclaim to all the children of the generation two steps down from mine that the possessive "my" followed by whatever name that comes to mind creates a glorious state of being.

~Patty S. Sullivan
Chicken Soup for the Soul Celebrates Grandmothers

83

Babies, Boredom and Bliss

"We're not going in there, are we?" I asked, appalled, looking inside the baby store my friend was determined to enter. I'd come a long way to visit... hundreds of miles, and she wanted to shop in a baby store? Quite frankly, I found those kinds of stores boring, the way I found most babies boring. I'd never been accused of being enthusiastic over little creatures who couldn't walk, talk or do anything except scream, make a mess and demand all of one's attention.

Turning on the well-worn heel of her running shoe, my friend shot me a steely look. "We won't be long," she promised, striding into the store.

Unhappily I trailed after her. She's changed, I thought grumpily as I stifled a yawn and tottered through the crammed aisles on my high heels. Definitely changed, I thought sourly as she spent the next two hours oohing and aahing over everything to do with infants until I thought I'd go insane.

What can I say in defense of my once-glamorous friend, who now smelled of spit-up and stumbled tiredly through the store misty-eyed with joy?

She'd become a grandmother.

That fact was responsible for her gleeful preoccupation with the world of little things, the reason she didn't have time to dye the gray in her hair, the reason she'd traded in her classic clothing for jogging gear, the reason she didn't seem able to talk about anything. Except babies. And most particularly, one little grandbaby.

After helping cram purchases into every nook and cranny of her car, I reminded my friend of a lunch date with our high school girlfriends at a hot new restaurant that featured elegant dining in an atmosphere that catered to people like me—tourists with hard-earned time and money to spend, who wanted to be pampered in a child-free environment.

I squeezed into the passenger side of the car, holding a huge teddy bear on my lap, thankful that soon I'd be in a world of my peers where conversation would veer toward spas, salons and shopping.

But I was sadly, pathetically mistaken. No sooner did we get to the restaurant than my friend took out her wallet and proceeded to spread pictures of her grandson over the gleaming table, expecting us to ooh and aah over the bald-headed tyke with the toothless smile. Every woman did. Including the waitress.

But not me.

What's the matter? I thought, depressed. Am I the only woman on the planet who dislikes baby talk? It wasn't that I didn't like babies. I did. I'd borne and raised one myself. Lisa had turned into a lovely young woman. Intelligent, kind, ambitious. We had a good relationship based on respect, love and mutual interests. But I had never been what one could call maternal. And what's more, my friend never had been either, I thought, glaring at her over a glass of wine. I couldn't understand what had happened to her.

We'd been teenage mothers together. We'd married and grown up with our daughters together. Together as single mothers we'd struggled in a world where we tried to fit work and relationships and parenting all in one. We'd been the best of friends.

What had happened to bring us apart?

I could only think of one thing. One word. Actually, two words. Grand. Mother.

What was so grand about that? I thought irately.

Months later, my daughter called. "Mom, guess what?"

I was filing my nails with one hand and juggling the phone with the other, trying not to smear my facial pack.

"I'm going to have a baby!"

The phone slid down my face as visions of gray hair and sweatpants filled my mind, and the sounds of squawking at all hours of the day and night filled my ears. I tasted weariness as I imagined trundling after an infant who needed smelly diapers changed while testing formula to feed a hungry, wailing new soul.

New soul.

I burst into tears.

"Are you glad? Or are you mad?" Lisa shouted into the phone. With trembling fingers I juggled the receiver and said through a throat suddenly gone dry, "I'm not sure." Silently I tried out the unfamiliar label. Grandma. "When's the due date?" I whispered hoarsely.

"Christmas day!"

Christmas in Seattle.

I flew over on the twenty-third. Lisa met me at the airport. Beaming. Huge. I remembered how that felt. Remembered how... how wonderful it was! How joyful! How expectant! For the second time since I heard the news I burst into tears.

On December twenty-sixth, Bronwyn entered the world and stole my breath, my heart, my soul. My entire identity. "Let Grandma hold her!" I shouted, almost knocking my poor son-in-law off his feet as I snatched my granddaughter out of his arms. I looked down into her precious, angelic face and... burst into tears.

Over the next few days, I fought like a dragon to hold her, feed her, change her. I shopped in the local supermarket with my hair pulled into an untidy ponytail, dark smudges under my eyes from day-old mascara, sleepless nights and sentimental weeping.

As I sat in the market's deli, rocking Bronwyn in my arms and trying not to get spit-up on my jogging suit, I reflected on my new heart, new eyes, new senses. And I knew that up until the day she'd come into the world, I had been blind. The miracle of her birth had wrought a miracle in me, one I could not get enough of. Babies. I planned to call my friend to see if she'd be available to go shopping next time I was in town. There were some baby stores I was eager to visit. I hoped she'd bring photos.

I couldn't wait to show her mine.

~Janet Hall Wigler
Chicken Soup for the Grandma's Soul

84

Beach Talk

I t's countdown time. In a month, more or less, my daughter is due to give birth. "Do you think I'll stay like this forever?" she asks as we walk the beach.

"The condition isn't permanent," I assure her.

She feels as if she's going to explode, as I felt back in August of 1965 when my due date came and no baby arrived. Six days later, Elizabeth bounced red-faced into the world, and my stomach, which had gotten as huge as my daughter's is now, began to deflate.

Elizabeth parades her pregnancy proudly. Clad only in a two-piece black swimsuit, her belly protruding over the bottom half, she reminds me of photos one might see among the pages of National Geographic.

The last two days have been special for us, our time, my daughter's and mine. She has invited me to her summer house, where we put our busy lives on hold for a mother/daughter mini-vacation. Now, we walk the beach, filling in the blank spaces of our lives, usually relegated to brief, late-night phone calls assuring each other we are both well.

This morning we have time to linger as we savor that rare gift of togetherness. Walking along with my child who is carrying her child in utero, I note silently that our lives, as if by magic, will change in a heartbeat.

Soon, these lazy summer days that run smoothly into each other will be interrupted by the demands of a newborn, and knowing this, Elizabeth has invited me to Fire Island to share in these few remaining quiet moments. Aside from an occasional seagull and a few early morning walkers like us, Liz and I are alone.

Our talk turns to practical matters that have to do with her pregnancy: Lamaze classes, Liz's work schedule, and how she plans to combine her job with motherhood. We discuss breast-feeding, the intricacies of the labor process, her fear of the pain and the security of knowing if it gets too difficult there are positive alternatives. Her doctor from Manhattan also has a house on Fire Island. "If you go into labor on the island," he joked, "I'll simply throw you in my boat and deliver the baby on board."

"You call me the minute a contraction hits," I remind her, "so I can get to the hospital. That's part of the deal."

"You also promise to behave," she warns me. "You promise to sit in the waiting room and not bug anyone."

I agree to be the model mother, waiting patiently until my grandchild arrives. If it were up to me, I would be with her every step of the way. I even offered to be her Lamaze coach.

"Really, Mom!" she said. "That's why God invented husbands."

We talk about motherhood, and I recall my pediatrician telling me thirty years ago, "The best thing you can do is enjoy your baby. Have fun. Everything else will fall into place."

It sounded good even though it wasn't always possible. New parents are bound up in tending to the needs of their infants. Fun takes a back seat to new responsibilities. Sleep-deprived and edgy, parents respond to every cry, every nuance, walking through these early days in a zombie-like trance.

"Will I be a good mother?" Elizabeth asks suddenly. "How will I know what to do? How do I know if I'm doing it right? What if I make mistakes?" Her barrage of questions comes pouring out as a last-minute, urgent attempt to gather up my secrets of mothering, and the fact is, even now, I don't have the answers.

"You will make mistakes," I say. "You won't always know what to do, but it won't matter. All you need to do is love your child." I echo my pediatrician's words: "The rest will fall into place."

I feel a bit smug as I offer these words of wisdom, but they are the only ones I have. The rest will follow on their own. Liz and her husband, Noel, will find answers through their own parenting techniques, and years later, they may be as stymied as I am now when their children seek for the responses she looks for from me this morning.

What I do tell her is that I was more unprepared than she is and: "It's the loving that always makes it work." She seems satisfied with that. We walk back holding hands and looking forward to breakfast.

"The baby just kicked really hard!" Liz says.

I reach out to touch the fleshy belly that houses my grandchild. Today I think it's a boy. Yesterday I was convinced it was a girl. The suspense is killing me.

"Whatever it is, I think I'm going to explode," Liz says.

I brush a strand of hair from her eyes. "I love you," I say.

"Me, too, Mom," she whispers.

The clouds part, giving birth to sunshine as a new day stretches out before us. We walk the rest of the way arm in arm, alone together, mother and daughter in one shadow.

~Judith Marks-White
Chicken Soup for the Mother & Daughter Soul

Chapter
9

Like Mother, Like Daughter

Special Mother-Daughter Moments

*I am convinced that the greatest legacy
we can leave our children is happy memories.
~Og Mandino*

85

Thumbs-Up Smiley Face

How we remember, and what we remember,
and why we remember form the most personal map of our individuality.
~Christina Baldwin

Long before "single parent" became a coined term, I was one. In retrospect, I didn't fully realize the overall impact that my husband's sudden death would have on our life. His passing happened shortly after our daughter, Kathy, had celebrated her ninth birthday. As any grieving person would do, from time to time, I silently questioned God's wisdom in having called my husband to himself at such an early age. Because there were no answers to my questions, I blindly chose to dedicate myself to the joys of raising a daughter, and immersed myself in my job at the nearby high school.

Being a bright-eyed, active kid, Kathy instinctively helped in many ways to "perk me up," doing her part to keep our home life from being too sad. She was relentless in her ongoing efforts to make me smile, no matter where we were or who was with us. She innocently discovered a surefire method of achieving her goal: when she detected that I was "down," she would simply take a pen, and on the rounded part of her thumb, inscribe a smiley face. Then she would proudly stick her thumbs-up smiley face directly in front of my eyes and as close to my nose as possible.

She was persistent in her efforts, amazing me by always having a pen available, and using her private signal to me everywhere and in any situation. I was the recipient of her thumbs-up smiley face while driving in the car, shopping at the grocery store, attending church services, trying to bravely celebrate holidays, visiting relatives, and on and on.

Her special signal always brought an immediate smile to my face, so much so that I began doing it for her as well. Of course, the first time I tried it on her, it evoked a loud, long laugh and a "You finally caught on, Mom!" look on her face.

I can't remember exactly how long this thumbs-up-smiley-face ritual continued. From time to time throughout the years, it still comes in handy, whenever Kathy or I seem to need it.

During her high school years and the ups and downs of getting to know the difference between boyfriends and just plain boys, the thumbs-up smiley face was used by both of us—when a boyfriend had told her he found a new girlfriend, I used it; and when certain boyfriends brought her home too late at night, she used it.

After she graduated from college, having obtained a dental hygiene degree but subsequently failing the comprehensive exam on her first try, the thumbs-up smiley face did its job.

When she asked that I escort her down the aisle on her wedding day, we both cried as she told me I had been both her father and mother for so long that no one else could do the job. And again, the thumbs-up smiley face worked its magic.

Now that she is married with children of her own, and valiantly facing the joys and dilemmas of parenthood, we continue to find occasions when the thumbs-up smiley face still strengthens the special bond between us.

~Patricia Buck
Chicken Soup for the Single Parent's Soul

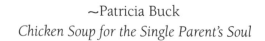

86

Light

It was only two weeks before Christmas, but fear, not cold, made my hands shake as I stood in the darkness of the hotel parking lot, trying to unlock my rental car. The Texas predawn air was balmy, and if I'd bothered to ask them, my relatives and friends would have assured me that I was about to set out on an errand as balmy as the weather. I was heading out to navigate my way alone, through a city of unfamiliar streets, to drive a nine-months-pregnant woman I'd met only the previous night to the hospital to deliver... my child.

A widow for one year, a mother of four—three sons under twelve and a stepdaughter just starting college—a freelance writer with a hole in her kitchen floor the size of Lake Michigan, and a hole in her heart the size of an ocean, I had decided that what I needed to do was not to fix my linoleum or get a steady job—but to become a single mother to a baby daughter. This choice I'd made against all reason. It was a choice so controversial even among people who truly loved me that it had prompted more than one serious breach of friendship. After all, I was hardly fossilized, just enough past the age of forty to feel it in my knees. I could and would love and raise another child, a daughter.

But alone?

With my husband, who'd died of colon cancer at forty-four the previous year, I had joshed longingly about another child, but I struggled with infertility. Adoption, our only possible route to parenthood, was both risky and expensive. My dreams of another child should have faded in the cold light of reality. But though many of the illusions of youth had indeed died with Dan, the idea that one day I'd sit myself down and write a big, fat bestselling novel and my fantasy of a baby daughter had not. I was determined. Since I knew for certain that over-forty moms (particularly those with big fannies and big families) were not exactly the dream dates of the millennium, I was reasonably sure I wouldn't marry again.

I wondered why it was so dark. I searched the frontage roads for a bank clock, and to my horror, realized it was only two o'clock in the morning, instead of six. In my confusion, I'd set the alarm wrong! So I spent the next few hours in an all-night diner, slugging down cups of coffee, regarding my reflection in the window and wondering who I was.

How had all this happened?

I'd found out about the adoption agency from a friend. We'd met at a holiday craft fair, and delighted as I was to see my pal, it was the occupant of her shoulder backpack I couldn't take my eyes off. He had a thick shock of dark hair and fine chiseled features of a baby Byron. His name was Jack, and my pal and her hubby had adopted him through an agency in San Antonio. I thought the agency would laugh so hard when I called that they'd never get to the point of sending me the application.

But the agency director had no problem with single parents, even widows with big holes in their floors. A few months later, I was filling out voluminous applications. And a few months after that, in the middle of Thanksgiving dinner, I got a phone call. There was a nineteen-year-old birth mother who, against all reason, seemed to think I had the right stuff. Until just a week before, she'd been "matched" with the perfect couple, but they'd left her in the lurch when an ultrasound exam proved that the baby she was carrying was not the boy they dreamed of, but a girl.

That had been my only qualification. I wanted a girl. I figured luck would favor a little girl with three older brothers to protect her. The birth mother, whose name was Luz, thought the same thing.

I pulled the car up close to the stairs of the second-floor apartment where Luz, pretty and shy and grindingly poor, but already a good and proud mother to two unplanned babies, was watching for me through a crack in the window blinds. Luz had chosen me over dozens of other two-parent families. She'd even asked me to coach her labor. She believed in me.

Luz waved to me. She'd be down in a moment. The nanny the agency had sent to mind Luz's children had just arrived. I had five more minutes alone with my doubts.

This was the first really huge decision I'd ever made entirely on my own in my adult life. It made refinancing my house look like a game of beach volleyball and starting my own business seem like getting a perm.

Now, as I watched Luz open her apartment door and negotiate the slick pavement like a tightrope walker carrying a bowling ball, I let my smile show more confidence than I felt. For the moment, the lifetime commitment wasn't all I was worried about. There was the immediate future to contend with. For though I'd given birth myself, I'd never seen a baby born.

In the hospital, as Luz was hooked up to lines and monitors that would attend the induction of labor, I noticed shafts of watery winter light sliding through the blinds. It had been a cloudy morning, but the sun would shine today, after all. I took it as a sign. I was ready to accept any tiding of comfort and joy.

The medicine began to drip into the tubes, and quickly, contractions commenced. Luz breathed and blew; I counted. The hours crawled past. I looked up at the clock. I called my son and my friend at the hotel, and the director at the adoption agency. No, no one new was in the world yet. The contractions became more commanding, their clench gathering speed like a runaway sled. I phoned my older sons and daughter, and a sweetly intuitive nurse placed the receiver against the fetal heart monitor so that my nine-year-old son, Dan, a thousand miles due north in Wisconsin, could hear his baby sister's beating heart. The light was changing. The sun was bright at the west window; it was late afternoon and time for Luz, soothed by pain medication, to rest before pushing. I sat beside her as she moaned and slept, my cheek resting on her extended hand.

We were two single mothers—one probably too old for this and one certainly too young. It was December 8th, in Catholic tradition the Feast of the Immaculate Conception, and outside in the hall an Army choir was singing ancient songs about another single mother and the baby in the barn.

Soon it was time for Luz to push, and she gathered herself, silent and stoic, her clenched face like the image on an Aztec coin. Twice, she told me, "I can't go on." Twice, I told her she had no choice—neither of us did. I put my arms around her and we held on to one another, and in the light of that one bedside lamp, its cone the shape of a golden trumpet, in the whole universe, there were only the two of us.

And then, suddenly, slippery, just one minute after the doctor came rushing into the room, there were three—the third a baby woman who would grow up to understand all this and someday to endure it.

Together, Luz and I marveled over her tiny, flossy dark head. Our daughter for this moment. My daughter ever after. "Let Mom hold the baby," the doctor said gently. And Luz slowly raised one hand and pointed to me.

So I stood up alone and held her for the first time. And there she was, fairest of the fair she was, seven pounds and fifteen ounces of earth angel and nobody's baby but mine. I named her Francie Nolen, for a little girl in an old book, *A Tree Grows in Brooklyn*, a little girl who came up strong and sure in circumstances that might have daunted a lesser spirit.

Francie might not have the inestimable benefit of a father. Her mother would have a crinkly smile and creaky knees, not bounce and sparkle. But there was some wisdom and not a little patience behind that crinkly smile. Francie would have siblings to champion her, as well as the support and comfort of all those doubters back home who'd be converted as soon as they laid eyes on her. Let them say I already had my hands full—weren't these big hands? I would not let any of my children down, nor let them feel that raising them had strained me past my limits.

As I looked down at Francie, I could feel those limits stretch and grow. I made a promise to her and the gallant girl who had given her life and given her up. My little girl would have laughs. She would have stories, good pasta twice a week, a house full of comforting noise. And most importantly, she would never, ever go to sleep except in the knowledge that she was loved beyond... beyond reason.

That December night was five years ago. And indeed, Francie has grown up unique in many ways, but most especially in her boldness. She has the stride of a tiny prizefighter and the will of a lion cub.

Six months after her birth, my first novel, *The Deep End of the Ocean*, was published, and suddenly, we got not only a new floor where there had once been a hole, but a new chance at life. And as for the hole in our hearts, Francie's personality helped shrink it to bearable proportions, and one day, along came a brave young man who wanted not only me, squeaky knees and all, but all my brood, for his very own.

My husband and I were married just weeks after my second novel was published. It was called *The Most Wanted*, and it was in part about a young teenager who gave birth to a baby girl in terrible circumstances, but who, because of the intervention of an older woman who longed for a child, got a second chance. It was my attempt, in fiction, to correct what I could not correct in life for the birth mother of my little girl. I dedicated that book to my daughters, and also to Luz, whose name, in Spanish, means "light."

~Jacquelyn Mitchard
Chicken Soup for the Mother & Daughter Soul

Looking for Love(s)

"I t's all your fault," I screamed, throwing my hairbrush down on the chipped walnut laminate. Here I was—at what I'd been told was a "magic moment" in my life—about to go out on my first date. I was fifteen years old; the year was 1962. And my mother—my mother—was getting ready to go out on her "first date," too.

"You'll really like my friend Walter," my mother said in a soothing tone. Then, with more emphasis, "The fact that I'm divorced is not why this boy waited until now to ask you out. And it's certainly not Walter's fault that all your friends have been dating since the fall." Her tone softened again: "It's been longer than that for me, hon. I just want to have a good time again."

But I knew she was wrong. I knew everyone else in my class looked at me with a combination of pity and disgust. Besides, Mom didn't deserve to have a "good time." I was the one who was supposed to be having the time of my life.

I found myself nervously twisting a lock of my hair, and with trembling fingers, I quickly patted it back in place. I wondered how anyone could see the situation except as it was: My mother was so inadequate that my father had been forced to look elsewhere. And now she was desperately trying to find a "replacement." How utterly humiliating.

"When is your date picking you up?" asked my mother, in an attempt to get things smoothed over.

"Hopefully, before that man comes for you," I said, tossing back my head and refusing to look at her. I didn't want Dave to witness how low my mother had sunk, how shamelessly she could flaunt her singleness—her differentness from all my friends' parents. It was most definitely her fault that no self-respecting boy would want to be seen with me.

Standing behind me at the full-length mirror and leaning to one side to peer past me at her own reflection, Mom asked, "Well, how do I look?"

"Old... fat... disgusting!!" I screeched, tears springing to my eyes. I rushed from the room and clambered up the stairs to the attic. I had to get away from her for a while. Then, just maybe, I wouldn't hate her quite so much. I fled to the refuge that had always helped me sort things out before: the trunk.

For years I'd come up to the attic to lose myself by going through the old clothes I found in the trunk. Often I tried them on. Mom had shown me the jacket she loved when she was not much older than I was. Looking at the jacket, I wondered why she had loved it so. I imagined her at age seventeen, huddled on the high-school bleachers nervously rubbing the edges of her bunny-fur bolero. I modeled a couple of old hats, but couldn't really get into the spirit. While digging out a pair of rusty old figure skates, I found that the bottom of the trunk could fold up. Under it, I discovered a little compartment, and hidden inside it were some old crusty newspaper clippings and some letters.

"Dearest Marge," the first one began. "I can't believe how I miss you. I'm here in France, and, I'd never tell anyone but you, my squad actually got lost in the forest. It was so awful. God! I wish I was back there in Oblong with you, after the Friday night game. I love you so very much, and I just don't know if I can wait till we actually tie the knot. XOXO, Charlie." Attached was a clipping showing a picture of Mom, looking so young and slim—kind of like the old movie star Greta Garbo—and a man identified as Charles Somner. It was an announcement of their upcoming wedding!

But, that wasn't right. Charlie wasn't my father. My dad was Dad. My mother's husband was never a boyfriend who got killed in the war... was he? Mom had never whispered a word of this previous relationship to me. What if she had married Charlie? Would I be here? Would I be me? I wrapped myself in the bunny-fur bolero and began to cry again, just a little. Why did it all have to be so horribly difficult?

I sniffed, but widened my eyes, worried about making them red before my date, and started absently rubbing the bunny fur. Now that my mom and dad were divorced, I only had more questions, more problems. What if Mom fell in love and married some third guy? Would I ever think of him as Dad? He couldn't be! Apparently she'd loved Charlie, the guy in the uniform, and I think she had loved my dad, too — once. But neither love had lasted. Could she, could any woman, ever truly love so many different men? What is it about love that makes you keep looking for it, over and over again?

My thoughts were interrupted when the doorbell rang.

My mother went downstairs to answer it. I tore off the bolero, ran down from the attic and peered — secretively and ashamedly — from around the corner upstairs. "Oh, my God!" I whispered to myself. They were there. Both of them were there. Our "first dates" had arrived at the same time! What a horrible, mortifying coincidence!

As I hurriedly wiped my eyes and pinched my cheeks, I heard Dave say, "Mrs. Kersch, I just couldn't believe it. We were almost out of the house when I figured out that my dad had a date with my date's mother tonight! Incredible, huh?!"

Walter was Dave's dad! My mother was going out with my date's father, and it was okay with Dave? He actually rode over here with his dad? His probably divorced dad!

I took a breath so deep it hurt, then descended the stairs, shyly peered up at my first date and said, "Dave, I'd like you to meet my mom." Then I paused, slipped my arm around her waist and added, "She looks kinda like Greta Garbo, don't you think?"

I grew up quite a bit that night. And although my first date would not be my last, my first relationship — the imperfect bond I'd formed with my mother — would last forever.

~Kathleen Kersch Simandl
Chicken Soup for the Single Parent's Soul

88

Teddy Bear Tonic

It was my fortieth birthday, an event some women dread, but others celebrate. For me, it was time for my first mammogram. I always made sure I followed the guidelines for preventative health care. This year, the kind woman at my gynecologist's office told me that it was time to add mammograms to the annual checkup.

As luck would have it, the first available appointment was on my birthday. I hesitated. After all, who wants to spend her birthday at the doctor's office? Then I recalled some advice that I'd once heard: your birthday is a perfect reminder for annual physicals.

While I was feeling somewhat intimidated by my first mammogram, the staff made every effort to put me at ease. Just when I thought I was done, however, the nurse came in and told me they needed to repeat the films. There was a thickening, she said. Nothing to worry about though, large-breasted women sometimes needed to be repositioned.

I waited again. The nurse came back and told me that the doctor would be right in. I thought, That's nice — the doctor takes the time to see everyone who comes in for a mammogram. It gave me a feeling of confidence.

But my confidence vanished when the doctor informed me there was a suspicious area that required further study. "Not to worry," she said. "Everything's fine."

So down the hall I marched for an ultrasound. The room was dark. The doctor was serious. Trying some humor, I said, "The last time I had an ultrasound, there was a baby."

But there was no baby this time, and soon I was asking the dreaded question. "Is it cancer?"

The doctor was noncommittal, "This concerns me," was all she said. She suggested a biopsy. Right then and there.

I was not ready for that. My simple mammogram had turned into a six-hour marathon session. I had been shuffled back and forth for one test after another, now culminating in the biopsy.

I drove home on automatic pilot. Luckily, the doctor's office was a mere five minutes from my house. I drove through traffic wearing my sunglasses, which hid the tears pouring from my eyes. I stifled the screams I felt rising in my gut, as I thought, I am forty years old, too young. It's my birthday. Why is this happening to me?

Unfortunately, my three kids were already home from school when I arrived. I didn't know how I was going to deal with this cancer scare, but one thing I did know was that I could not deal with the kids at that moment.

I had to pass through the family room to go upstairs to the sanctuary of my bedroom. Hoping the kids were completely enthralled by the television, I went through the room quickly, then ran upstairs and threw myself on the bed, unleashing all my pent-up rage and fear.

A knock on the door heralded the arrival of my oldest daughter, fourteen-year-old Robyn. I couldn't let her in because my distress was too obvious. "I'll be right down," I shouted through the door.

Robyn went away, and I breathed a sigh of thanks.

It seemed just a few minutes later when the door opened. My husband, Paul, walked in, and looked on helplessly as I dissolved into a puddle. He gathered me in his arms to offer what comfort he could.

"Robyn called me. She thinks you have breast cancer," he said simply.

How could she possibly have known? It turned out that resourceful little Robyn had not been convinced by my assurances that I was okay. She had known something was wrong when I walked through the house with my sunglasses on. Evidently the sound of my wracking sobs had scared her. (I thought I'd muffled them so that no one would hear.) Young Detective Robyn then consulted my Day-Timer and noted that I had been to the doctor's office. Not recognizing the name of my usual physician, she looked the name up in the phone book. The large advertisement for the breast center told her all she needed to know. Fearing the worst, she called her dad at work.

I told Paul the whole story of my six-hour ordeal, and he suggested we better face the troops. Letting their suspicions grow would be worse than the truth.

We both went downstairs, and Paul lined the kids up on the couch. It was our first family summit. I cleared my throat. I can do this, I told myself.

Then I looked at the fear plastered all over the young faces of my three children: Robyn, on the brink of womanhood; John, a brave soldier, not quite twelve; and Lisa, still my baby at ten.

I couldn't do it. Paul took over. Sitting next to me, clutching my hand, he explained very succinctly that I was having a problem. Yes, breast cancer was suspected, but we wouldn't know until the results of the tests came back.

Robyn, so resourceful and perceptive in spotting the problem, didn't say a word. She has always been hard to read. John was full of questions; he needed the details. Lisa cried, clinging to me.

Somehow we got through a hastily prepared dinner. It was all I could do to retain my composure. Afterwards, I made an abrupt retreat to my room.

After a while, there was a timid knock on the door. Robyn, my quiet one, entered, clutching the teddy bear she'd had since childhood. She sat down next to me on the bed and handed me the teddy bear. "He's always made me feel better," she said.

Such simple words, such heartfelt sentiments. My daughter was trying to comfort me in the only way she knew. I opened my arms to receive the token of my daughter's love. And yes, that teddy bear did make me feel better at the end of that long and difficult day.

During subsequent days, I traveled a tortuous road. The diagnosis was indeed cancer, but I made it through surgery, chemotherapy and radiation.

Although Robyn is now too old to give me teddy bears, Lisa, our youngest, still bestows familiar bear-shaped tokens of love on me, with pink ribbons attached.

I call it Teddy Bear Power. It really does make everything all better.

~Bonnie Walsh Davidson
Chicken Soup for Every Mom's Soul

89

She Did It Her Way

Mother's love grows by giving.
~Charles Lamb

"**M**om, we're getting married... sometime in June." This from my hippie daughter calling on a pay phone in Maine. (No phone or electricity at her house — or perhaps cabin is a better word.)

"We don't want a fancy wedding or dressy clothes or a lot of guests. We just want to be married in your backyard. I'll let you know the date."

Long ago, her father and I made up our minds to listen to her and do things the way she wanted as much as we could. And of course, I was thrilled she was getting married. I was always secretly worried that marriage was too "old-fashioned" for her. She was a child of the '60s, eager to right the wrongs of the world, to live life on the edge and to never be part of the "establishment."

Well, backyard weddings can be lovely, I thought. It's not our beautiful church with a majestic organ, flowing white dress or bridesmaids. But, still... I took an upbeat approach, which was really the only sensible thing to do under the circumstances.

Later with dates arranged, a guest list of sorts (our family and best friends and "a bunch of friends... we'll let you know how many") and the food decided on ("only veggie stuff and some champagne"), she agreed I could ask the minister of our church to perform the ceremony "for legal purposes."

All negotiations were going well until I mentioned the wedding gown.

"No special dress, Mom. Sorry. Your first daughter, your good daughter (said with a wry smile, a favorite family joke) did the white dress and veil thing. Not me. I have lots of clothes that would do for a wedding."

I thought of all her dresses (short, wild, braless) and realized that she mostly wore jeans or cut-offs. Nothing I had seen her wear in years even whispered "wedding" to me.

So in the following days, ignoring my own good advice to let her do it her way, I wandered around different stores and looked at dresses that might do for my bride-to-be daughter. Then I saw it: simple, unbleached muslin with a shirred waist, scooped neckline with just a bit of Irish lace and little capped sleeves. It was long, but not floor-length. It was graceful, but not formal. It was lovely and simple, and it was my daughter.

Envisioning her wearing it, I bought the dress and took it home.

Later that day, I placed the box on her bed with a little note stating: "I just happened upon this while shopping (okay, a small white lie). This looks like you. Would you try it on for me?"

When she came in that evening, she went to her room and all was quiet. A bit worried I had hurt her feelings with my purchase, I went upstairs to her room where she sat on the bed holding the dress on her lap while tears rained down her cheeks—and she was smiling.

"I never knew you thought of me like this, Mom. The dress is so lovely and soft and simple. I love it. And I'll love wearing it for the wedding. Thanks for knowing me so well."

Two weeks later, on a sun-filled afternoon, friends gathered in our backyard. Our daughter walked down the steps—to the strum of a guitar—smiling proudly in her surprise dress. She looked wonderful, as I knew she would.

It was a perfect wedding... almost.

Had I known her fiancé would be wearing yellow paisley bell-bottoms, I might have shopped for him as well!

~Julie Firman
Chicken Soup for the Bride's Soul

The Queen of Coleslaw

Do not anticipate trouble or worry about what may never happen.
~Benjamin Franklin

To my mother, the four basic food groups are meat, dairy, grain and coleslaw. She thinks if it's not used in coleslaw, it's not a vegetable, it's a nuisance, and not worth growing in the first place. In our house, the slaw goes on the table in a bowl that — well, let's just say if we made a batch of punch we'd have nothing to put it in. Poking out of the top is a huge stainless steel cafeteria-style spoon, dubbed the "institution spoon" by my brother, who often acted as if he belonged in one.

I love my mother's coleslaw, but I remember a time when it provoked absolute panic in me.

Early on in first grade, I raced home from school at lunchtime with a collection of papers handed to me by the teacher. As I burst through the front door I immediately ran to the kitchen where my mother stood at the stove stirring a pot of chicken noodle soup. Pulling on her apron with one hand and holding a fist full of papers in the other, I pleaded with her, "Read them to me, Mom — please!"

Mom took the papers as we sat at the kitchen table. Slowly she started reading aloud. I listened intently to every word, paying no attention to the bowl of soup in front of me. I squealed with delight as she read to me what seemed an almost endless list of exciting adventures awaiting me in the coming year.

And then it happened.

"It's customary for mothers to bring a homemade treat for the class to share on each child's birthday," she read. "It needn't be anything fancy, just something you enjoy making."

The words floated through the air in agonizing slow motion, hovering over my head in the mist of the steamy chicken soup.

"Just something you enjoy making... enjoy making... enjoy making." The phrase echoed loudly inside of me, conjuring up the same stomach churning feeling that accompanies the ominous phrase: "You have a cavity... a cavity... a cavity."

My mother's standard response to anyone who paid her coleslaw a compliment was this: "It's nothing fancy, it's just something I enjoy making." Oh, how those words wreaked havoc with me.

Until my birthday in April, I lived in dread that mother would show up at school pushing a wheelbarrow full of her famous coleslaw for everyone to share. I pictured that old stainless steel spoon protruding from a mountain of cabbage while she navigated the wheelbarrow up and down the aisles. As she maneuvered, a stack of "Happy Birthday" Dixie cups would be dangling from her wrist in a drawstring plastic bag.

When I left for school on the morning of my birthday, there were two large heads of cabbage in the refrigerator and a curious grin on my mother's face. Full-blown panic swept me into its sturdy grip.

Much to my relief, Mom showed up promptly at 1:30 in the afternoon with a tray full of yummy chocolate cupcakes. Each one had two M&Ms for eyes and a string of four or five more in a semicircle to make a smile. All except mine. On mine, one of the "eye" M&Ms was cut in half so that my cupcake was winking at me. To this day Mom says it was just a coincidence but I am not convinced.

I owe my mother a thank you for the cupcakes and the coleslaw. But mostly I owe her a thank you for the memory of her standing at the kitchen table with her apron tied in a big old bow in the back. Mom always shredded the cabbage in time to the tune playing on the radio. I wonder if she knows I noticed that. I did, you know.

My mother not only makes the best coleslaw, she makes the best memories, too.

~ Annmarie Tait
Chicken Soup for the Mother & Daughter Soul

The Impossible Dream

Accept challenges, so that you may feel the exhilaration of victory.
~George S. Patton

In 1968, my daughter, Carrie, was in fifth grade, and her teacher was Mr. Kennedy, the most avid Cleveland Indian fan in Tucson, the winter home of the team. Every year Mr. Kennedy took a class field trip to see the Indians play, and this year's game was sure to be special. Willie Mays and the San Francisco Giants were coming to town.

Carrie was absolutely sure, as only a ten-year-old can be, that she would catch a fly ball—maybe even a home run—and get all the Cleveland players to sign it. "And I'm gonna get Willie's autograph, too," she announced.

How does a parent prepare a child for inevitable failure and disappointment without destroying the faith that spawned the dream? We tried. "That'd be wonderful, Honey, but well, there'll be hundreds of kids, maybe even thousands, at Hi Corbett Field."

"That's okay," she answered, totally undeterred.

But her dad and I knew that every kid there would be scrambling for autographs. Willie Mays would be swamped—maybe even surrounded by a police escort. We assured her that we'd be proud of her if she brought home a signature or two on her game program.

"Nope!" she told us. "Mr. Kennedy says the only sure way to get autographs is to catch a ball. The players will autograph that, but they mostly ignore the programs. So I'm going to catch a ball."

We suggested that fly balls were traveling so fast that even grown-ups had trouble landing one. We told her there wouldn't be many pop-ups and maybe no home runs, and such big stands spread out all over. She didn't hesitate. "One of those flies will find me," she said confidently. "Where's Dad's old mitt? I want to practice."

So, in the three days we had before the big game, her dad and I took turns hitting easy pop-ups and shaking our heads. It was hopeless. Carrie had never been interested in baseball and had only played softball in the once-a-week P.E. classes at her elementary school. Every time a ball headed toward her, she held out the mitt and closed her eyes.

At least we could help her with that. I yelled at her to keep her eyes open. Her dad kept telling her, "Watch the ball. Eyes on the ball!"

On the day of the game, she stood poised at the door—a bright-eyed little girl with a Cleveland Indians cap on her curls and her dad's old mitt in her hands. I wanted to hold her, to warn her about the real world, to tell her there would be no pop ball, no autographs—certainly not Willie Mays'! Instead, I said, "Give it your best shot, Honey!"

Her dad added, "Go, girl!"

All day I stewed and fretted, until around lunchtime when I decided worrying was useless. I couldn't fly over the field and drop a baseball into my daughter's hands. I could do nothing except.... "Please, dear God," I prayed, "give me the words to comfort her, to help her understand that wanting and getting don't always go together, that there are many things in life that we can't control."

When she got off the school bus that afternoon, I could see she had had a wonderful time. She was a blur of leaping, bouncing motion. Obviously, the other kids were excited, too. They yelled and cheered and waved at Carrie, and she waved back before jumping into the car.

"I caught one, Mom!" she announced breathlessly. "Willie popped one up, and it came right at me, and I held up my mitt and kept my eyes open, and it just plopped right in!"

In her outstretched hands lay a baseball—a baseball covered

with scrawled signatures. I took it tenderly and turned it slowly. Most of the autographs were unrecognizable, but there was one in large, bold letters that stood out from the rest—Willie Mays!

"How...?" I began.

"It was the ball, Mom, like Mr. Kennedy said. All the kids were pushing and shoving, holding out their programs, but Willie stopped signing those. Then he looked up and saw me hanging over the fence, holding out the ball I caught. He walked right over and grinned at me. Mom, Willie Mays grinned at me and took my baseball and signed it right across the middle."

Carrie still has that ball and the game program, keepsakes of a truly special time in her life. For me, there was an intangible lesson in my daughter's unlikely catch—You gotta believe.

~Peggy Spence
Chicken Soup for the Baseball Fan's Soul

92

A Family Christmas Carol

While we try to teach our children all about life,
Our children teach us what life is all about.
~Angela Schwindt

It had been snowing since two o'clock that afternoon, and the transmission on my car had been locked into "sled" since I had pulled out of the office parking lot. Time was slipping away, and as I watched the giant flakes tumble out of the sky onto my windshield, I really began to wonder if I was going to make it on time. Of course I would make it. There was no option.

For weeks now, all my daughter, Alexandra, had talked about was the Christmas concert and the usual third grade scuttlebutt that surrounded it. "Mom, Rachel was supposed to do a solo, but guess what? She's not! Lindsay gets to do it instead." "Mom, I get to stand next to Tyler for the whole concert!" "Mom, you won't believe it, but Lexie's whole family is coming to the concert, even from another state!" This last comment was the one she dwelled on most — making a pilgrimage all the way from out of state to see third graders sing Christmas carols was a pretty big deal. (It had to have been, to eclipse the excitement of standing next to Tyler.)

As I sat in traffic I thought about all the school events I had attended — alone. Alexandra never mentioned it, but I wondered how she felt about me being the only one who ever came to her events. My own family lived out of town, and her father and his family never quite managed to fit those things into their schedules. I wondered if it bothered her.

The concert was scheduled to begin at seven o'clock sharp. With only a minute to spare, I found myself running: first, through the snow-drifted parking lot, then through the school corridor, with my wet scarf flapping behind me. I entered the crowded auditorium and spied a lone seat near the front. From her place onstage, Alexandra saw me dash for the chair, and she smiled. I was close enough to hear the loud, prepageant chatter of the children onstage.

"Look, Alexandra, there is my aunt and my cousin. They came all the way from West Virginia. I can't believe my whole family is here!"

Alex smiled at Lexie and said, "My whole family is here, too! Look, there she is!" Alex gave me a big smile and an enthusiastic wave. I waved back at her, never once noticing the melting snow dripping off my head.

~Michelle Anzelone
Chicken Soup for the Single Parent's Soul

93

Honey's Greatest Gift

L ike most families with a dog, we loved our yellow Lab and treasured the gifts she brought into our lives. From the time she joined our family at the age of seven weeks, Honey enlivened our household with her boundless enthusiasm, happiness and love. Her powerful "helicopter" tail wagged in a circle; she loved to play hide-and-seek with us and readily allowed visiting children to crawl all over her—and to play with her tennis balls and squeaky toys.

When our oldest son, Josh, began kindergarten, our youngest son, Daniel, found an eager playmate in Honey. When Daniel began school, she became my companion, often sitting next to me, head resting on my lap as I did paperwork for our fledgling business. But it was her companionship with my mother that led to what was, perhaps, her greatest gift.

Growing up in Germany, Mom's life had been difficult. A stern older couple adopted her when she was about three years old. At sixteen, the town she lived in, Wuerzburg, was leveled during a World War II air strike. She fled from town to town on her own, trying to survive and suffering repeated rejections by people who could have helped her, but instead looked after their own interests. Then she married my father, an American soldier. Their marriage was not a happy one, and Mom struggled in her role as a mother of four. Between my mother's unhappiness and my father's quiet and distant nature, there wasn't a lot of emotional nurturing in our family.

When Mom—a widow—moved to our city as a senior citizen, I was concerned. Would we relate? Could I deal with the emotional distance between us? To top it off, once again Mom felt lonely and displaced. In an effort to ease her loneliness, Mom often drove the mile to our house to walk Honey. They were perfect for each other. Mom walked slowly, and by this time, so did Honey, also a senior citizen. Together they explored the trails that interlace our neighborhood. The gentle yellow dog brought out a softness in Mom. My mother babied Honey, sometimes sneaking her forbidden foods despite my protests. Although I considered Honey a family member, to me she was still a dog, but to Mom she was nearly human; as a result, we occasionally clashed over our differing "dog-parenting" styles.

It was about a year after Mom's arrival that my husband, Steve, and I knew Honey's end was near. Honey, now fourteen, could no longer curl up to sleep. Her joints were stiff, and though we gave her daily anti-inflammatory drugs, we suspected she continued to suffer. But we didn't have the heart to put her to sleep. In spite of her physical ailments, Honey still fetched the paper daily and turned into a puppy at the prospect of a walk. Her enthusiasm for life masked what should have been obvious.

Then one sunny Tuesday in March, I finally understood that our stoic pet had had enough. She was clearly suffering, and I knew it was time. Before I could change my mind about doing what we had put off for too long, I called the vet. They made arrangements for Honey's favorite veterinarian, Dr. Jane, to come in on her day off. Steve met me at the vet's office and together we comforted Honey as she slipped away from this world.

Her loss affected me far more than I could have imagined. I moped around the house, restless and overcome by sudden bursts of tears. My grieving was heightened by the fact that just a few months before we had also become empty nesters. Without Honey to fill her customary space in our kitchen, our house now seemed bigger and emptier than before.

I resisted telling Mom that we had put her walking buddy to sleep. How could I cope with her emotional reaction, which I anticipated would be greater than my own? So, I hatched a plan: Steve had to work late on Thursday night. Mom and I could have dinner together; after dinner I would reveal my secret.

"Okay," Mom said when I telephoned. "I'll come over."

"No, no," I countered, realizing she would wonder where Honey was as soon as she walked through the door. "Why don't you cook for us? I'd like to eat at your house."

Mom agreed. I don't remember the conversation we had or what we ate because the whole time I was distracted by the secret I was keeping. Finally, it was time to leave, and I still couldn't tell Mom about Honey. Mom made herself cozy on her sofa. I said goodbye, pulled on my coat and was at the door when I forced myself to turn around.

Sitting stiffly near Mom with my coat on, I blurted: "Mom, we put Honey to sleep on Tuesday."

"Oh, no!" Mom cried out. "I didn't get to say goodbye."

To my surprise, I was the one who started to cry. Through my tears I explained why we had put Honey to sleep. With more honesty and vulnerability than I had ever shown to my mother, I blubbered, "I miss her so much."

"But you carried on with her so," she said, referring to our differences concerning Honey's "parenting."

"I know, but I loved her. We did so much together."

Mom scooted closer to me on the couch. "I'm so sorry," she said, wrapping her arms around me. Then she cradled me while I rested my head on her chest and sobbed.

For the first time in forty-six years, I experienced the calm reassurance of a mother's love. Soaking up my mother's tenderness, I marveled that it had its root in her relationship with Honey. And, although crying in my mother's arms didn't take away my pain, I was deeply comforted. I lost a loving companion that week, but I also gained something rich and beautiful. My mom and I finally made an emotional connection, which has continued to expand—thanks to Honey and her last and greatest gift.

~B. J. Reinhard
Chicken Soup for the Dog Lover's Soul

94

The Green Pajamas

I can no other answer make, but, thanks, and thanks.
~William Shakespeare

I often watched from inside the house as my mother lugged a bucket of coal up the back steps. There were seventeen steps, and she usually brought up three loads of coal. She'd smile at me when she passed the window. Many times I'd shout through the glass, "Let me help!"

Her answer remained the same. "No. You stay inside where it's warm, Mannie. This only takes a minute. Besides, there's only one bucket." I must have been about nine years old.

You shouldn't have to do this, Mama. You've already worked all day in an office. I know you are tired.

Sometimes I wouldn't watch out the window. I'd busy myself in some other part of the house until I knew the coal for the next day had been brought up. Often I'd think about my friends who had fathers who could bring coal in. My own father had died before I was two.

Yet, even though my mother had to go to work each day and I missed not having a father, our life together in our small house included a lot of happiness.

As I grew older, I'd bring up the coal some days before my mother got home from work. It was terribly heavy, and I could never seem to get an adequate supply. I longed to find some way to make things better for her.

Unexpectedly, when I was about thirteen, I got a temporary job wrapping Christmas gifts at a local department store on the weekends. Although I was young and inexperienced, I worked quickly and earned twenty-three cents an hour. I was to get paid just before Christmas.

I wanted to get my mother something special that year—something to make life easier for her. After work one evening, I went window-shopping. I saw what my mother must have. A dark-haired mannequin modeled it. She had a radiant smile, and there were no tired lines on her face. She appeared pampered and relaxed in the moss-green satin lounging pajamas and short matching robe. She was about the size of my mother, I thought. I strained to see the price tag, turning my head almost upside down.

Twenty-five dollars and ninety-five cents. It was a fortune in 1950!

I had no idea if I would earn that much money. And even if I did, someone else might buy the beautiful set before I did. "Dear God," I prayed, looking intently at the pajamas, "hold them for me. Don't let anyone buy them, and let me make $25.95 at least."

Many evenings after work I stood in front of the shop window looking at the pajamas, smiling with deep satisfaction, relieved that they were still there.

Two nights before Christmas, I got paid. I poured the money out of my pay envelope and counted it. Twenty-seven dollars and thirteen cents! I had more than enough. I ran to the store with the money in my pocket. I entered out of breath and said to the saleslady, "I want to buy the beautiful pajamas set in the window. It's $25.95."

The saleswoman knew my mother and me. She smiled warmly, but suggested, "Marion, don't you think your mother would rather have something more... practical?"

I shook my head. I didn't even understand her subtle and kindly meant suggestion. Nothing on earth could have changed my mind. Those pajamas were for my mother. God had kept everyone from buying them, and I had the money to pay for them. I watched almost breathlessly as the woman took the pajamas and robe out of the window. While she got a box, I reached out and touched the soft satin. It was an exquisite moment. She wrapped the gift in soft tissue paper first, then in Christmas paper.

Finally, with the large package under my arm, I headed home. I put my mother's gift under the tree wondering how I'd wait until Christmas morning.

When it dawned, I couldn't open any of my gifts until my mother opened hers. I watched with a pounding heart.

She pulled back the tissue paper and her mouth formed a silent "O." She touched the pajamas with one finger—then held up the robe. She looked at me and said, "Oh, Mannie! It's the most beautiful thing I've ever seen. I don't know how you managed it, but I love it!"

I smiled and said, "Put it on, Mama."

She did and cooked breakfast in the outfit. All morning and afternoon she told me how much she loved the gift. I knew she would. She showed it to everyone who came by.

Through the years, even after they'd fallen apart, my mother would still tell people about those pajamas.

I reasoned that somehow my gift had made up for her having to bring in coal, build fires and walk to work. Each evening my mother would put on her satin pajamas and we'd sit by the fire listening to the radio, reading or talking.

As a child, I never realized that I should have gotten her a sweater or boots. No one could have talked me into it, for the green satin pajamas seemed to transport us into another world, just as I knew they would.

Many years later, after I had children of my own, my mother was visiting with us one Christmas. Despite the joy of the season, I was a bit weary. It seemed like I'd been tired for months—maybe years. I'd finally come to realize that motherhood is a full-time, often mundane job, every day. The demands of raising a family had begun to show on my face and in my attitude.

The children squealed and tore into their presents. We were knee-deep in paper, which, I thought with irritation, I'd later have to clean up. Just then my mother handed me a present. "Merry Christmas, Mannie," she said softly.

She hadn't opened her gifts. She watched me as I carefully opened the large golden package. I folded back pink tissue paper and caught my breath. Slowly I lifted out the most beautiful, elegant pink-and-gold silk lounging robe I'd ever seen. I ran my hand over the gold-embossed design. "Ohhh," was all I could manage for a few moments. Then I said, "I can't believe it's for me. It's not something a mother would wear." I looked down at my worn flannel robe through a blur of tears.

"Put it on," my mother urged.

As I threw off the old robe, it seemed that I shed discouragement and weariness, too. I stood up wrapped in the lovely silk robe, knowing fully how Cinderella must have felt.

"Hey," one of the children said, "look at Mama. She's pretty." Everyone looked at me. My husband smiled.

Standing there that Christmas morning in the elegant robe, I suddenly remembered back through the years and recalled those green satin pajamas. I looked at my mother. I believe she remembered them, too. She must have, to have known how desperately I needed that robe. There was no need to say anything. We both understood the gifts too well.

~Marion Bond West
Chicken Soup for the Mother's Soul 2

95

Secret Weapon

In 1965, when I was a little girl, my family moved to a picturesque neighborhood in Pennsylvania. We were stunned to find a petition had been circulating to bar us from settling there. The neighbors, upon learning that a family with seven kids was elbowing its way into their territory, feared the worst. Perhaps they had envisioned seven times the mischief—churned-up flowerbeds, battered mailboxes, their sleepy lives unraveled by gleeful shrieks of children peppering cars with rocks and tripping up the elderly.

The petition was denied.

And so we moved into the colonial-style house, my parents' first home after fifteen years of transitioning from one army housing complex to another. What a luxury it was, owning a brick structure with two stories that we did not have to share with other families. The backyard, stretching on for what seemed like miles, tugged at my exploring spirit.

As one month flowed into the next, the neighbors held their breath. Finally, there was a collective sigh of relief as they began to see that their world would remain intact after all.

Then they began to wonder why. Why was such a large family so quiet? Even during Dad's tour in Vietnam, there was not a single hiccup.

What the neighbors didn't bank on was Mom's secret weapon—a weapon that would have brought Genghis Khan to his knees. Flattened evil empires. Rewritten history.

Her secret weapon, for lack of a more technical term, was "the look."

I believe there was a patent pending on it at the time.

This is how it worked.

First, the eyebrows arched. Then the lips tightened into one thin, rigid line. The eyes, narrowed and unflinching, turned to glass.

Whenever I was caught in mid-mischief, there she was, armed with that baleful stare. I was a fish about to be slapped onto butcher paper if I dared twitch. None of my brothers and sisters had the nerve to challenge "the look," so I could only imagine the consequences of crossing that line. I was certain that it meant being hauled away to a dark, damp place for bad kids, where a cackling witch pinched their fingers to see if they were plump enough to be on the menu. You can be assured that I never once attempted to confirm this.

There were even times Mom had the eerie ability to foresee mischief barely hatching in my brain. One look in my direction whittled my plans, along with my constitution, to sawdust. Like the Nat King Cole song, my only alternative was to straighten up and fly right — for the time being.

As it always is with army life, after three years and one more sibling added to the family, we followed Dad to his new assignment, where we were once again placed in generic housing on post. To this day, my parents cherish the friendships they collected while living on that tree-lined street in Pennsylvania. I've never forgotten the sweet man next door who always seemed to have a pocketful of butterscotch candy for us when he mowed his lawn.

A few years ago, my three-year-old niece was acting bratty at the dinner table, which solicited a five-star glare from her grandmother. Our forks poised in midair, we waited awkwardly for the little girl's reaction. Then...

"Grandma!" she said, giggling. "You're funny!"

We gasped.

She had breached the rules and... and she was still living!

Even more shocking, though, was what I detected on my mother's face. A trace of defeat. Just enough to make me appreciate how precious that tool must have been to her all these years, the pride she must have felt to be able to discipline a caravan of kids in church, in the store, the park, libraries and museums—all with just one look. Especially in one particular neighborhood that dreaded our arrival.

It's been said that Mom was the only one in her family who successfully adopted her mother's glare to control the kids. It must be genetic. The other day my two-year-old was whizzing around at top speed on the Sit-N-Spin during naptime when I opened the door quietly and zeroed in on him with that look. He braked with his heels, hopped off and quickly crawled into bed.

Hmmm. Maybe it's not too late for that patent after all.

~Jennifer Oliver
Chicken Soup for the Grandma's Soul

Chapter 10

Like Mother, Like Mother, Like Daughter

Funny Mother-Daughter Moments

My mother had a great deal of trouble with me,
but I think she enjoyed it.
~Mark Twain

96

The Littlest Daughter

The toughest part of motherhood is the inner worrying and not showing it.
~Audrey Hepburn

They were a happy family: four Pogue daughters all in the same school in different grades. They were talented and friendly girls. The youngest, Janice, who was in my class, seemed to be glued to her mother's skirts. The three older girls took the bus to school every morning and gaily rushed to their classrooms, but Janice was always driven to school by her mother, arriving just in time for the kindergarten morning song. Her mother usually stayed around until Janice seemed to be content and was involved in some activity, and then she would tiptoe out. But she would return in time to take Janice home.

One Friday, Janice's mother called and asked for a conference with me. She entered in an agitated and fragile way. She almost seemed to wring her hands in distress. She said in a too-soft voice, "My husband is going to Europe on business for two weeks, and he insists that I go with him. I have tried to explain over and over that Janice needs me here. But he is equally adamant that she will be fine without me so I have no choice; I have to go. I have told the babysitter that she is to drive her every morning and watch her until she is settled into the classroom. She has explicit instructions about picking her up and getting to school early so Janice won't worry. Will you please give Janice special attention and help her during this time of our separation? We have never been apart a single day since she was born five years ago. She is so young and fragile, and I want to be sure everything goes well for her."

She stopped for a quick breath, but I stepped in and assured her that we would make every effort to support Janice and see that she was happy and healthy while her mother was away. I even volunteered to meet Janice at her car so she would see a familiar face. Janice's mother thanked me for our understanding and reassurance. As she left we talked about the logistics of watching for Janice and agreed that it would present some extra effort on my part but was worth the time it might take.

Monday morning, anticipating a tearful, anxious child, I planned a special program of fun and games. I waited outside to greet Janice, but just then the bus arrived and not three, but four Pogue girls got off of it. Janice skipped along joyfully, yelling "goodbye" to her sisters as she ran with two friends into the classroom. I walked slowly into the classroom and called Janice over to ask how the bus ride went. Impatiently she said, "Oh, I always wanted to take the bus with the other kids, but Mother needs to be with me. You see there won't be any more babies, and so I have to be a baby a little longer. While she is away, I'll just ride the bus every day. I am five, you know."

~Julie Firman
Chicken Soup for the Mother & Daughter Soul

97

Starring on the Six O'Clock News

It is almost impossible to smile on the outside without feeling better on the inside.
~Anonymous

"Erin," my mom sighed, "why don't you ever finish what you start?"

I did have a restless nature, but the real truth was that I never quite felt that I fit in. My brother had graduated from high school the year before and was both athletically gifted and popular. He was a head taller than all the other guys and had a diamond smile. Everyone gravitated toward his down-to-earth quiet charm. His perfection was maddening. At fourteen, it was painfully obvious to me that I would never walk in his shoes, only his shadow.

I was plump and moody, and I felt dreadfully average. And, despite the messages teenagers get about self-confidence and individuality, despite the fact that he no longer attended my school, I was insanely jealous of my brother. I knew it was up to me to make my own mark in high school.

I worked hard at developing my own unique style. I built a collection of dark clothes and weird jean skirts made from old Levis I picked up from Goodwill. However, I knew that I could not complete my look unless I was properly pierced. I knew of no one of any status who didn't have at least double-pierced ears. My single-pierced ears were far too conservative for the look I was going for.

"Mom?" I asked one morning. "Could I get my ears double-pierced?"

"Absolutely not. You have enough holes in your head already," she said.

Of course, I wasn't at all surprised at her response. I was notorious for taking a mile when I got an inch, and she probably thought I would pierce every part of flesh exposed to daylight when she wasn't looking. So rather than take no for an answer, I decided to take the task into my own hands. With a gigantic sewing needle from the closet, an unbaked potato and some ice cubes, I went into the bathroom and began the task of transforming myself from an ordinary person to an absolute rebel. I nearly passed out when the needle popped partway through my left earlobe. I waited for the dizzy spell to pass before finishing the job and popping it the rest of the way through. My old gold posts seemed to get stuck and had to be twisted awkwardly through my ear but I managed. I drizzled hydrogen peroxide across my wound. In the grand tradition of not finishing what I started, I made a decision. No way was I piercing the other. One ear was cool enough.

For the next six weeks, I was grateful for the camouflage of my hair. I would leave home with the piercing carefully concealed beneath my curls and pull my hair up once I reached the bus stop. I was absolutely sure that everyone at school noticed my ears. It didn't take too long though, before the whole world noticed.

A week later, our football team won the state championship. We were a Class B school, little more than a bunch of farm kids who took time out from baling hay and milking cows to toss a football around, so it was a surprise to everyone that our underdog team had won. The school was on fire with anticipation! The local news channel got wind of our school's recent victory and showed up with news vans, cameras and well-dressed reporters to do a story on our team. They spotted me with my bouncy ponytail and uniquely pierced ears and decided to interview me. I was going to be a star!

I said stuff like, "Awesome!" "Powerful!" and "Really, really cool!" before the cameras left. My little brother Adam wanted to chat about the interview all the way home. Because I was now famous, I graciously answered his questions.

When we arrived home, Andy was there for a visit. My parents quickly gathered around the TV when my little brother announced that I was going to be on the six o'clock news. Dad scrambled for a VCR tape, and then... there I was in living color. The first thing I noticed was my new gold post in my left ear. It was like the North Star glinting in the light of the news camera. My brother Andy spotted it too. He looked at me and grinned knowingly.

"Um..." I said. "I have some homework to do."

"Wait," my mom said. "Sit down. Adam honey, will you rewind that again so we can all watch it once more?" He did, and my earring was now the size of a baseball glinting in the sunlight. I got up and bolted for the stairs. I only made it halfway up before I felt hands grasp my ankles and pull. Before I could catch my footing I was flat on my back staring up into my mother's face. I was busted.

"I don't believe it!" she said. "How long have you been hiding this?"

"A month or so," I admitted. Her eyes narrowed and I knew I was in for it. But then suddenly the corners of her mouth creased and she laughed.

"You know I have to ground you for disobeying," she said through giggles and snorts. "Let me see the other one," she said.

"I couldn't finish it. The first one made me really dizzy," I confessed. This was too much for her, and she burst into peals of laughter. Before long, I was laughing too.

In that moment it didn't matter what anyone else thought of me. It didn't matter that I lost driving privileges for a week, or that I was being laughed at. What mattered was that deep down I knew that Mom understood and she liked me. She liked me despite my insecurities, my oddities and my restlessness and yes, even my rebelliousness. And somehow, getting that other ear pierced didn't matter to me anymore.

~Erin K. Kilby
Chicken Soup for the Preteen Soul 2

Mommy Needs a Raise!

Make your optimism come true.
~Author Unknown

As a single parent, I know that my ten-year-old daughter has learned to do without many extras. Some time ago, to make things up to her, I promised to buy her toys as soon as I got a raise. A while later, my boss went on vacation and arranged for me to watch his dog, cats and parrot. The night before he was due back, we went to feed the animals for the last time. As my daughter busied herself with the parrot, I couldn't believe my ears. She was bombarding the hapless bird with: "Mommy needs a raise! Mommy needs a raise! Mommy needs a raise!"

I got the raise; she got the toys.

~Regina Wiegand
Chicken Soup for the Working Woman's Soul

Clothes Closet Reflections

The quickest way to know a woman is to go shopping with her.
~Marcelene Cox

All mothers of teenage daughters know what it's like. Clothes shopping with that age group is a test of patience, physical endurance, restraint and basic human kindness.

"Mother, give it up! These pants are way too baggy!"

"They're skin tight!"

"Well, these shoes are okay and they look just like the name-brand ones and they fit okay, but Mother, they don't have that little aardvark on the label and everybody will know! I'll pay the twenty-dollar difference myself for the name-brand ones, okay?"

"When donkeys fly, you will."

"Mom! Do you actually think I'd be caught dead in a dress like that?"

"No, I was thinking more in terms of the homecoming dance, but if you keep talking to me like this..."

Oh Lord, give me patience. Direct me out of this store and over to the place where they sell warm chocolate-chip cookies. Quickly.

After a few dismal, distressing shopping trips with my daughters, trips that practically brutalized me with teenage logic, I decided to let them shop alone from then on with money they earned themselves.

Thanks, Lord, for that brilliant idea. I may survive single motherhood, after all.

Then one day, a few years later, it happened.

"Mom," Julie asked sweetly, "may I borrow your yellow blouse to wear to school tomorrow? And maybe that brown print skirt?"

"Sure, honey!" I practically fell off the stool at the kitchen counter. At last my daughters were growing up. Our taste in clothes was starting to meld. I suddenly felt ten years younger.

A few minutes later, Jeanne passed through the kitchen.

"Mom, could I try on some of your clothes? I might like to borrow your plaid skirt and one of your scarves."

"Help yourself, my dear," I smiled smugly.

Either I'm getting really hip when it comes to clothes, or they've finally discovered sensible fashion, I mused.

Single parenthood was suddenly fun. Instead of fighting over the cost of clothes and the styles my daughters chose versus those that actually made sense in the real world, suddenly visions of new, exciting mother-daughter shopping sprees danced in my head. I saw the three of us lunching together after our shopping adventures, discussing our bargains and look-alike fashions, while dining on quiche and croissants.

Right then Jeanne and Julie emerged from my bedroom dressed practically head-to-toe in fashions from my wardrobe, including jewelry and accessories.

"Thanks, Mom! These are great!" they bubbled.

I wasn't so sure about the combinations they'd chosen, but I certainly wasn't about to criticize. After all, I didn't want to ruin this special moment, this tender passage from teendom to adulthood.

"Yeah, they're perfect Mom," Jeanne nodded. "It's nerd day at school tomorrow... you know, everybody dresses up like the fifties, real dorky-like. These things are perfect."

"Oh...."

Lord, are you there? I need more patience. Lots more. Right this minute, Lord. Are you listening?

~Patricia Lorenz
Chicken Soup for the Mother & Daughter Soul

Catfishing with Mama

My mother was a fishing fanatic, despite her Charleston, South Carolina, blue-blood upbringing. When she was twenty, she graduated magna cum laude from the College of Charleston and left that city of history and suffocating social rules forever. With the twenty-dollar gold piece she got for the Math Prize, she bought a railroad ticket for as far west as it would get her. Austin, Texas, was $19.02 away.

There she met my father and proceeded to have seven children — all girls. She also took up fishing, and by the time I was born, she had enough tackle, lawn chairs and fishing hats to fill a steamer trunk. To my father's horror, her favorite lure was blood bait. Bass and catfish were her prey.

Every summer it was my mother's custom to pack the seven of us girls into the DeSoto and drive from Austin to Charleston to visit our grandparents. We camped and fished the whole way.

Mama's preparations for the fifteen-hundred-mile trip consisted of packing the car with seven army cots, a basket of Stonewall peaches and sixteen gallons of live bait, with her tackle box and assorted rods and reels thrown in. Her idea of successful traveling was to get us all in the car without one of us sitting on the blood bait or being left at a gas station. Once she'd done a head count and ascertained the security of the bait, she'd drive like A. J. Foyt until it was too dark to go any farther. This meant we were usually tired, hungry and lost on some back road in the middle of Louisiana or Mississippi when we stopped to camp.

"Stopping to camp" in our case meant suddenly swerving off the road when my mother spied a river or lake that stirred her sporting blood. She never once planned our stops like normal people do, timing themselves to arrive at a campsite or park around dusk. But this was the 1950s, when people still slept with the screen door unlocked and left the keys in the car. We felt perfectly safe at any roadside area, and we were.

The trip that brought us face to face with history was the one we took in the summer of 1958 when I was ten.

Three days into the journey found us somewhere in the mountains of Kentucky. I was never quite sure where we were at any given point on these trips, since I knew only one landmark—the tree-lined road to my grandparents' house—the finish line. But again, we had driven for hours into the night futilely looking for water. When we finally pulled off the road, the hills around us were black as midnight under a skillet. Then a slice of a quarter moon slid out from behind a cloud and delicately illuminated a rock gate in front of us.

"Oh, look," Mama cried, "a national park!"

There was an audible sigh of relief from the back seat. "Let's camp here, Mama!" we clamored urgently.

Since she had been slapping her cheeks for the last hour to stay awake, she agreed.

We cruised down a black dirt road into the parking area. Nestled nearby was the outline of a log cabin. Beyond that, the glint of water.

"See that!" Mama said excitedly. "A sleeping cabin. By some kind of lake. This is paradise."

We parked and unloaded the car, dragging our stuff into the log cabin.

It was open and empty. We could see it was very old and rudimentary, but it had a bathroom with running water. For us it was luxury quarters. We bathed and ate our dinner of kipper snacks and soda crackers, with Moon Pies for dessert. Then we snuggled into the cots that we'd fixed up in the one bare room.

Mama set off with long strides toward the water, gear in hand.

The faint murmur of her voice as she conversed with her tackle box drifted through the open windows. With that and a cozy roof overhead, my sisters curled up and fell to sleep like a litter of puppies.

I picked up my rod and reel and, still in my pajamas, slipped quietly out the door. Across the damp grass I could see my mother's silhouette making casting motions. For a moment I felt the thrill of anticipation inherent in fishing: There was a fat catfish with my name on it waiting out there, I just knew it.

I joined my mother, and we fished together, just us — the water and the quarter moon. It was one of those moments that form a permanent part in the book of parent-child memories, although it was destined to be brief.

Mama could practically conjure up fish to her, and sure enough, within half an hour she got a strike and brought in a fourteen-pound cat.

Probably my Fat-Cat, I thought irritably.

"Look," she said, bending around me, her hands grasping mine as I held my rod. "Let me show you..."

She made a deft flicking motion, and suddenly my line shot across the water. The light of the moon made it look like the trail of a shooting star. It fell silently on the dark water and disappeared.

"Right there," she said lowly. "Hold tight to it."

She turned away and began cleaning her fish. I gripped the rod until my knuckles were white. I had a feeling for what was coming. Suddenly, the line lurched tight, and my arms shot forward. I almost flew into the black water of the lake.

"It's a big one, Mama!" I yelled. "I don't think I can hold it." My feet were slipping down the bank, and the mud had oozed up to my ankles. "Mama, quick!"

She grasped me around the waist and yanked me back up the bank. The pull on the line lessened.

"Now! Bring it in now!" she shouted.

I reeled in as hard as I could. Suddenly, the fish was right there below me, lying in shallow water. It was a big one, all right. Almost as big as Mama's.

"Good work," she said, leaning over and carefully pulling the catfish onto the bank. It slapped the wet grass angrily. I was exhausted. We took our fish back to the cabin and fell into a deep sleep.

It seemed only minutes later that our sleep was penetrated by voices. Lots of voices. Suddenly, the door of the cabin burst open, and sunlight and a large group of people led by a woman in a uniform flowed into the room. The uniformed person was in the middle of a speech.

"And here we have the boyhood home of President Abraham Lincoln — aagghhhhh!"

We all screamed at once. My mother, protective in her own quixotic way, leapt off the cot, her chenille bathrobe flapping, and shouted at the intruders, "Who do you think you are, bursting in on a sleeping family like this?"

The guide was struck speechless. She gathered herself with visible effort. "Ma'am, I don't know who you are, but this is the Abraham Lincoln Birthplace National Historic Site," she reported tersely.

Her eyes quickly shifted sideways to take in two huge catfish lying on the floor. Although she tried to conceal it, her lips pursed with disgust. I knew right off she wasn't a fisherman.

"And his lost cabin," she continued, "is not an overnight stopover for fishing expeditions. This is a restricted area with guided tours beginning at 7:00 A.M. and..."

"Oh my God, we overslept!" Mama shouted. "Pack the car, girls. We've got to get on the road!"

We lurched into a flurry of experienced cot-folding and were out the door in seconds.

"But ma'am," the guide called at my mother's disappearing back, "you weren't supposed to sleep in here. This is Lincoln's Log Cabin. It's a National Treasure!"

"We treasure our night here," my mother shouted back, as she gunned the car around. "Abe wouldn't have minded."

With that we roared off in the direction of South Carolina. I saw a sign as we left: "Leaving Hodgenville, Kentucky, Abraham Lincoln's Birthplace. Y'all Come Back."

"Not likely," my mother laughed. "A good fishing spot, but I hate to do anything twice, don't you?"

And that's how it happened that, during the summer I was ten, the course of history was changed. Unofficially, to be sure, but if there had been a historical marker by that lake, it would now have to read: "Abe Lincoln Fished Here... and So Did I."

~Lin Sutherland
Chicken Soup for the Nature Lover's Soul

Heave Ho

Carry laughter with you wherever you go.
~Hugh Sidey

Well, I'm not a lot of the things I used to be, but I'm sure of a lot of things I didn't used to be. Some of those things are good, some bad, some are just what they are, different. Like they say: nothing ever stays the same.

MS (multiple sclerosis) has become a part of who I am, just a part. Having lived with the culprit for over half of my life, I'm getting used to the adversities presented to me. I've learned that laughter can go a long way in dealing with hardships and difficulties. It seems as if my life is becoming quite a comic routine!

The other day my daughter came to get me. Driving is one thing I don't do anymore. Since she had no lift in her SUV, it was determined I would take my wheelchair instead of my motorized scooter. That wasn't the problem. The problem was her vehicle.

We'd recently moved into the neighborhood and had not gotten acquainted with our neighbors. Of all days, the neighbors across the street were out in the front visiting with company. They are a young couple with two little girls. And I am an old lady. I don't feel like an old lady, but that's beside the point. To a young couple, I'm an old lady. Well, really to be truthful, a fat old lady.

My daughter has an Eddie Bauer Ford Expedition, whatever that is. It looks like a green tank when you're an old lady, especially when you're an old lady in a wheelchair. She pushed me up next to that monster, and I eyeballed it and knew that this was going to be one gigantic challenge. "Now, Ronda, this is not going to be easy," I comment.

"We can do it," she says.

Oh sure, I think to myself, what is this we stuff?

"Just put your foot up here, and get a hold of that."

"Oh yeah, sure!"

"Come on, I'll help you," she assures me.

She takes my foot and places it on the running board or whatever in the world they call them these days—that's what they called them in my day.

"Now get a hold of that strap up there, Mom, and pull!"

This is where I begin to snicker and my foot slips off whatever that dang thing my foot was on. She lets out a giggle behind me, and we start all over again. Now my daughter is a petite little thing and I am, well—old. We get my foot up on that thing again, I grab hold and holler, "Shove!" She gives me a nudge, and I holler again, "I said shove!" She starts laughing and down I come! By this time, we are both laughing and creating quite a scene.

"Now, Ronda, you have to butt your shoulder to me and shove hard, like your dad does," I say between my laughter and her giggles. "Don't be afraid to push hard."

I have plenty of padding so it's not like she was going to hurt herself on my bones or anything. A big part of my body is numb so it wasn't like I could feel her bouncing off my blubber either. So we began again.

"I don't want to hurt you, Mom," she giggles.

"Don't worry; you're not going to hurt me; your dad does it all the time," I assure her. My comments don't bring any sympathy, just more giggles. As we start again she gets serious and so do I, as I become aware that I am making quite an impression on our neighbors.

"Now shove!" I scream.

"Heave ho!" she shouts.

We both break out in hysterical laughter as the steering wheel gets acquainted with my face, leaving my feet and legs sticking out the door. I'm prone on the front seat and the neighbors are getting free entertainment. By this time my face is in excruciating pain, not from the steering wheel, but from the muscles being strained from so much laughter. Ronda helps me, and I finally get pushed, pulled and tucked into my seat, and we drive away leaving my neighbors wondering about the circus act that has moved in across the street.

Yeah, things have changed, I've changed; nothing ever stays the same, not even circus acts. I hope my neighbors are prepared, because I've become a three-ringer!

~Betty A. King
Chicken Soup for the Mother & Daughter Soul

More

Chicken Soup for the Soul®

Chicken Soup for the Soul

Share with Us

We would like to know how these stories affected you and which ones were your favorites. Please write to us and let us know.

We also would like to share your stories with future readers. You may be able to help another reader, and become a published author at the same time. Please send us your own stories and poems for our future books. Some of our past contributors have launched writing and speaking careers from the publication of their stories in our books!

The best way to submit your stories is through our web site, at:

www.chickensoup.com

If you do not have access to the Internet,
you may submit your stories by mail or by facsimile.

Chicken Soup for the Soul
P.O. Box 700
Cos Cob, CT 06807-0700
Fax 203-861-7194

Chicken Soup for the Soul®

Enjoy these additional fine books for Women:

Chicken Soup for the Woman's Soul
Chicken Soup for the Mother's Soul
A Second Chicken Soup for the Woman's Soul
Chicken Soup for the Parent's Soul
Chicken Soup for the Expectant Mother's Soul
Chicken Soup for the Christian Family Soul
Chicken Soup for the Mother's Soul 2
Chicken Soup for the Grandparent's Soul
Chicken Soup for the Christian Woman's Soul
Chicken Soup for the Mother & Daughter Soul
Chicken Soup for Every Mom's Soul
Chicken Soup for the Grandma's Soul
Chicken Soup for the Single Parent's Soul
Chicken Soup for the Mother and Son Soul
Chicken Soup for the Working Mom's Soul
Chicken Soup for the Soul: Celebrating Mothers and Daughters
Chicken Soup for the New Mom's Soul
Chicken Soup for the Soul: A Tribute to Moms

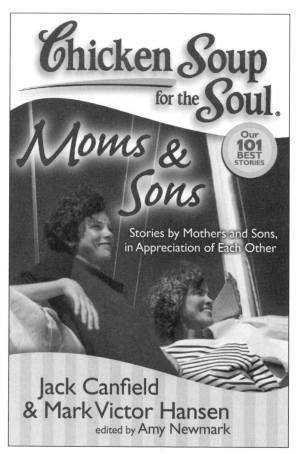

There is a special bond between mothers and their sons and it never goes away. This new book contains the 101 best stories and poems from Chicken Soup's library honoring that lifelong relationship between mothers and their male offspring. These heartfelt stories written by mothers, grandmothers, and sons, about each other, span generations and show how the mother-son bond transcends time. Some of these stories will make readers laugh and some will make them cry, but they all will warm their hearts and remind them of the things they love about each other.

978-1-935096-16-0

*C*heck out the other books in the

Mom will know where it is…what to say…how to fix it." This Chicken Soup book focuses on the pervasive wisdom of mothers everywhere, and includes the 101 best stories from Chicken Soup's library on our perceptive, understanding, and insightful mothers. These stories celebrate the special bond between mothers and children, our mothers' unerring wisdom about everything from the mundane to the life-changing, and the hard work that goes into being a mother every day.

978-1-935096-02-3

Books for Moms Series

The Wisdom of Dads

Stories about Fathers and Being a Father

978-1-935096-18-4

Children view their fathers with awe from the day they are born. Fathers are big and strong and seem to know everything, except for a few teenage years when fathers are perceived to know nothing! This book represents a new theme for Chicken Soup – 101 stories selected from forty past books, all stories focusing on the wisdom of dads. Stories are written by sons and daughters about their fathers, and by fathers relating stories about their children.

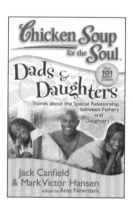

Dads & Daughters

Stories about the Special Relationship between Fathers and Daughters

978-1-935096-19-1

The day a girl is born she starts a special relationship with her father. It doesn't matter whether she is ten years old or fifty – she will always be his little girl. And daughters take care of their dads too, whether it is a tea party for two at age five or loving care fifty years later. This wide-ranging exploration of the relationship between fathers and daughters provides an entirely new reading experience for Chicken Soup fans, with selections from forty past Chicken Soup books. Stories were written by fathers about their daughters and by daughters about their fathers, celebrating the special bond between fathers and daughters as they move through life's phases, from birth to childhood, to those sometimes difficult teen years, to marriage and grandchildren, and to end of life issues.

Books for Families

On Being a Parent

Inspirational, Humorous, and Heartwarming Stories about Parenthood

978-1-935096-20-7

Parenting is the hardest and most rewarding job in the world. This upbeat and compelling new book includes the best selections on parenting from Chicken Soup's rich history, with 101 stories carefully selected to appeal to both mothers and fathers. This is a great book for couples to share, whether they are just embarking on their new adventure as parents or reflecting on their lifetime experience.

Grand and Great

Grandparents and Grandchildren Share Their Stories of Love and Wisdom

978-1-935096-09-2

A parent becomes a new person the day the first grandchild is born. Formerly serious and responsible adults go on shopping sprees for toys and baby clothing, smile incessantly, pull out photo albums that they "just happen to have" with them, and proudly display baby seats in their cars. Grandparents dote on their grandchildren, and grandchildren love them back with all their hearts. This new book includes the best stories on being a grandparent from 33 past Chicken Soup books, representing a new reading experience for even the most devoted Chicken Soup fan.

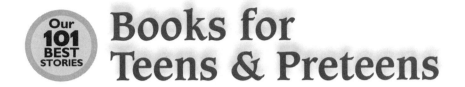

Books for Teens & Preteens

Our 101 BEST STORIES

Chicken Soup for the Soul: Preteens Talk
Inspiration and Support for Preteens from Kids Just Like Them
978-1-935096-00-9

Chicken Soup for the Soul: Teens Talk Growing Up
Stories about Growing Up, Meeting Challenges, and Learning from Life
978-1-935096-01-6

Chicken Soup for the Soul: Teens Talk Tough Times
Stories about the Hardest Parts of Being a Teenager
978-1-935096-03-0

Chicken Soup for the Soul: Teens Talk Relationships
Stories about Family, Friends, and Love
978-1-935096-06-1

Chicken Soup for the Soul: Christian Teen Talk
Christian Teens Share Their Stories of Support, Inspiration and Growing Up
978-1-935096-12-2

Chicken Soup for the Soul: Christian Kids
Stories to Inspire, Amuse, and Warm the Hearts of Christian Kids and
Their Parents
978-1-935096-13-9

Chicken Soup for the Soul
Loving Our Dogs
Heartwarming and Humorous Stories about Our Companions and Best Friends
Jack Canfield & Mark Victor Hansen
edited by Amy Newmark

Chicken Soup for the Soul
Loving Our Cats
Heartwarming and Humorous Stories about Our Feline Family Members
Jack Canfield & Mark Victor Hansen
edited by Amy Newmark

Chicken Soup for the Soul
Women to Women
Women Sharing Their Stories of Hope, Humor, and Inspiration
Jack Canfield & Mark Victor Hansen
edited by

Chicken Soup for the Soul
Older & Wiser
Stories of Inspiration, Humor, and Wisdom about Life at a Certain Age
Jack Canfield & Mark Victor Hansen
edited by Amy Newmark

Chicken Soup for the Soul
Happily Ever After
Fun and Heartwarming Stories about Finding and Enjoying Your Ma
Jack Canfield & Mark Victor Hansen
edited by Amy Newmark

Chicken Soup for the Soul
Tales of Golf and Sport
The Joy, Frustration, and Humor of Golf and Sport
Jack Canfield & Mark Victor Hansen
edited by Amy Newmark

Chicken Soup for the Soul
Christmas Cheer
Stories about the Love, Inspiration, and Joy of Christmas
Jack Canfield & Mark Victor Hansen
edited by Amy Newmark

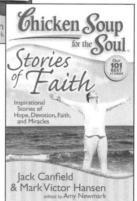

Chicken Soup for the Soul
Stories of Faith
Inspirational Stories of Hope, Devotion, Faith, and Miracles
Jack Canfield & Mark Victor Hansen
edited by Amy Newmark

More Great  Books

Chicken Soup for the Soul: Loving Our Dogs
Heartwarming and Humorous Stories about our Companions and
Best Friends
978-1-935096-05-4

Chicken Soup for the Soul: Loving Our Cats
Heartwarming and Humorous Stories about our Feline Family Members
978-1-935096-08-5

Chicken Soup for the Soul: Woman to Woman
Women Sharing Their Stories of Hope, Humor, and Inspiration
978-1-935096-04-7

Chicken Soup for the Soul: Older & Wiser
Stories of Inspiration, Humor, and Wisdom about Life at a Certain Age
978-1-935096-17-7

Chicken Soup for the Soul: Happily Ever After
Fun and Heartwarming Stories about Finding and Enjoying Your Mate
978-1-935096-10-8

Chicken Soup for the Soul: Tales of Golf and Sport
The Joy, Frustration, and Humor of Golf and Sport
978-1-935096-11-5

Chicken Soup for the Soul: Christmas Cheer
Stories about the Love, Inspiration, and Joy of Christmas
978-1-935096-15-3

Chicken Soup for the Soul: Stories of Faith
Inspirational Stories of Hope, Devotion, Faith and Miracles
978-1-935096-14-6

Chicken Soup for the Soul

Who Is
Jack Canfield?

Jack Canfield is the co-creator and editor of the *Chicken Soup for the Soul* series, which *Time* magazine has called "the publishing phenomenon of the decade." Jack is also the co-author of eight other bestselling books including *The Success Principles™: How to Get from Where You Are to Where You Want to Be, Dare to Win, The Aladdin Factor, You've Got to Read This Book*, and *The Power of Focus: How to Hit Your Business and Personal and Financial Targets with Absolute Certainty*.

Jack has recently developed a telephone coaching program and an online coaching program based on his most recent book *The Success Principles*. He also offers a seven-day *Breakthrough to Success* seminar every summer, which attracts 400 people from fifteen countries around the world.

Jack is the CEO of the Canfield Training Group in Santa Barbara, California, and founder of the Foundation for Self-Esteem in Culver City, California. He has conducted intensive personal and professional development seminars on the principles of success for over a million people in twenty-three countries. Jack is a dynamic keynote speaker and he has spoken to hundreds of thousands of others at more than 1,000 corporations, universities, professional conferences and conventions, and has been seen by millions more on national television shows such as *The Today Show, Fox and Friends, Inside Edition, Hard Copy, CNN's Talk Back Live, 20/20, Eye to Eye*, and the *NBC Nightly News* and the *CBS Evening News*.

Jack is the recipient of many awards and honors, including three honorary doctorates and a *Guinness World Records Certificate* for having seven books from the *Chicken Soup for the Soul* series appearing on the *New York Times* bestseller list on May 24, 1998.

To write to Jack or for inquiries about Jack as a speaker, his coaching programs, trainings or seminars, use the following contact information:

Jack Canfield
The Canfield Companies
P.O. Box 30880 • Santa Barbara, CA 93130
phone: 805-563-2935 • fax: 805-563-2945
E-mail: info@jackcanfield.com
www.jackcanfield.com

Who Is
Mark Victor Hansen?

Mark Victor Hansen is the co-founder of *Chicken Soup for the Soul*, along with Jack Canfield. He is also a sought-after keynote speaker, bestselling author, and marketing maven.

For more than thirty years, Mark has focused solely on helping people from all walks of life reshape their personal vision of what's possible. His powerful messages of possibility, opportunity, and action have created powerful change in thousands of organizations and millions of individuals worldwide.

Mark's credentials include a lifetime of entrepreneurial success. He is a prolific writer with many bestselling books, such as *The One Minute Millionaire*, *Cracking the Millionaire Code*, *How to Make the Rest of Your Life the Best of Your Life*, *The Power of Focus*, *The Aladdin Factor*, and *Dare to Win*, in addition to the *Chicken Soup for the Soul* series. Mark has had a profound influence in the field of human potential through his library of audios, videos, and articles in the areas of big thinking, sales achievement, wealth building, publishing success, and personal and professional development.

Mark is the founder of the *MEGA Seminar Series*. *MEGA Book Marketing University* and *Building Your MEGA Speaking Empire* are annual conferences where Mark coaches and teaches new and aspiring authors, speakers, and experts on building lucrative publishing and speaking careers. Other MEGA events include *MEGA Info-Marketing* and *My MEGA Life*.

He has appeared on *Oprah, CNN,* and *The Today Show.* He has been quoted in *Time, U.S. News & World Report, USA Today, New York Times,* and *Entrepreneur* and has had countless radio interviews, assuring our planet's people that "You can easily create the life you deserve."

As a philanthropist and humanitarian, Mark works tirelessly for organizations such as Habitat for Humanity, American Red Cross, March of Dimes, Childhelp USA, and many others. He is the recipient of numerous awards that honor his entrepreneurial spirit, philanthropic heart, and business acumen. He is a lifetime member of the Horatio Alger Association of Distinguished Americans, an organization that honored Mark with the prestigious Horatio Alger Award for his extraordinary life achievements.

Mark Victor Hansen is an enthusiastic crusader of what's possible and is driven to make the world a better place.

Mark Victor Hansen & Associates, Inc.
P.O. Box 7665 • Newport Beach, CA 92658
phone: 949-764-2640 • fax: 949-722-6912
www.markvictorhansen.com

Who Is
Amy Newmark?

Amy Newmark was recently named publisher of Chicken Soup for the Soul, after a thirty-year career as a writer, speaker, financial analyst, and business executive in the worlds of finance and telecommunications.

Amy is a graduate of Harvard College, where she majored in Portuguese, minored in French, and traveled extensively. She is also the mother of two children in college and has two grown stepchildren.

After a long career writing books on telecommunications, voluminous financial reports, business plans, and corporate press releases, Chicken Soup for the Soul is a breath of fresh air for Amy. She has fallen in love with Chicken Soup for the Soul and its life-changing books, and found it a true pleasure to conceptualize, compile, and edit the "101 Best Stories" books for our readers.

The best way to contact Chicken Soup for the Soul is through our web site, at www.chickensoup.com. This will always get the fastest attention.

If you do not have access to the Internet, please contact us by mail or by facsimile.

Chicken Soup for the Soul
P.O. Box 700
Cos Cob, CT 06807-0700
Fax 203-861-7194

Chicken Soup for the Soul

ˉThank You!

O
Our first thanks go to our loyal readers who have inspired the entire Chicken Soup team for the past fifteen years. Your appreciative letters and e-mails have reminded us why we work so hard on these books.

We owe huge thanks to all of our contributors as well. We know that you pour your hearts and souls into the stories and poems that you share with us, and ultimately with each other. We appreciate your willingness to open up your lives to other Chicken Soup readers.

We can only publish a small percentage of the stories that are submitted, but we read every single one and even the ones that do not appear in a book have an influence on us and on the final manuscripts.

As always, we would like to thank the entire staff of Chicken Soup for the Soul for their help on this project and the 101 Best series in general.

Among our California staff, we would especially like to single out the following people:

- D'ette Corona, who is the heart and soul of the Chicken Soup publishing operation, and who put together the first draft of this manuscript

- Barbara LoMonaco for invaluable assistance in obtaining the fabulous quotations that add depth and meaning to this book

- Patty Hansen for her extra special help with the permissions for these fabulous stories and for her amazing knowledge of the Chicken Soup library and Patti Clement for her help with permissions and other organizational matters.

In our Connecticut office, we would like to thank our able editorial assistants, Valerie Howlett and Madeline Clapps, for their assistance in setting up our new offices, editing, and helping us put together the best possible books.

We would also like to thank our master of design, Creative Director and book producer Brian Taylor at Pneuma Books, LLC, for his brilliant vision for our covers and interiors.

Finally, none of this would be possible without the business and creative leadership of our CEO, Bill Rouhana, and our president, Bob Jacobs.

Chicken Soup for the Soul

www.chickensoup.com